LIBERTY'S
REFUGE

LIBERTY'S REFUGE

THE FORGOTTEN

FREEDOM OF ASSEMBLY

John D. Inazu

Yale

UNIVERSITY PRESS

New Haven & London

Yale University Press books may be purchased in
quantity for educational, business, or promotional use.
For information, please e-mail sales.press@yale.edu
(U.S. office) or sales@yaleup.co.uk (U.K. office).

Set in Baskerville type by IDS Infotech Ltd., Chandigarh, India.
Printed in the United States of America.

Library of Congress Cataloging-in-Publication Data

Inazu, John D.
Library's refuge : the forgotten freedom of assembly / John D. Inazu.
p.cm.
Includes bibliographical references and index.
ISBN 978-0-300-17315-4 (cloth : alk. paper) 1. Assembly, Right of—United States.
2. Freedom of association—United States. I. Title.
KF4778.I53 2012
342.7308'54—dc23
2011021414

A catalogue record for this book is available from the British Library.

This paper meets the requirements of
ANSI/NISO Z39.48–1992 (Permanence of Paper).

10 9 8 7 6 5 4 3 2 1

For Byrd and Taizo

CONTENTS

ACKNOWLEDGMENTS

I am grateful for substantial advice and comments from Jeff Spinner-Halev, Mike Lienesch, Stanley Hauerwas, Jeff Powell, Susan Bickford, Amin Aminfar, Rick Garnett, Guy-Uriel Charles, and James Boyle. I owe a particular note of thanks to Andy Koppelman for his generous engagement with a book with which he has many disagreements. Thanks also to Rob Vischer, Gerald Postema, Jim Skillen, Bob Cochran, Kristen Johnson, Max Eichner, Tabatha Abu El-Haj, Roman Hoyos, Neil Siegel, Nathan Chapman, Bill English, Kim Krawiec, Jed Purdy, Bill Marshall, Larry Helfer, Stuart Benjamin, Jack Knight, Joseph Blocher, Sara Beale, David Lange, Ryan Messmore, Jonathan Mitchell, Ernie Young, Steve Smith, Paul Haagen, Michael Curtis, Dan Blinka, and Jason Mazzone. This book benefited from audiences at the Harvard Graduate Conference in Political Theory and faculty workshops at Duke University School of Law and the University of North Carolina School of Law. Thanks to the library staffs at Duke University School of Law (especially Jennifer Behrens, Molly Brownfield, and Kelly Leong), the University of North Carolina, and Syracuse University. The final stages of this manuscript benefited from exceptional research assistance from Chase Anderson, Ellie Poole, and Josh Roling.

My completion of this book was made possible through the generous financial support of Dr. and Mrs. Thomas S. Royster during my graduate work at the University of North Carolina and by a number of people at Duke University School of Law and the Program in Public Law, especially Neil Siegel, Liz Gustafson, and David Levi. Chapters 2 and 3 draw heavily from "The Forgotten Freedom of Assembly," *Tulane Law Review* 84 (2010): 565–612, and "The Strange Origins of the Constitutional Right of Association," *Tennessee Law Review* 77 (2010): 485–562. Portions of Chapter 4 are taken from "The Unsettling 'Well-Settled' Law of Freedom of Association," *Connecticut Law Review* 43 (2011): 149–208. I am grateful to the editors for their permission to rely upon these publications. Some of my arguments about intimate and expressive association are summarized in the *Amicus* Brief of Pacific Justice Institute and Christian Service Charities in Support of Petitioner Christian Legal Society in *Christian Legal Society v. Martinez*, No. 08–1371 (February 2010). Thanks to Pete Lepiscopo for his work on that brief.

Mike O'Malley at Yale University Press believed in this manuscript, and Bill Frucht, Piyali Bhattacharya, Ann-Marie Imbornoni, and Otto Bohlmann helped see it through to completion. Thanks also to the three reviewers whose insightful critiques have made this manuscript a better book and its author a better scholar.

Scott Davis, Tod Laursen, Rich Schmalbeck, Scott Silliman, Joel Fleishman, Mike Broadway, Roger Wollman, and Curtis Freeman encouraged me in important ways at earlier stages of my academic training. Allan Poole, Cleve May, Seth Dowland, Evan Gurney, Alex Hartemink, and Greg Mitchell endured many conversations about the arguments contained in this book. Jeff Powell has been a mentor since my days as a law student at Duke—no one has been more influential to my development as a lawyer and a scholar.

I am blessed beyond measure by my wife, Caroline, and our two daughters, Lauren and Hana. My parents, Willie and Sandy Inazu, have modeled life for me in ways that I hope to do for my own children. Caroline's parents, Skip and Melissa Young, have been a consistent presence in our lives (and have also served as faithful babysitters).

ACKNOWLEDGMENTS

This book is dedicated to my grandfathers. In 1945, as the United States Supreme Court issued one of its most important opinions about the freedom of assembly in *Thomas v. Collins,* Byrd Curtis sat captive in a Nazi prisoner-of-war camp and Taizo Inazu stood behind the barbed wire of Tule Lake Relocation Camp. We work out the theory and practice of assembly between the poles of abuse to which they testify.[1]

CHAPTER 1

OVERVIEW OF THE ARGUMENT

Congress shall make no law respecting an establishment of religion, or
prohibiting the free exercise thereof; or abridging the freedom of speech,
or of the press; *or the right of the people peaceably to assemble,* and to petition
the Government for a redress of grievances.
—*United States Constitution, Amendment I*

The freedom of assembly has been at the heart of some of the most
important social movements in American history: antebellum aboli-
tionism, women's suffrage in the nineteenth and twentieth centuries, the
labor movement in the Progressive Era and the New Deal, and the Civil
Rights Movement. Claims of assembly stood against the ideological
tyranny that exploded during the first Red Scare in the years surrounding
the First World War and the Second Red Scare of 1950s' McCarthyism.
Abraham Lincoln once called "the right of the people peaceably to
assemble" part of "the Constitutional substitute for revolution." In 1939,
the popular press heralded assembly as one of the "four freedoms"
central to the Bill of Rights. Even as late as 1973, John Rawls characterized it as one of the "basic liberties." But in the past thirty years, the
freedom of assembly has become little more than a historical footnote in

American law and political theory. Why has assembly so utterly disappeared from our democratic fabric? And, as important, what has been lost with the loss of assembly?[1]

One might, with good reason, think that the right of assembly has been subsumed into the rights of speech and association and that these two rights adequately protect the boundaries of group autonomy. On this account, contemporary free speech doctrine guards the best-known form of assembly—the occasional, temporal gathering that often takes the form of a protest, parade, or demonstration. Meanwhile, the right of association, or, more precisely, the right of *expressive association*, shelters assemblies that extend across time and place—groups like clubs, churches, and civic organizations. In other words, the free speech framework focuses on the message that a group conveys at the moment of its gathering (the words on a placard, the shouts of a protester, the physical presence of a sit-in), while the expressive association framework focuses on the group that enables a message by ensuring that people can "associate for the purpose of engaging in those activities protected by the First Amendment—speech, assembly, petition for the redress of grievances, and the exercise of religion."[2]

The idea that the rights of speech and association adequately guard the groups that the right of assembly might otherwise have protected is not implausible, and a number of scholars appear to have adopted it. Indeed, most modern constitutional arguments involving questions of group autonomy invoke the right of expressive association. Andrew Koppelman, a well-respected constitutional scholar, has argued that expressive association has come to represent "a well-settled law of freedom of association," an "*ancien regime.*"[3]

I believe that this turn to speech and association to protect the boundaries of group autonomy—and therefore pluralism and dissent—is misguided. The central argument of this book is that something important is lost when we fail to grasp the connection between a group's formation, composition, and existence and its expression. Many group expressions are only intelligible against the lived practices that give them meaning. The rituals and liturgy of religious worship often embody deeper meaning than an outside observer would ascribe to them. The political significance of a women's pageant in the 1920s would be lost without knowing why these women gathered. And the creeds and songs recited by members of groups ranging from Alcoholics Anonymous to the Boy Scouts reflect a way of living that cannot be captured by a text or its utterance at any one event.[4]

The right of expressive association elides this connection between a group's practices and its message. Consider the following examples: a gay social club, a prayer or meditation group, and a college fraternity. Each of these groups conveys a message by its very existence. Each of these groups bears witness to a social practice that, to varying degrees and at various times, disrupts social norms and consensus thinking. Those sound like important First Amendment interests. But none of these groups qualifies as an expressive association—none of these groups is "expressive enough" under current constitutional doctrine.[5]

What is more, even when the right of expressive association does show up, it doesn't offer very rigorous protections, at least when confronted with antidiscrimination norms. Civic organizations, social clubs, and religious student groups have all been found to be expressive associations— and all have been left utterly unprotected by the right of expressive association. The Ninth Circuit recently illustrated this trend—and the logical end of antidiscrimination norms unchecked by principles of group autonomy—in the reasoning underlying its denial of constitutional protections to a high school Bible club that sought to limit its membership to Christians: "States have the constitutional authority to enact legislation prohibiting invidious discrimination. . . . We hold that the requirement that members [of a high school Bible club] possess a 'true desire to . . . grow in a relationship with Jesus Christ' inherently excludes non-Christians . . ., [thus violating] the District's non-discrimination policies." In other words, a Christian group that excludes non-Christians is for that reason invidiously discriminating.[6]

There is another problem with the right of association—it is not actually in the text of the Constitution. This will come as a surprise to some, including dozens of federal judges and their law clerks who have referred to a nonexistent "freedom of association clause" in the First Amendment. Look again at the epigraph to this introductory chapter—there is no such clause. In fact, the right of association was absent from our constitutionalism for most of our nation's history—the Supreme Court first announced it in its 1958 decision *NAACP v. Alabama ex rel. Patterson.*[7]

Of course, any written document requires some level of interpretation, and the Supreme Court has long recognized other rights not in the text of the Constitution, most notably a right to privacy. But unlike privacy, association has an obvious antecedent in the text of the Constitution: the right of assembly. We should not supplant assembly with the invented right of association—or at least the version of that right that the Court has embraced over the past fifty years—without understanding why we have done so and what we have given up in the process.

This book offers assembly as an alternative to the enfeebled right of expressive association. The history of assembly reveals four principles that help us see its contours and its contemporary applications. First, assembly extends not only to groups that further the common good but also to dissident groups that act against the common good. Second, this right extends to a vast array of religious and social groups. Third, just as the freedom of speech guards against restrictions imposed prior to an act of speaking, assembly guards against restrictions imposed prior to an act of assembling—it protects a group's autonomy, composition, and existence. Fourth, assembly is a form of expression—the existence of a group and its selection of members and leaders convey a message. Collectively, these four principles counsel for strong protections for the formation, composition, expression, and gathering of groups, especially those groups that dissent from majoritarian standards.

The judicially recognized right of association advances neither these principles nor the values that underlie them. The shift in the constitutional framework from assembly to association (1) diminished protections for dissenting and destabilizing groups; (2) marginalized political practices of these groups by narrowing the scope of what counts as "political"; and (3) obscured the relationship between the practices and expression of these groups. The forgetting of assembly and the embrace of association thus marked the loss of meaningful protections for the dissenting, political, and expressive group.[8]

While today's cultural and legal climate raises the most serious challenges to practices at odds with liberal democratic values, the eclectic collection of groups that have been silenced and stilled by the state cuts across political and ideological boundaries. The freedom of assembly once opposed these incursions. As C. Edwin Baker has argued: "The function of constitutional rights, and more specifically the role of the right of assembly, is to protect self-expressive, nonviolent, noncoercive conduct from majority norms or political balancing and even to permit people to be offensive, annoying, or challenging to dominant norms."[9]

But the social vision of assembly does more than enable meaningful dissent. It provides a buffer between the individual and the state that facilitates a check against centralized power. It acknowledges the importance of groups to the shaping and forming of identity. And it facilitates a kind of flourishing that recognizes the good and the beautiful sometimes grow out of the unfamiliar and the mundane. Indeed, almost every important social movement in our nation's history began not as an organized political party but as an informal group that formed as much around ordinary social activity as extraordinary political activity. We lose more than the shared experience of cheese fries and cheap beer when we bowl alone.[10]

Recovering the vision of assembly remains an urgent task. In June 2010, the Court dealt a twofold blow to the principles of group autonomy by relying on attenuated conceptions of the rights of speech and association. In *Holder v. Humanitarian Law Project*, the Court curtailed in the name of national security interests the right of individuals to associate with and advocate on behalf of certain foreign political groups. And in *Christian Legal Society v. Martinez*, the Court relied on a muddied area of free speech doctrine to deny the right of a religious student group to limit its membership to those of its choosing, the right to retain control over its own message—the right to exist.[11]

Holder and *Martinez* hinder the group autonomy upon which democracy depends. As Stephen Carter has argued, "Democracy advances through dissent, difference, and dialogue. The idea that the state should not only create a set of meanings, but try to alter the structure of institutions that do not match it, is ultimately destructive of democracy because it destroys the differences that create the dialectic."[12] Beginning from a very different perspective, William Eskridge arrives at a similar conclusion: "The state must allow individual nomic communities to flourish or wither as they may, and the state cannot as a normal matter become the means for the triumph of one community over all others."[13] The Court's doctrinal reliance on the right of association in *Holder* and the right of speech in *Martinez* ignores the important views that Carter and Eskridge raise.

Holder and *Martinez* are lamentable, but they are unsurprising. They reflect the unprincipled development of the Court's approach to questions of group autonomy over the past fifty years. This book proposes an alternative. It tells a different story about the constitutional protections for groups and argues that we need to reinvigorate these protections. The following pages provide an overview of the next four chapters: (1) the history of the right of assembly; (2) the invention of the right of association in the 1950s and 1960s; (3) the transformation of the right of association in the 1970s and 1980s; and (4) a theory of assembly.

The Right Peaceably to Assemble

There has been some debate as to whether "the right of the people peaceably to assemble, and to petition the government for a redress of grievances" in the First Amendment recognizes a single right to assemble for the purpose of petitioning the government or establishes both an unencumbered right of assembly and a separate right of petition. Contrary to interpretations advanced in some scholarship, the text of the First Amendment and the corresponding debates over the Bill of Rights suggest that the framers understood assembly to encompass more than petition. The first groups to invoke the freedom of assembly also construed it broadly. At the end of the eighteenth century, the Democratic-Republican Societies emerging out of the increasingly partisan divide between Federalists and Republicans repeatedly invoked the right of assembly. During the antebellum era, policymakers in southern states recognized the significance of free assembly to public opinion and routinely prohibited its exercise among slaves and free blacks. Meanwhile, female abolitionists and suffragists in the North organized their efforts around a particular form of assembly, the convention. As Akhil Amar has observed, the nineteenth-century movements of the disenfranchised brought "a different lived experience" to the words of the First Amendment's assembly clause. They were political movements, to be sure, but they embodied and symbolized even larger societal and cultural challenges.[14]

At the end of the nineteenth century, the Supreme Court misconstrued the text of the First Amendment in suggesting that the right of assembly was limited to the purposes of petitioning for a redress of grievances. But while some commentators accepted this narrow interpretation, state courts interpreting parallel state constitutional provisions of assembly articulated far broader protections. This more expansive sense of assembly was also represented in three social movements during the Progressive Era: a revitalized women's movement, a surge in political activity among African Americans, and an increasingly agitated labor movement.

The Supreme Court made the federal right of assembly applicable to the states in its 1937 opinion *De Jonge v. Oregon*. The newly expanded right gained traction in subsequent cases. But these advances proved evanescent, and later cases involving the rights of "speech and assembly" routinely resolved the latter within the framework of the former. Although the right of assembly remained important in several decisions overturning convictions of African Americans who participated in peaceful civil rights demonstrations in the 1960s, courts resolved most cases involving group autonomy without considering assembly. The Supreme Court, in fact, has not addressed an assembly claim in thirty years.[15]

The Right of Association in the National Security Era

Around the time that assembly began falling out of political and legal discourse, the Supreme Court shifted its constitutional focus to a new concept: association. The development of the constitutional right of association—and with it, the disappearance of assembly—in many ways depended upon surrounding contexts. I divide these contexts into two eras. The first, which I call the national security era, began in the late 1940s and lasted until the early 1960s. It formed the background for the Court's initial recognition of the right of association in *NAACP v. Alabama*. The second, which I call the equality era, began in the 1960s and included an important reinterpretation of the right of association in *Roberts v. United States Jaycees*.[16]

Political, jurisprudential, and theoretical factors shaped the right of association in each of these eras. In the national security era, the primary

7

political factor was the historical coincidence of the Second Red Scare and the Civil Rights Movement. From the late 1940s to the early 1960s, the government's response to the communist threat pitted national security interests against group autonomy. Segregationists in the South capitalized on these tensions by analogizing the unrest stirred by the NAACP to the threats posed by communist organizations; segregationists even charged that communist influences had infiltrated the NAACP. The Supreme Court responded unevenly, suppressing communist groups in the name of order and stability but extending broad protections to civil rights groups.

The jurisprudential factor shaping the right of association involved disagreement on the Court over the constitutional source of that right. This disagreement was most evident when the Court applied the right to limit state (as opposed to federal) law. Justices Frankfurter and Harlan argued that association constrained state action because like other rights, it could be derived from the "liberty" of the Due Process Clause of the Fourteenth Amendment. Justices Black, Douglas, Brennan, and Warren insisted that association was located in some aspect of the First Amendment and argued that it be given the same "preferred position" as other First Amendment rights. On their view, association applied to the states because the Fourteenth Amendment had incorporated the provisions of the First Amendment. These differences encompassed not only the *source* of the constitutional limits on state action but also the *extent* of those limits. For Black, the rights in the First Amendment were "absolute" and could not be restricted by state action. Frankfurter argued instead for a "balancing" that weighed the interests of the government against the liberty of the Fourteenth Amendment. The result of these two perspectives was that the Court was more likely to uphold a state law restricting expressive freedom if it followed the liberty argument and more likely to strike down the law if it followed the incorporation argument.

The theoretical factor influencing the shaping of association was the pluralism popularized by David Truman and Robert Dahl in the 1950s and 1960s. Earlier pluralists had advanced "the conviction that government must recognize that it is not the sole possessor of sovereignty, and that private groups within the community are entitled to lead their own free lives and exercise within the area of their competence an authority so effective as to justify labeling it a sovereign authority." But mid-twentieth-century pluralism merged these insights with currents from Arthur Bentley's "science of politics" and Louis Hartz's "Lockean consensus." The resulting political theory emphasized the balance and consensus among groups rather than the juxtaposition of groups against the state. These assumptions laid the foundation for the freedom of association in two ways. First, they established a normative presumption that groups were valuable to democracy only to the extent that they reinforced and guaranteed democratic premises and, conversely, that groups antithetical to these premises were neither valuable to democracy nor worthy of its protections. Second, because this normative presumption excluded groups beyond the margins of consensus, pluralists saw the possibility of harmony and balance among those groups that remained.[17]

The Transformation of Association in the Equality Era

The second constitutional period of the right of association is the equality era, which began in the mid-1960s. The equality era introduced its own political, jurisprudential, and theoretical factors to the right of association. The primary political factor involved ongoing efforts to attain meaningful civil rights for African Americans. As the Civil Rights Movement gained traction, the focus of activists shifted from protecting their own associational freedom (as represented in cases like *NAACP v. Alabama*) to challenging segregationists' right to exclude African Americans from group membership. Questions over the limits of this right to exclude became increasingly complex when civil rights litigation moved from public accommodations to private groups.

The jurisprudential factor in the equality era involved the right to privacy. Although privacy and association had been linked in some of the Court's earliest cases on the freedom of association, new connections emerged when the Court first recognized a constitutional right to privacy in its 1965 decision *Griswold v. Connecticut*. Because privacy, like association, appeared nowhere in the text of the Constitution, the Court's earlier recognition of the right of association in *NAACP v. Alabama* became an important example of the kind of "penumbral" reasoning underlying

Griswold. But there was a definitional problem with the Court's understanding of associational privacy. In contrast to the view of privacy as the guarantor of *individual* autonomy that *Griswold* came to represent, privacy in the early right of association cases had more to do with protecting the boundaries of *group* autonomy.[18]

The theoretical factor in the equality era was the rise of Rawlsian liberalism. Rawlsian questions about the relationship between liberty and equality and the meaning of justice dominated scholarly discussions about associational freedom. Rawlsian premises also permeated the work of legal scholars like Kenneth Karst and Ronald Dworkin. Dworkin's recognition of "rights as trumps" revealed that Rawlsian-inspired thought shared concerns about majoritarianism voiced by earlier theorists like Madison and Tocqueville. But unlike Madison's factions and Tocqueville's associations, the ostensibly neutral procedural devices of Rawls's "public reason" and Dworkin's "law as integrity" didn't merely counter majoritarian influence—they constrained the autonomy of groups that failed to comport with liberal values.[19]

The influence of Rawlsian liberalism and the two lines of cases that emerged over the right to exclude and the right to privacy coalesced in *Roberts v. United States Jaycees*. Justice Brennan's opinion for the Court identified two separate constitutional sources for the right of association in earlier cases. One line of decisions protected "intimate association" as "a fundamental element of personal liberty." Another set of decisions guarded "expressive association," which was "a right to associate for the purpose of engaging in those activities protected by the First Amendment—speech, assembly, petition for the redress of grievances, and the exercise of religion." Sixteen years later, the Court reaffirmed this fundamental distinction in *Boy Scouts of America v. Dale*.[20]

A Theory of Assembly

This book suggests that the loss of assembly and the uncritical embrace of the constitutional right of association have weakened group autonomy by suppressing dissent, depoliticizing action, and constraining expression. These changes are related to each other: they are all methods of control. They deny that "the activity of rendering the world a meaningful place by generating narratives and norms requires space for groups of people gathered apart from the state and bound to come into conflict with it." In other words, they open the door for the state to impose meaning, purpose, and value on groups and their activities.[21]

The thin protections of the right of association are underwritten by a political theory of *consensus liberalism*, which purports to be "procedural" or "neutral" but whose espoused tolerance extends only to groups that endorse the fundamental assumptions of liberal democratic theory. Consensus liberalism paves the way for the state to demand what Nancy Rosenblum has called a "logic of congruence" requiring "that the internal life and organization of associations mirror liberal democratic principles and practices." It leaves us without all-male fraternities, all-male Jaycees, and all-Christian student groups. Taken seriously, it also leaves us without all-female sororities, all-female health clubs, and all-gay social clubs. In other words, it leaves us without a meaningful pluralism.[22]

Consensus liberalism is objectionable from at least four distinct strands of political theory: contemporary liberalism, communitarianism, classical liberalism (and its contemporary libertarian successors), and radical democracy. *Contemporary liberalism* (or at least some versions) objects to consensus liberalism's privileging of certain liberal values over others. Since the work of Isaiah Berlin, contemporary liberalism has recognized the necessity of balancing a plurality of values—one value cannot uniformly trump others. More recently, William Galston has argued that "value pluralism" means that "liberalism requires a robust though rebuttable presumption in favor of individuals and groups leading their lives as they see fit, within a broad range of legitimate variation, in accordance with their own understanding of what gives life meaning and value."[23]

Communitarianism, which emerged during the 1980s and 1990s in response to some of the claims of Rawlsian liberalism, objects to the idea that the equality upon which consensus liberalism depends can be given a coherent meaning apart from the practices of a particular community. "Liberal equality" begs the question of "whose equality, which liberalism."[24]

Classical liberalism objects to consensus liberalism's push to eliminate the private sphere. Much of the theoretical work traces back to John Locke's divide between public and private. Locke has become the patron saint of one of the modern heirs to classical liberalism, *libertarianism*. For example, Robert Nozick's *Anarchy, State, and Utopia* employs Lockean arguments against Rawls's theory of justice. Similar libertarian arguments have also been raised in the specific context of the boundaries of group autonomy.[25]

An absolute libertarianism is implausible today. Employment discrimination, public accommodation, and other laws that emerged out of the civil rights era routinely curtail the autonomy of commercial enterprises, and few people object to these restrictions. For this reason, most recent libertarian arguments defend the autonomy of "noncommercial" groups rather than private groups more generally. Andrew Koppelman has called these arguments *neolibertarian*. According to Koppelman, neolibertarian arguments are "only slightly modified versions of old, discredited libertarian objections."[26]

Koppelman links neolibertarian arguments not only to segregrationist objections to the Civil Rights Act of 1964 but also to rampant racism following the Civil War that led private businesses to refuse to serve African Americans. His objection to the neolibertarian position is politically salient and intellectually rigorous. It ties some arguments for greater group autonomy to a virulent racism that most people—including most of those who fall under Koppelman's neolibertarian label—condemn as reprehensible. But Koppelman's historical and normative argument falls short in one important respect: it leaves unaddressed the competing narrative of the protections our country has long granted to groups that dissent from majoritarian control. Like "the idea of a legal prohibition against discrimination," the legal recognition of the importance of group autonomy "is as old as the United States."[27]

The latter, in fact, long precedes the founding, having taken root in the political practices of William Penn and Roger Williams, who between them founded four of the original thirteen colonies. As Richard Hofstadter has noted:

> Madisonian pluralism owes a great deal to the example of religious toleration and religious liberty that had already been established in eighteenth-century America. The traditions of dissenting Protestantism had made an essential contribution to political pluralism. That fear of arbitrary power

which is so marked in American political expression had been shaped to a large degree by the experience men of dissenting sections had had with persecution. Freedom of religion became for them a central example of freedom in general, and it was hardly accidental that the libertarian writers who meant so much to the colonials so often stemmed from the tradition of religious dissent.[28]

This other history that Koppelman omits points toward yet another political theory that objects to consensus liberalism: radical democracy. My book locates the right of assembly in the political theory of Sheldon Wolin, who both fears the expansion of power in unforeseen and uncontrolled channels and offers a counternarrative to the stories perpetuated by consensus liberals like Dahl and Rawls. Wolin's work illuminates neglected constitutional values and highlights the importance of challenging the ways in which consensus liberalism characterizes groups and their forms of expression.[29]

After laying out a political theory of assembly, I revisit the historical and jurispurdential developments that locate theory in the actual politics of the United States. The call for greater group autonomy through the right of assembly is not without limiting principles. The text of the First Amendment offers one: assemblies must be peaceable. Our constitutional, social, and economic history suggests another: antidiscrimination norms should typically prevail when applied to commercial entities.

Other questions are more difficult to answer. Among the most difficult is whether the right of assembly tolerates racial discrimination by peaceable, noncommercial groups. Our constitutional history supports a plausible argument that "race is just different," that the state's interest in eliminating racial discrimination justifies a nearly total ban on racially segregated private groups. As Justice Stewart wrote in *Jones v. Alfred H. Mayer Co.*, "Congress has the power under the Thirteenth Amendment rationally to determine what are the badges and the incidents of slavery, and the authority to translate that determination into effective legislation. . . . When racial discrimination herds men into ghettos and makes their ability to buy property turn on the color of their skin, then it too is a relic of slavery."[30] We might plausibly treat race differently when considering the boundaries of group autonomy. I would be quick to do so as a matter of personal preference—I can think of no racially discriminatory group to which I attach personal value or worth. But treating race differently in all areas ultimately undercuts a vision of assembly that protects pluralism and dissent against state-enforced orthodoxy. We cannot move from the premise that genuine pluralism matters to an effort to rid ourselves of the groups that we don't like.

The question of racial discrimination, specifically discrimination by whites against African Americans, is one of the most difficult issues confronting any argument for greater group autonomy. As I explain in Chapter 5, my proposal permits some racially discriminatory groups. It is an argument rooted in social change—the belief that today we are a society different from the one we were in 1960 and that we will continue to hold the ground that has been won. I do not mean to suggest that we have solved the problem of race. I do argue that in this, as in many other areas of the law, we recognize that the structural politics today are different from what they were fifty years ago.[31]

On the other hand, the right of assembly will not always trump competing interests. Courts will have to draw lines and balance interests, just as they do with the freedom of speech. As I suggest in Chapter 5, the protections for assembly ought to be constrained when a private group wields so much power in a given situation that it prevents other groups from meaningfully pursuing their own visions of pluralism and dissent— as private groups did in the American South from the decades following the Civil War to the end of the civil rights era.[32]

Toward a Contextual Analysis

In light of the constraints described above and the social and constitutional history of the right of assembly, I propose the following definition:

The right of assembly is a presumptive right of individuals to form and participate in peaceable, noncommercial groups. This right is rebuttable when there is a compelling reason for thinking that the justifications for protecting assembly do not apply (as when the group prospers under monopolistic or near-monopolistic conditions).

This proposal differs from two competing alternatives. The first is the neolibertarian proposal. I reject this approach because it fails to account for the way in which the dynamics of power operate in some noncommercial groups. The second is what Koppelman calls the message-based approach, the Court's current framework for analyzing claims of the right of association. I critique the theory, doctrine, and history of the message-based approach throughout this book, but in Chapter 5, I pay particular attention to Koppelman's arguments. Koppelman believes that a requirement that a group self-identify as "stridently prejudiced" is "desirable," because "discrimination is not so cheap as it was before, and a group will have to decide whether discrimination is worth the added cost." I explain why this approach is misguided as a matter of First Amendment doctrine, workability, and efficiency.[33]

In my view, we are better off with a contextual analysis that allows courts to examine how power operates on the ground. This approach would ask courts to evaluate challenges to the exercise of the right of assembly in the specific contexts in which those assemblies exist. Sometimes—albeit rarely—the power exerted by peaceable, noncommercial assemblies will overreach to such an extent that the right will give way to the interests of the state. Let me offer a few other examples of the kind of contextual analysis that I have in mind. In the 1950s, African American voters in Fort Bend County, Texas, challenged their exclusion from the Jaybird Democratic Association—a private group not governed by state election laws. The Jaybird Association held an election among its members every year prior to the Democratic primary. For more than sixty years, the candidate selected by the Jaybirds went on to win the Democratic primary and the general election. Most people would recognize that the Jaybirds would qualify under my definition as a peaceable, noncommercial assembly. Most people would also recognize that the Jaybirds had so skewed the balance of power in Fort Bend County that they deserved to be denied the protections of assembly.[34]

Or take a more contemporary example. Suppose that membership in the Christian Legal Society at Hastings College of the Law was a prerequisite to the most desirable legal jobs—a feather in the cap surpassing even membership on the *Hastings Law Journal*. If that were the case, the Christian Legal Society may well lose the protections of assembly. Of course, membership in the Christian Legal Society at Hastings College of the Law did not provide these kinds of advantages. A closer case may have existed with the Minneapolis and St. Paul Jaycees when the Court decided *Roberts v. United States Jaycees* in 1984. The problem is that we simply don't know. The opinions in *Roberts* lack any contextual analysis. Nothing in Justice Brennan's majority opinion or Justice O'Connor's concurrence tells us anything about how the Jaycees in Minneapolis and St. Paul had overreached their private power to the detriment of women or why compelling the Jaycees to accept women as full members rather than as associate members would have remedied that power disparity. The justices simply assumed that the state's interest in eradicating gender discrimination warranted trumping the autonomy of the Jaycees. Nobody offered any explanation of why *this* remedy helped to eradicate gender discrimination in *these* circumstances sufficient to trump the autonomy of *this* group.

Having mentioned these examples, let me be quick to note that I find aspects of my own proposed drawing of lines incomplete and imprecise. For example, I am unsure how a theory of assembly would address highly regulated groups like political parties, labor unions, and professional associations. As Steven Calabresi notes, these kinds of groups present a particular challenge to questions of group autonomy: "Some so-called mediating institutions may truly mediate between the private individual and the state. Synagogues, churches, temples, families, and voluntary community and civic associations and groups often fall readily into this category. Other groups, however, such as political parties, labor unions, bar associations, and other modern-day corporate 'guilds' may not. It may often be the case that these kinds of groups do not so much 'mediate' *between* the individual and the state, as that they try actually *to enlist the state* on their side of some otherwise-private competitive struggle." On the other hand, some highly regulated groups embody the very values and purposes that I defend throughout this book. In fact, in recent decades, the Court appears to have developed a distinct right of "political association" applicable to political parties.[35]

It may be that the principles of assembly that I have sketched here are capacious enough to encompass some highly regulated groups. It may be that the "highly regulated" distinction is itself problematic—after all, the state could simply start to regulate more groups more extensively. More pointedly, this kind of ambiguity is inherent in all line-drawing and to some extent plagues the distinction that I have proposed between commercial and noncommercial groups. As James Boyle has argued with respect to the related divide between public and private, the process of marking these boundaries "is one of contentious moral and political decision making about the distribution of wealth, power, and information" and "the supposedly settled landscape is in fact an ever-changing scene."[36]

I believe that the contextual analysis that I recommend—which accounts for some of the realities of the changing dynamics of power— addresses some of these concerns. But I hope that critics who disagree with my reasoning on this point will nonetheless take seriously the critiques in the rest of the book and either sharpen my proposed alternative or strengthen the explanations for the neolibertarian and message-based proposals. We need to find a better way forward in this area of the law. The aspiration of this book is to get us thinking in that direction, not to insist that I have arrived at the best possible solution.

My inquiry into a theory of assembly ends with an illustration: the "missing dissent" in *Roberts v. United States Jaycees*. One reason for engaging in this exercise is to demonstrate the plausible fit of assembly in American constitutionalism. Our constitutional rights unfold within a discourse shaped by judicial decisions, most especially those decisions of the United States Supreme Court. This doesn't mean that the Court's opinions do or should assume an infallible place in our constitutionalism. But they do have *a* place, and arguments from history and political theory must at some point intersect and engage with law to make "connections to possible and plausible states of affairs" and to "integrate not only the 'is' and the 'ought,' but the 'is,' the 'ought,' and the 'what might be.'"[37]

On Method (and Substance)

This book confronts contentious issues of political theory and constitutional interpretation. The latter in particular exposes me to a number of methodological critiques. Do I reject or embrace an originalist argument? Am I consistent with a textualist approach? Am I more or less faithful to the kind of interpretive "dynamism" that supports contemporary social values? Even after this brief introduction, it should be apparent that my method of constitutional interpretation does not fit neatly within any one of these perspectives. It aligns most closely with the eclectic vision set forth in Philip Bobbitt's *Constitutional Fate* but draws as well from the kind of tradition-based arguments employed by Alasdair MacIntyre.[38] Although I will return briefly to Bobbitt's modalities in Chapter 5, I will have little else to say explicitly about methods of constitutional interpretation. The lack of direct theoretical engagement should not be mistaken for a lack of awareness or concern. This book argues that the current approach to constitutional protections for group autonomy fails historically, theoretically, and doctrinally. The skeptical reader will need to answer each of these arguments, even if he or she remains wedded to a particular interpretive methodology.

Some people will be unpersuaded by a constitutional vision that gives greater protections to dissenting groups, particularly one that limits the reach of antidiscrimination laws. They will push instead for greater congruence and less difference. That is the logic underlying the Court's decision in *Martinez*. It is the fundamental tenet of the Ninth Circuit's decision in *Truth v. Kent* that equates a Christian club's desire to limit its members to Christians to invidious discrimination. Those who endorse decisions like *Martinez* and *Kent* and reject the constitutional vision set forth in this book need to provide a better justification for their normative preferences. They should articulate a convincing constitutional doctrine and ethos that legitimates the jurispathic silencing of "those who would make a *nomos* other than that of the state."[39] This area of the law deserves greater respect—and a more coherent jurisprudential approach—than we have given it thus far.

Our efforts to address these challenges should be guided by an interdisciplinary awareness. The important issues surrounding the boundaries of group autonomy cannot be addressed through a theoretical lens that forgets legal history or a doctrinal legal lens that ignores political context. Resources within history and political theory can help sharpen the ways in which we explore the meaning of constitutionalism. Yet this openness to other resources introduces problems of its own. The greatest challenge to an interdisciplinary conversation is the same one that complicates our ability to render sympathetic readings of groups not our own: the ease and frequency with which we gloss over and caricature unfamiliar ways of knowing and doing. Part of the value of engaging in this kind of interdisciplinary work is the reminder that the meaning and significance of texts and events is not exhausted by a parochial or canonical reading from a specific discipline; so too, the meaning and significance of a group's practices to its expression cannot adequately be captured by the uncharitable or monolithic description of a court, government official, or scholar. *Liberty's Refuge* argues that the best protection against this danger is the forgotten freedom of assembly.

CHAPTER 2

THE RIGHT PEACEABLY TO ASSEMBLE

The following pages trace the story of the freedom of assembly. This is the right of assembly "violently wrested" from slave and free African Americans in the South and denied to abolitionist William Lloyd Garrison in the North. It is the freedom recognized in tributes to the Bill of Rights across the nation as America entered the Second World War— at the very time it was denied to 120,000 Japanese Americans. It is the right placed at the core of democracy by many eminent twentieth-century Americans, including Dorothy Thompson, Zechariah Chafee, Louis Brandeis, John Dewey, Orson Welles, and Eleanor Roosevelt.

After examining the constitutional grounding of assembly in the Bill of Rights, I explore its use in legal and political discourse in six periods of American history: (1) the closing years of the eighteenth century that brought its first test through the Democratic-Republican Societies; (2) assembly in the antebellum era; (3) federal and state understandings of assembly following the Civil War; (4) the claims of assembly by suffragists, civil rights activists, and organized labor during the Progressive Era; (5) the rhetorical high point of assembly between the two world wars; and (6) the end of assembly in the midst of mid-twentieth-century liberalism and the Court's initial recognition of the freedom of association. The diverse contexts through which I trace appeals to and denials of the right of assembly inevitably present a textured understanding of what is meant by "assembly." In some cases, the people claiming assembly focused solely on a particular gathering—something akin to a protest or demonstration. But in many other instances, the right of assembly extended beyond an expressive moment to protect the group that made that expression possible. Similarly, while some claims of assembly came from tradition-ally conceived political groups, others arose from more surprising sources.

As I recount the role of assembly in the political history of the United States, I pay particular attention to three characteristics. First, groups invoking the right of assembly have usually been those that dissent from the majoritarian standards endorsed by government. Second, claims of assembly have insisted on a political mode of existence that is separate from the politics of the state. Finally, practices of assembly have them-selves been forms of expression—parades, strikes, and meetings, but also more creative means of engagement like pageants, religious worship, and the sharing of meals. The diverse groups that have gathered throughout our nation's history embody these three themes of assembly: the dissenting, the political, and the expressive. Theirs is the story of the forgotten freedom of assembly.[1]

The Constitutional Right of Assembly

I begin with the text of the First Amendment, and with a textual obser-vation. While we should not make too much of slight variations in wording, grammar, and punctuation in constitutional clauses (there is little indication that the framers applied our level of exegetical scrutiny to the texts that they considered and created), our current arguments are constrained by the precise text handed down to us because modern constitutional law sometimes parses wording more carefully. And so it is for this reason a useful exercise to consider forensically the text that survived and the text that did not.[2]

The most important aspect of the clause containing the constitutional right of assembly may be three words missing from its final formulation: *the common good*. Had antecedent versions of the assembly clause prevailed in the debates over the Bill of Rights and assembly been limited to purposes serving the common good, the kinds of dissenting and disfavored groups that have sought refuge in its protections may have met with far less success. That understanding of assembly would have foreshadowed the consensus narrative advanced by mid-twentieth-century pluralism: we tolerate groups only to the extent that they serve the public interest and thereby strengthen the stability and vitality of the nation. The framers decided otherwise.

When the First Congress convened in 1789 to draft amendments to the Constitution, it took under consideration proposals submitted by the several states. Virginia and North Carolina offered identical amendments covering the rights of assembly and petition: "That the people have a right peaceably to assemble together to consult for the common good, or to instruct their representatives; and that every freeman has a right to petition or apply to the legislature for redress of grievances." New York and Rhode Island offered slightly different wording, emphasizing that the people assembled for "their" common good rather than "the" common good: "That the People have a right peaceably to assemble together to consult for their common good, or to instruct their Representatives; and that every person has a right to Petition or apply to the Legislature for redress of Grievances." On June 8, 1789, James Madison's proposal to the House favored the possessive pronoun over the definite article: "The people shall not be restrained from peaceably assembling and consulting for their common good; nor from applying to the legislature by petitions, or remonstrances for redress of their grievances." Whether intentional or not, the recognition of the common good of the people who assemble rather than the common good of the state signaled that the interests of the people assembled need not align with the interests of those in power.[3]

The point was not lost during the House debates. When Thomas Hartley of Pennsylvania contended that, with respect to assembly, "every thing that was not incompatible with the general good ought to be granted," Elbridge Gerry of Massachusetts replied that if Hartley "supposed that the people had a right to consult for the common good" but "could not consult unless they met for that purpose," he was in fact "contend[ing] for nothing." In other words, if the right of assembly encompassed only the common good as defined by the state, then assembly as a means of protest or dissent would be eviscerated.[4]

On August 24, 1789, the House approved a version of the amendment that retained the reference to "their common good" and also incorporated the rights of speech and the press: "The freedom of speech, and of the press, and the right of the people peaceably to assemble and consult for their common good, and to apply to the government for redress of grievances shall not be infringed." Eleven days later, the Senate defeated a motion to strike the reference to the common good. But the following week, the text was inexplicably dropped when the Senate merged language pertaining to religion into the draft amendment.[5]

Striking the reference to the common good may have been intended to broaden the scope of the assembly clause, but it also introduced a textual ambiguity. Without the prepositional "for their common good" following the mention of assembly, the text now described "the right of the people peaceably to assemble, and to petition the government for a redress of grievances." This left unclear whether the amendment recognized a single right to assemble for the purpose of petitioning the government or whether it established both an unencumbered right of assembly and a separate right of petition. In one of the only recent considerations of assembly in the First Amendment, Jason Mazzone argues in favor of the former: "There are two clues that we should understand assembly and petition to belong together. The first clue is the use of 'and to petition,' which contrasts with the use of 'or' in the remainder of the First Amendment's language. The second clue is the use of 'right,' in the singular (as in 'the right of the people peaceably to assemble, and to petition'), rather than the plural 'rights' (as in 'the rights of the people peaceably to assemble, and to petition'). The prohibitions on Congress' power can therefore be understood as prohibitions with respect to speech, press, and assembly in order to petition the government."[6]

Mazzone's interpretation is problematic because the comma preceding the phrase "and to petition" is residual from the earlier text that had described the "right of the people peaceably to assemble and consult for their common good, and to petition the government for a redress of grievances." Whether left in deliberately or inadvertently, the comma relates back to a distinction between a right to peaceable assembly and a right to petition.[7] Moreover, at least some members of the First Congress conceived of a broader notion of assembly, as evidenced by an exchange between Theodore Sedgwick of Massachusetts and John Page of Virginia during the House debates over the language of the Bill of Rights. Sedgwick criticized the proposed right of assembly as redundant in light of the freedom of speech: "If people freely converse together, they must assemble for that purpose; it is a self-evident, unalienable right which the people possess; it is certainly a thing that never would be called in question; it is derogatory to the dignity of the House to descend to such minutiae." Page responded: "[Sedgwick] supposes [the right of assembly] no more essential than whether a man has a right to wear his hat or not, but let me observe to him that such rights have been opposed, and a man has been obliged to pull off his hat when he appeared before the face of authority; people have also been prevented from assembling together on their lawful occasions, therefore it is well to guard against such stretches of authority, by inserting the privilege in the declaration of rights; if the people could be deprived of the power of assembling under any pretext whatsoever, they might be deprived of every other privilege contained in the clause." Irving Brant notes that while Page's allusion to a man without a hat is lost on a contemporary audience, "the mere reference to it was equivalent to half an hour of oratory" before the First Congress. Page was referring to the trial of William Penn.[8]

On August 14, 1670, Penn and other Quakers had attempted to gather for worship at their meeting-house on Gracechurch Street in London, in violation of the 1664 Conventicle Act that forbade "any Nonconformists attending a religious meeting, or assembling themselves together to the number of more than five persons in addition to members of the family, for any religious purpose not according to the rules of the Church of England." Prevented from entering by a company of soldiers, Penn began delivering a sermon to the Quakers assembled in the street. Penn and a fellow Quaker, William Mead, were arrested and brought to trial in a dramatic sequence of events that included a contempt of court charge because they wore hats in the courtroom. A jury acquitted the two men on the charge that their public worship constituted an unlawful assembly. The case gained renown throughout England and the American colonies. Brant reports that "every Quaker in America knew of the ordeal suffered by the founder of Pennsylvania and its bearing on freedom of religion, of speech, and the right of assembly" and "every American lawyer with a practice in the appellate courts was familiar with it, either directly or through its connection with its still more famous aftermath." According to Brant:

> William Penn loomed large in American history, but even if he had never crossed the Atlantic, bringing the Quaker religion with him, Americans would have known about his "tumultuous assembly" *and his hat.* Few pamphlets of the seventeenth century had more avid readers than the one entitled "The People's Ancient and Just Liberties, asserted, in the Trial of William Penn and William Mead at the Old Bailey, 22 Charles II 1670, written by themselves." Congressman Page had known the story from boyhood, reproduced in Emlyn's *State Trials* to which his father subscribed in 1730. It was available, both in the *State Trials* and as a pamphlet, to the numerous congressmen who had used the facilities of the City Library of Philadelphia. Madison had an account of it written by Sir John Hawles, a libertarian lawyer who became Solicitor General after the overthrow of the Stuarts in 1688.[9]

Congressman Page's allusion to Penn made clear that the right of assembly under discussion in the House encompassed more than meeting to petition for a redress of grievances: Penn's gathering had nothing to do with petition; it was an act of religious worship. After Page spoke, the House defeated Sedgwick's motion to strike assembly from the draft amendment by a "considerable majority." On September 24, 1789, the Senate approved the amendment in its final form, and the subsequent ratification of the Bill of Rights in 1791 enacted "the right of the people peaceably to assemble."[10]

The text handed down to us thus conveys a broad notion of assembly in two ways. First, it does not limit the purposes of assembly to the common good, thereby implicitly allowing assembly for purposes that might be antithetical to that good (although constraining assembly to peaceable means). Second, it does not limit assembly to the purposes of petitioning the government. As we will see in this and later chapters, both of these interpretations have at times been neglected in legal and political discourse. But the dissenting, political, and expressive assembly is consistently displayed in the practices of the people who have gathered throughout American history. It is to these practices that I now turn.

The First Test of Assembly: The Democratic-Republican Societies

The freedom of assembly faced an early challenge when the first sustained political dissent in the new republic emerged out of the increasingly partisan divide between Federalists and Republicans. By the summer of 1792, Republican concern over the Federalist administration and its perceived support of the British in their conflict with the French had reached new levels of agitation. The Republican-leaning *National Gazette* began calling for the creation of voluntary "constitutional" and "political" societies to critique the Washington administration.[11]

The first of these societies was organized in Philadelphia in March of 1793. Over the next three years, dozens more emerged in most of the major cities in the United States. The Democratic-Republican Societies consisted largely of farmers and laborers wary of the aristocratic leanings of Hamilton and other Federalists, but they also included lawyers, doctors, publishers, and government employees. The largest society—the Democratic Society of Pennsylvania—boasted more than three hundred members.[12]

The societies "invariably claimed the right of citizens to assemble." A 1794 resolution from a society in Washington, North Carolina, asserted: "It is the unalienable right of a free and independent people to assemble together in a peaceable manner to discuss with firmness and freedom all subjects of public concern." That same year, the Boston *Independent Chronicle* declared: "Under a Constitution which expressly provides '*That the people have a right in an orderly and peaceable manner to assemble and consult upon the common good*,' there can be no necessity for an apology to the public for an Association of a number of citizens to promote and cherish the social virtues, the love of their country, and a respect for its Laws and Constitutions." The Democratic Society of Pinckneyville similarly insisted: "One of our essential rights, we consider that of assembling, at all times, to discuss, with freedom, friendship and temper, all subjects of public concern."[13]

The societies usually met monthly, and more frequently during elections or times of political crisis. Philip Foner reports that a large part of their activities consisted of "creating public discussions; composing, adopting, and issuing circulars, memorials, resolutions, and addresses to the people; and remonstrances to the President and the Congress—all expressing the feelings of the assembled groups on current political issues." In Robert Chesney's characterization, the societies "embodied an understanding of popular sovereignty and representation in which the role of the citizen was not limited to periodic voting, but instead entailed active and constant engagement in political life." But the societies that represented some of the earliest lived expressions of dissenting groups also recognized that their assembly—their existence—extended far beyond simple meetings or political discussion. They joined in the "extraordinarily diverse array of . . . feasts, festivals, and parades" that unfolded in the streets and public places of American cities. As Simon Newman's study of popular celebrations observes more generally, gatherings of this era were self-consciously political expressions: "Festive culture required both participants and an audience, and by printing and reprinting accounts of July Fourth celebrations and the like newspapers contributed to a greatly enlarged sense of audience: by the end of the 1790s those who participated in these events knew that their actions were quite likely going to be read about and interpreted by citizens far beyond the confines of their own community."[14]

Celebrations of the French Revolution assumed an especially partisan character when members and supporters of the Federalist party refused to participate in them. Without the endorsement of the Federalist government, Republicans "were forced to foster alternative ways of validating celebrations that were often explicitly oppositional." In doing so, they characterized their tributes as representing the unified views of the entire community rather than political elites. Newman writes: "The result of the Democratic Republican stratagem was that members of subordinate groups—including women, the poor, and black Americans, all of whom were excluded from or had strictly circumscribed roles in the white male contests over July Fourth and Washington's birthday celebrations—found a larger role for themselves in French Revolutionary celebrations than in any of the other rites and festivals of the early American republic." The relatively egalitarian gestures of these celebrations were not well received by Federalists, who berated the women who participated in them with sarcasm and derision and raised fears about black participation in public events.[15]

Federalists became increasingly agitated with the growing popular appeal of the societies. The pages of the pro-Federalist *Gazette of the United States* repeatedly warned that they were fostering disruptive tendencies and instigating rebellion. The Federalist press also highlighted that several members of societies in western Pennsylvania had been actively involved in the Whiskey Rebellion. President Washington had been incensed by organized opposition to the whiskey tax, writing in a personal letter that while "no one denies the right of the people to meet occasionally, to petition for, or to remonstrate against, any Act of the Legislature," nothing could be "more absurd, more arrogant, or more pernicious to the peace of Society, than for . . . a self-created *permanent* body" that would pass judgment on such acts. He came to believe that the widespread public condemnation of the Whiskey Rebellion had created a political opportunity for the "annihilation" of the societies. Washington took aim at them in his annual address to Congress on November 19, 1794, asserting that "associations of men" and "certain self-created societies" had fostered the violent rebellion. Chesney suggests that "the speech was widely understood at the time not as ordinary political criticism, but instead as a denial of the legality of organized and sustained political dissent." And Irving Brant observes that "the damning epithet 'self-created' indorsed the current notion that ordinary people had no right to come together for political purposes."[16]

Following Washington's address, the Federalist-controlled Senate quickly censured the societies. The House, in contrast, entered an extended debate about the wording of its response, and assigned James Madison, Theodore Sedgwick, and Thomas Scott to draft a reply. The Federalist Sedgwick, who years earlier had suggested that the freedom of assembly was so "self-evident" and "unalienable" that its inclusion in the constitutional amendments was unnecessary, now argued in spite of the First Amendment that the societies' efforts to organize were effectively illegal. But after four days of debate, Madison maintained that a House censure would be a "severe punishment" and have dire consequences for the future of free expression. The final language in the House response was substantially more muted than that issued by the Senate.[17]

After Washington's address and the congressional responses, "spirited debates concerning the legitimacy of the societies were conducted in every community where a society existed." Responding to Washington's charge that the societies were "self-created," the Democratic Society of New York asked: "Is it for assembling, that we are accused; what law forbids it?" The Patriotic Society of the County of New Castle noted more tersely: "The right of the people to assemble and consult for their common good, has been questioned by some; to such we disdain any reply."[18]

Due in part to Washington's wide popularity, public opinion turned the corner against the societies. Many of them folded within a year of the president's speech, and by the end of the decade, all had been driven out of existence. But despite their short tenure, the societies' influence was not inconsequential. According to Foner, "as a center of Republican agitation and propaganda . . . the societies did much to forge the sword that defeated Federalism and put Jefferson in the presidency." They also resisted majoritarian conceptions of the common good, practiced a different form of politics in their planned and spontaneous gatherings, and expressed their message through their composition as well as their words—*who* these societies included signaled much about *what* they represented as a group.[19]

Assembly in the Antebellum Era

In spite of the fate of the Democratic-Republican Societies, the idea that the people could assemble apart from the state continued to take hold in early America. Benjamin Oliver's 1832 treatise *The Rights of an American Citizen* called the right of assembly "one of the strongest safeguards, against any usurpation or tyrannical abuse of power, so long as the people collectively have sufficient discernment to perceive what is best for the public interest, and individually have independence enough, to express an opinion in opposition to a popular but designing leader."[20] Writing in 1838, the state theorist Francis Lieber described "those many extra-constitutional, not unconstitutional, meetings, in which the citizens either unite their scattered means for the obtaining of some common end, social in general, or political in particular; or express their opinion in definite resolutions upon some important point before the people." These "public meetings" were undertaken for a variety of purposes:

They are of great importance in order to direct public attention to subjects of magnitude, to test the opinion of the community, to inform persons at a distance, for instance, representatives, or the administration, of the state of public opinion respecting certain measures, whether yet depending or adopted; to resolve upon and adopt petitions, to encourage individuals or bodies of men in arduous undertakings, requiring the moral support of well-expressed public approbation; to effect a contract and connexion with others, striving for the same ends; to disseminate knowledge by way of reports of committees; to form societies for charitable purposes or the melioration of laws or institutions; to sanction by the spontaneous expression of the opinion of the community measures not strictly agreeing with the letter of the law, but enforced by necessity; to call upon the services of individuals who otherwise would not feel warranted to appear before the public and invite its attention, or feel authorized to interfere with a subject not strictly lying within their proper sphere of action; to concert upon more or less extensive measures of public utility, and whatever else their object may be.[21]

The antebellum era also produced several state court decisions upholding the right of religious groups to exclude unwanted members. Although not specifically invoking the right of assembly, these cases recognized that a group's control of its membership mattered to its autonomy—a principle that remains crucial today. In the 1832 case of *Leavitt v. Truair*, the Supreme Judicial Court of Massachusetts noted that pursuant to the state's religious freedom act: "To form an original society several persons must agree to unite; the society then exists to some purposes, and may be called together and organized under the statute. Under a warrant of a justice of the peace, calling a meeting of such society, all those persons who had thus agreed and associated, would have a right to assemble and act, *and no others*."[22] Six years later, the court revisited the autonomy of religious societies in *First Parish in Sudbury v. Stearns* and stressed that while "no person can be made or become a member of any such corporation, without his consent," it was equally true that "no person can thrust himself into any such body against its will."[23]

Citizens in southern states recognized the significance of assembly and routinely sought to prohibit its exercise among slaves and free blacks. Throughout the antebellum era, white citizens petitioned state legislatures to intensify restrictions on assembly against African Americans. In 1818, citizens in North Carolina petitioned for restrictions against "the Numerous quantity of Negroes which generally assemble," and forty years later sought "to relieve the people of the State from the evils arising from numbers of free negroes in our midst." In South Carolina, citizens petitioned in 1820 to ban churches established "for the exclusive worship of negroes and coloured people." And in Mississippi, citizens distraught over "crowds of negroes, drinking, fiddling, dancing, singing, cursing, swearing, whooping, and yelling, to the great annoyance and scandal of all respectable and order loving persons," sought in 1852 to restrict "any noisy or clamorous assembly of negroes." Similar petitions unfolded in Virginia and Delaware.[24]

Southern legislatures embraced these restrictions. A 1792 Georgia law restricted slaves from assembling "on pretense of feasting." In South Carolina, an 1800 law forbade "slaves, free negroes, mulattoes, and mestizoes" from assembling for "mental instruction or religious worship." An 1804 Virginia statute made any meeting of slaves at night an unlawful assembly. In 1831, the Virginia legislature declared "all meetings of free Negroes or mulattoes at any school house, church, meeting house or other place for teaching them reading or writing, either in the day or the night," to be an unlawful assembly.[25]

The restrictions on assembly intensified following Nat Turner's 1831 rebellion in Southampton County, Virginia. Turner's insurrection sent Virginia and other southern states into a panic. Virginia governor John Floyd made the rebellion the central theme of his December 5, 1831, address to the legislature. Floyd believed that black preachers were behind a broader conspiracy for insurrection and had acquired "great ascendancy over the minds of their fellows." He argued that these preachers had to be silenced "because, full of ignorance, they were incapable of inculcating anything but notions of the wildest superstition, thus preparing fit instruments in the hands of crafty agitators, to destroy the public tranquility." In response, the legislature strengthened Virginia's black code by imposing additional restrictions on assembly for religious worship.[26]

Concern over Turner's rebellion also spawned additional restrictions on the assembly of slaves and free blacks in Maryland, Tennessee, Georgia,

North Carolina, and Alabama. By 1835, "most southern states had outlawed the right of assembly and organization by free blacks, prohibited them from holding church services without a white clergyman present, required their adherence to slave curfews, and minimized their contact with slaves." The following year, Theodore Dwight Weld aptly referred to the oppressive restrictions on blacks as "'the right of peaceably assembling' violently wrested."[27]

The extent of restrictions on the assembly of African Americans is evident in an 1860 opinion of the Louisiana Supreme Court, *African Methodist Episcopal Church v. City of New Orleans*. In 1848, a group of ten free blacks had established the African Methodist Episcopal Church as "a private corporation having a religious object," pursuant to the state's statute governing the organization of corporations. Two years later, the Louisiana legislature amended the relevant statute to provide that "in no case shall the provisions of this Act be construed to apply to free persons of color in this State, incorporated for religious purposes or secret associations, and any corporations that may have been organized by such persons under this Act for religious purposes, or secret associations, are hereby annulled and revoked." New Orleans then passed an ordinance that outlawed "assemblages of colored persons, free and slave" "for purposes of worship . . . unless such congregation be under the supervision and control of some recognized white congregation or church." In rejecting the claims of church members against the city, the Louisiana Supreme Court opined that "the African race are strangers to our Constitution."[28]

The importance of assembly to religious worship and the felt impact of its loss is captured in the words of James Smith, a Methodist minister whose 1881 narrative detailed his experiences as a slave in Virginia: "The way in which we worshiped is almost indescribable. The singing was accompanied by a certain ecstasy of motion, clapping of hands, tossing of heads, which would continue without cessation about half an hour; one would lead off in a kind of recitative style, others joining in the chorus. The old house partook of the ecstasy; it rang with their jubilant shouts, and shook in all its joints. . . . When Nat Turner's insurrection broke out, the colored people were forbidden to hold meetings among themselves." The restrictions on assembly did not simply silence political dissent in a narrow sense. They assaulted an entire way of life: suppressing worship, stifling education, and blocking community among slave and free African Americans. Conversely, the persistent pleas for a meaningful right of assembly by slave and free blacks claimed far more than a right to hold a meeting—they demanded a right to gather and exist in groups.[29]

While southern states increased their efforts to deny the freedom of assembly for African Americans, abolitionists in the North expanded their reliance on the right. And because many abolitionists were women, freedom of assembly was "indelibly linked with the woman's rights movement from its genesis in the abolition movement." Female abolitionists and suffragists organized their efforts around a particular form of assembly: the convention. The turn to the convention was not accidental. Between 1830 and 1860, official conventions accompanied revisions to constitutions in almost every state. The focus of these official conventions on rights and freedoms provided a natural springboard for "spontaneous conventions" to criticize the blatant racial and gender inequalities perpetuated by the state constitutions.[30]

Women held antislavery conventions in New York in 1837 and in Philadelphia in 1838 and 1839. Two years after the famous 1848 convention in Seneca Falls, New York, and less than a month before the official convention to revise the Ohio constitution, a group of women gathered in Salem, Ohio, to call for equal rights for all people "without distinction of sex or color." These early suffragist assemblies were in one sense narrowly "political," focusing on questions of rights and equality. But they also demonstrated the expressive significance of the group itself, quite apart from the spoken expression of its members. It mattered that these assemblies consisted of *women*. As Nancy Isenberg describes, "The Salem forum stood apart from the American political tradition. Activists used the meeting to critique politics as usual. Women occupied the floor and debated resolutions and gave speeches, while the men sat quietly in the gallery. Through a poignant reversal of gender roles, the women engaged in constitutional deliberation, and the men were relegated to the sidelines of political action." The very form of the convention conveyed the suffragist message of equality and disruption of the existing order.[31]

Women's conventions often met with harsh resistance. When Angelina and Sarah Grimké toured New England on a campaign for the American Anti Slavery Society in 1837, they were rebuked for lecturing before "promiscuous audiences." The following year, Philadelphia newspapers helped inspire a riotous disruption of the Convention of American Women Against Slavery that ended in the burning of Pennsylvania Hall. The participants of the 1850 Salem convention were denied the use of the local school and church. An 1853 women's rights convention at the Broadway Tabernacle in New York degenerated into a shouting match when hecklers interrupted the speakers. Rather than criticize the disruptive crowd, the *New York Herald* sardonically characterized the gathering as the "Women's Wrong Convention" and quipped that "the assemblage of rampant women which convened at the Tabernacle yesterday was an interesting phase in the comic history of the nineteenth century." The following year, the *Sunday Times* published an editorial describing the national women's rights convention in Philadelphia with racial and sexual slurs.[32] Isenberg intimates that proponents of these attacks believed that "women's unchecked freedom of assembly mocked all the restraints of civilized society."[33]

A striking example of the importance of free assembly to politically unpopular causes in the antebellum era occurred in 1835, when the Boston Female Anti-Slavery Society invited William Lloyd Garrison and the British abolitionist George Thompson to speak at its annual meeting. After the society had announced that the meeting would take place at the offices of Garrison's *Liberator*, antiabolitionists circulated a handbill, duly printed in the *Boston Commercial Gazette*: "That infamous foreign scoundrel THOMPSON, will hold forth *this afternoon*, at the Liberator Office, No. 46 Washington street. The present is a fair opportunity for the friends of the Union to *snake Thompson out*! It will be a contest between the abolitionists and the friends of the Union. A purse of $100 has been raised by a number of patriotic citizens to reward the individual who shall first lay violent hands on Thompson, so that he may be brought to the tar kettle before dark. Friends of the Union, be vigilant!" When the society proceeded with its meeting in spite of the threat, a large crowd gathered and soon turned riotous. Unable to locate Thompson, some of them called for Garrison's lynching. Garrison fled through a back entrance and barely escaped with his life. Reflecting on the harrowing experience in the November 7, 1835, edition of the *Liberator*, Garrison lambasted the instigators of the riot in an editorial entitled "Triumph of Mobocracy in Boston": "Yes, to accommodate their selfishness, they declared that the liberty of speech, and the right to assemble in an associated capacity peaceably together, should be unlawfully and forcibly taken away from an estimable portion of the community, by the officers of our city—the humble servants of the people! Benedict Arnold's treachery to the cause of liberty and his bleeding country was no worse than this."[34]

The Boston violence "became a cause célèbre among abolitionists who defended their right to free speech and assembly." But fifteen years later, when Thompson returned to Boston to address the Massachusetts Anti-Slavery Society in Faneuil Hall, he was again driven away by a mob. Frederick Douglass referred to this later incident as the "mobocratic violence" that had "disgraced the city of Boston." In an 1850 address delivered in Rochester, New York, Douglass decried "these violent demonstrations, these outrageous invasions of human rights" and argued that "it is a significant fact, that while meetings for almost any purpose under heaven may be held unmolested in the city of Boston, that in the same city, a meeting cannot be peaceably held for the purpose of preaching the doctrine of the American Declaration of Independence, 'that all men are created equal.'"[35]

Assembly at the Close of the Nineteenth Century

The right of assembly figured prominently in political rhetoric during the 1866 congressional campaign, which Michael Kent Curtis has called "a referendum on the plan of reconstruction embodied in the Fourteenth Amendment." According to Curtis, "The insistence on protecting constitutional rights to free speech, press, religion, and assembly throughout the nation was a recurring theme in the 1866 campaign. It was clearly expressed in the convention of Southern loyalists who assembled in Philadelphia in 1866. The convention was attended by a number of influential Republicans from the North, and its activities were reported in detail by the Republican press." When the call for the Philadelphia convention had been issued in July 1866, its organizers included an

"Appeal of the Loyal Men of the South to their Fellow Citizens," which was "widely reprinted in the Republican press." The appeal argued for the protection of First Amendment rights, contending that in the years since the founding, "statute books groaned under despotic laws against unlawful and insurrectionary assemblies aimed at the constitutional guarantees of the right to peaceably assemble and petition for redress of grievances."[36]

At the very time the Southern loyalists organized their Philadelphia convention, a different convention met with tragic results. After Republicans in Louisiana called a constitutional convention in New Orleans for the purpose of giving blacks the right to vote, Democrats convened a grand jury that indicted every member of the convention. But the commanding general of the federal troops in New Orleans refused to allow the arrests, writing to the mayor of the city that "if these persons assemble, as you say is intended, it will be, I presume, in virtue of the universally-conceded right of all loyal citizens of the United States to meet peaceably, and discuss freely questions concerning their civil governments." When the convention met on July 30, 1866, "the police and white Louisianans, in a paroxysm of hatred and fear, mobbed the delegates. Ignoring white handkerchiefs that [delegates] ran up the flagpole and waved from the windows . . ., the mob fired into the building, shot loyalists as they emerged, and pursued them through the streets, clubbing, beating, and shooting all they caught. Forty of the delegates and their supporters were killed, another one hundred and thirty-six wounded."[37]

The Louisiana massacre confirmed that the right of peaceable assembly remained vulnerable to violent suppression. A similar violence soon emerged elsewhere in the South, where widespread lawlessness and instability stifled political assemblies and empowered anarchic ones. The Ku Klux Klan formed in late 1865 in Pulaski, Tennessee, and within five years "most white men in [the southeastern United States] either belonged to the organization or sympathized with it." Charles Lane has chronicled the violence that immediately characterized Klan activities:

> In 1868, the Klan assassinated a Negro Republican congressman in
> Arkansas and three black Republican members of the South Carolina

legislature—and in Camilla, Georgia, four hundred Klansmen, led by the sheriff, fired on a black election parade and hunted the countryside for those who fled, eventually killing or wounding more than twenty people. A Klan-led "nigger chase" in Laurens County, South Carolina, claimed thirteen lives in the fall of 1870. Thanks in part to Klan intimidation of Republican voters—white and black—Democrats had returned to power in Alabama, Virginia, Tennessee, North Carolina, and Georgia in the 1870 elections. This only seemed to encourage more Klan terror elsewhere. In January 1871, five hundred masked men attacked the Union County jail in South Carolina and lynched eight black prisoners. In March 1871, the Klan killed thirty Negroes in Meridian, Mississippi.

These criminal acts fell outside the exercise of peaceable assembly, but they encountered little resistance in southern states where the rule of law itself was in question.[38]

Responding in part to the Klan offensives, Congress passed the Enforcement Act of 1870 to federalize crimes that were going unpunished in southern jurisdictions. The act relied on the powers granted Congress under the recently enacted Fourteenth and Fifteenth Amendments. Among other things, it prohibited conspiracy "to injure, oppress, threaten, or intimidate any citizen, with intent to prevent or hinder his free exercise and enjoyment of any right or privilege granted or secured to him by the constitution or laws of the United States." In October of 1870, the United States attorney in Alabama indicted a number of Klansmen who had killed four and wounded fifty-four in an assault on a Republican campaign meeting in Eutaw, Alabama. The indictment charged that the Klansmen had conspired to violate the Republicans' First Amendment rights of speech and assembly. Defense attorneys argued that the Bill of Rights applied to the federal government, not the states, and that the Fourteenth Amendment had not altered its scope. In any case, they pointed out, the violence had been carried out by private citizens, not state actors.[39]

In *United States v. Hall,* Fifth Circuit judge William Woods rejected both arguments. He concluded that the Fourteenth Amendment had made the rights of speech and assembly applicable to the states and had authorized Congress to enforce those rights against the states. Moreover, the state need not have itself endorsed or carried out the violence, because "denying the equal protection of the laws includes the omission to protect, as well as the omission to pass laws for protection." As Lane suggests, this meant that the federal government "had the power to protect freedmen not only from discriminatory state legislation but also from 'state inaction, or incompetency.'" Such a broad understanding of the right of assembly could have become one of the primary weapons to combat the Klan and other violent organizations set on suppressing the freedoms of blacks.[40]

Woods's interpretation would not last. Its unraveling began in Grant Parish, Louisiana, one of the crucibles of white supremacist violence. By the fall of 1871, whites in the area had formed a secret society "whose purpose was to kill or expel leading Republicans and prevent blacks from voting." One report indicated the group had 360 members, more than half of the adult white males in the parish. The unrest proved so unsettling that local Republican officials repeatedly requested the assistance of federal troops stationed in New Orleans. Tensions escalated further after Republicans challenged the results of the 1872 elections around the state. The contested elections led to a particularly volatile situation in Grant Parish, where racist candidates claimed landslide victories despite the fact that registered black voters outnumbered whites and Republicans had won handily just two years before. In March of 1873, Republicans sneaked into the parish courthouse in Colfax and swore in their candidates to the elected positions. White supremacists from Grant and nearby parishes converged on the courthouse, and black citizens moved in to defend it. On April 13, Easter Sunday, the whites attacked the courthouse. After a brief skirmish, the black citizens surrendered. In what became known as the Colfax Massacre, the white attackers then massacred dozens of their prisoners, including a number whom they marched into the woods and shot execution-style.[41]

The federal government tried nearly one hundred white perpetrators of the Colfax Massacre for violations of the Enforcement Act. Two counts of the indictments alleged that the defendants had prevented black citizens from enjoying their "lawful right and privilege to peaceably assemble together with each other and with other citizens of the United States for a peaceful and lawful purpose." William Cruikshank was one of only three defendants convicted. On appeal, Cruikshank and his co-defendants contended that the First Amendment did not guarantee the right of assembly against infringement by private citizens. The Supreme Court agreed, concluding in *United States v. Cruikshank* that the First Amendment "assumes the existence of the right of the people to assemble for lawful purposes, and protects it against encroachment by Congress. The right was not created by the amendment; neither was its continuance guaranteed, except as against congressional interference. For their protection in its enjoyment, therefore, the people must look to the States. The power for that purpose was originally placed there, and it has never been surrendered to the United States." The Court stopped short of declaring the Enforcement Act unconstitutional, but its ruling made further prosecutions practically impossible.[42]

Cruikshank's holding meant that private citizens could not be prosecuted for denying the First Amendment's freedom of assembly to other citizens. But the Court's dictum also proved significant. Reiterating that the First Amendment established a narrow right enforceable only against the federal government, Chief Justice Waite wrote: "The right of the people peaceably to assemble for the purpose of petitioning Congress for a redress of grievances, or for any thing else connected with the powers or the duties of the national government, is an attribute of national citizenship, and, as such, under the protection of, and guaranteed by, the United States." In context, it is likely that Waite was listing petition as an *example* of the kind of assembly that the First Amendment protected against infringement by the federal government; the Constitution also guaranteed assembly "for any thing else connected with the powers of the duties of the national government," which was as broadly as the right of assembly could be applied prior to its incorporation through the Fourteenth Amendment. But Waite's reference to "the right of the people peaceably to assemble for the purpose of petitioning Congress for a redress of grievances" came close to the text of the First Amendment. Read in isolation from his qualifying language, the dictum could erroneously be construed as limiting assembly to the purpose of petitioning Congress for a redress of grievances.[43]

Eleven years after *Cruikshank*, Justice William Woods made precisely this interpretive mistake in *Presser v. Illinois*. Woods, the same judge who prior to his elevation to the Supreme Court had held the right of assembly applicable to states and private actors in *Hall*, now reversed course and concluded that *Cruikshank* had announced that the First Amendment protected the right to assemble only if "the purpose of the assembly was to petition the government for a redress of grievances." *Presser* is the only time that the Supreme Court has expressly limited the right of assembly to the purpose of petition, and the Court has since indirectly contradicted the view that assembly and petition compose one right. But Woods's mistake has been followed in decades of scholarship.[44]

Despite the interpretative missteps by the Court and its commentators, the immediate effects of *Cruikshank* and *Presser* on the right of assembly were relatively minor. While the enactment of the Fourteenth Amendment laid the foundation for the eventual application of parts of the federal Constitution to the states, at the end of the nineteenth century neither the assembly clause nor any other provision of the Bill of Rights had yet been incorporated against the states. The more significant civil liberties protections were found in state constitutions. Although woefully inadequate in the protections they afforded African Americans, state court decisions and state constitutional provisions otherwise conveyed a broad sense of the scope and meaning of the right of assembly in at least two ways. First, they reinforced antebellum decisions signaling the importance of assembly and related political concepts to group autonomy. Second, they applied the right of assembly to purely social gatherings.

State recognition of the importance of membership decisions to group autonomy came in several forms. At least one court expressly adopted the principles set forth in *Leavitt* and *First Parish*, the Massachusetts antebellum cases that had endorsed the autonomy of religious societies. In 1877, the Supreme Court of New Hampshire cited both cases in *Richardson v. Union Congregational Society of Francestown*, observing that the idea that a society could not "be compelled to admit any one against its will" was a principle "inherent in every voluntary association."[45]

Similar ideas arose in other decisions upholding the rights of private societies to expel dissident members. In 1875, the Supreme Court of Illinois denied a challenge to a Chicago board of trade's decision to expel members of a certain firm. The board of trade had been chartered by the General Assembly, but the court explained:

It is true, that the body is organized under a statutory charter, and so are churches, masonic bodies, and odd fellow and temperance lodges; but we presume no one would imagine that a court could take cognizance of a case arising in either of those organizations, to compel them to restore to membership a person suspended or expelled from the privileges of the organization. They being organized by voluntary association, and not for the transaction of business, but for the purpose of inculcating their precepts and trusts, not for pecuniary gain, but for the advancement of morals and for the improvement of their members, they are left to adopt their constitutions, by-laws and regulations for admitting, suspending or expelling their members.[46]

Four years later, the St. Louis Court of Appeals rejected the appeal of four former members of the Grand Lodge of Missouri Independent Order of Odd Fellows. The court reasoned:

It is competent for the Baptist Church alone, through its proper officers (who do not derive their commissions from the State), and according to its established modes of procedure, to determine who is a Baptist; and it is, in like manner, competent for the Odd Fellows to determine who is an Odd Fellow; and these are questions into which the courts of this country have always refused to enter: holding that when men once associate themselves with others as organized bands, professing certain religious views, or holding themselves out as having certain ethical and social objects, and subject thus to a common discipline, they have voluntarily submitted themselves to the disciplinary power of the body of which they are members, and it is for that society to know its own. *To deny to it the power of discerning who constitute its members, is to deny the existence of such a society,* or that there is any meaning in the name which the Legislature recognizes when it grants the charter.[47]

Legal treatises from this era echoed these general principles. The 1894 edition of Frederick Bacon's *Treatise on the Law of Benefit Societies and Life Insurance* emphasized that when "the membership is recruited from a certain class, as Masons or Odd-fellows and the association is not for pecuniary gain, no person can compel the society to admit him."[48]

Legal commentators and state courts also applied the right of assembly to a broad array of gatherings. In 1867, John Alexander Jameson's treatise referred to "wholly unofficial" gatherings and "spontaneous assemblies" that were protected by the right of peaceable assembly, a "common and most invaluable provision of our constitutions, State and Federal." These assemblies were "at once the effects and the causes of social life and activity, doing for the state what the waves do for the sea: they prevent stagnation, the precursor of decay and death." They were "public opinion in the making,—public opinion fit to be the basis of political action, because sound and wise, and not a mere echo of party cries and plat-forms." Albert Wright's 1884 *Exposition of the Constitution of the United States* observed that under the right of assembly, "any number of people may come together in any sort of societies, religious, social or political, or even in treasonous conspiracies, and, so long as they behave themselves and do not hurt anybody or make any great disturbance, they may express themselves in public meetings by speeches and resolutions as they choose."[49]

In 1885, an Illinois state appellate court reviewed a village ordinance that restricted as nuisances "all public picnics and open air dances within the limits of the village." Rejecting the village's assertion that it could restrict these activities in any form, the court reasoned:

> It would be a startling proposition that under this general grant of power authorizing cities and villages to declare what shall be nuisances, they could prevent the people from assembling in a peaceable and orderly manner, on suitable occasions, to indulge in healthful recreations and innocent amuse-ments. It is difficult to perceive why dancing in the open air is per se any more reprehensible or more of a nuisance than playing at leap frog or lawn tennis. The groves and green woods are nature's own temples, to which the people have the right to repair with the consent of the owner, for rational sports and social intercourse, provided they do not disturb the public peace nor encroach upon private rights. The framers of the constitution inserted in that instru-ment a clause making inviolate the right of the people to assemble in a peace-able manner to consult for the common good, to make known their opinions to their representatives, and to apply for redress of their grievances. And it may well be supposed they would have added the right to assemble for open air amusements had any one imagined that the power to deny the exercise of such right would ever be asserted by a municipal corporation.

Assembly, in other words, encompassed far more than overtly political gatherings. It protected forms of expression that extended to "open air amusements"—even to dancing.[50]

Three years later, the Supreme Court of Kansas invalidated a Wellington city ordinance that prohibited parading without consent that involved "shouting, singing, or beating drums or tambourines, or playing upon any other musical instrument or instruments, or doing any other act or acts designed, intended, or calculated to attract or call together an unusual crowd or congregation of people upon any of said public streets, avenues, or alleys." A group of men and women making up a local branch of the Salvation Army and led by a female "captain" had intentionally transgressed the ordinance. In overturning their convictions, the court chastised the city for the reach of its restriction:

> This ordinance prevents any number of the people of the state attached to one of the several political parties from marching together with their party banners, and inspiring music, up and down the principal streets, without the written consent of some municipal officer. The Masonic and Odd Fellows organizations must first obtain consent before their charitable steps desecrate the sacred streets. Even the Sunday-School children cannot assemble at some central point in the city, and keep step to the music of the band as they march to the grove, without permission first had and obtained. The Grand Army of the Republic must be preceded in their march by the written consent of his honor, the mayor, or march without drums or fife, shouts or songs.

The court concluded:

> We do not believe that the legislative grant of power to the city council, as enumerated in the sections above cited, can be so construed as to authorize the city council to take from the people of a city and the surrounding country a privilege exercised by them in every locality throughout the land—to form their processions and parade the streets with banners, music, songs, and shouts. It is an abridgment of the rights of the people. It represses associated effort and action. It discourages united effort to attract public attention, and challenge public examination and criticism of the associated purposes. It discourages unity of feeling and expression on great public questions, economic, religious, and political. It practically destroys these great public demonstrations that are the most natural product of common aims and kindred purposes.

Other courts reached similar conclusions in challenges to restrictive ordinances by the Salvation Army.[51]

In 1897, the Supreme Court of Wisconsin interpreted a statutory grant of free assembly by specifying that: "Any person who shall, at any time, willfully interrupt or molest any assembly or meeting of people, for religious worship or for other purposes, lawfully and peaceably assembled, shall be punished by fine." Pointing to the right of assembly recognized under Wisconsin's constitution, the Court emphasized a broad interpretation of the "other purposes" specified in the statute: "The history and reason and spirit of the enactment show that any assembly or meeting of the people, lawfully and peaceably assembled, is within its protection." These broad interpretations of assembly also gestured toward the blurring of social and political lines that Aziz Rana describes in Populists of the time who "created lasting ties between party affiliation and ethnic, religious, or racial identity . . . through numerous social activities and popular spectacles, including parades and picnics."[52]

Assembly in the Progressive Era

As in many of the state court decisions at the turn of the century, the people claiming the right to assemble insisted on a far broader purpose and meaning than *Cruikshank* had signaled. During the Progressive Era, this thicker sense of assembly (as more than simply the right to gather to petition) is most evident in the practices of three political movements: a revitalized women's movement, a surge in political activity among African Americans, and an increasingly agitated labor movement. The histories of these movements are storied and complex, and even the most elementary treatment of them is beyond the scope of this book. But we can glean insights into the importance of assembly through snapshots of each.

The women's movement reemerged at the end of the nineteenth century, when "hundreds of thousands of women joined the thousands of clubs united under the auspices of the General Federation of Women's Clubs and the National Association of Colored Women." According to Linda Lumsden, these clubs "served as training grounds for the activist, articulate reformers who steered the suffrage movement in the 1910s." In 1908, various women's clubs began holding "open-air" campaigns to draw attention to their interests:

The success of the open-air campaigns helped prompt the organization of the first American suffrage parades, a more visible and assertive form of assembly. The spectacle of women marching shoulder to shoulder achieved many ends. One was that because of the press coverage parades attracted, suffrage became a nationwide issue. Women also acquired organizational and executive skills in the course of orchestrating extravaganzas featuring tens of thousands of marchers, floats, and bands. Better yet, parades showcased women's skills in these areas and emphasized their numbers and determination. Finally, and most crucially, marching together imbued women with a sense of solidarity that lifted the movement to the status of a crusade for many participants.[53]

As is often the case, the growth of local assemblies corresponded with the growth of the larger institutional structures that operated on a national level. The National American Woman Suffrage Association grew from forty-five thousand members in 1907, to one hundred thousand in 1915, to almost two million in 1917. But the core of assembly in the women's movement came through local networking and personal connections. Women's assemblies were not confined to traditional deliberative meetings but included banner meetings, balls, swimming races, potato sack races, baby shows, meals, pageants, and teatimes. Just as the Democratic-Republican Societies had earlier refused to limit their gatherings to formal meetings, the women's movement capitalized on an expanded conception of public political life. Their gatherings appealed not only to reason but also to the emotions of those before whom they assembled. As Harriot Stanton Blatch affirmed in 1912, men and women "are moved by seeing marching groups of people and by hearing music far more than by listening to the most careful argument."[54]

Important gatherings also unfolded among civil rights activists. Stirred by the brutal race riots in Atlanta in 1906 and in Springfield, Illinois, in 1908, Mary White Ovington joined Jane Addams, William Lloyd Garrison, John Dewey, W. E. B. Du Bois and other prominent Americans in calling for a conference to discuss "present evils, the voicing of protests, and the renewal of the struggle for civil and political liberty." The first National Negro Conference that ensued soon led to the formation of the NAACP. The new organization struggled, but in its early years, "the NAACP triumphed even in defeat." As Adam Fairclough writes: "Simply by creating public controversy, the Association forced whites to pay attention. Stung by the almighty row over *Birth of a Nation* [a racist film that the NAACP had campaigned against], Woodrow Wilson distanced himself from the film. Embarrassed by the dispute over segregation in the civil service, the federal government backed off from making racial segregation an official policy. Plans for a completely segregated postal service, for example, were quietly dropped." The NAACP's early efforts also aided membership drives, and a decade later, the group had more than 350 branches and one hundred thousand members.[55]

In addition to the rapid growth of the NAACP, Marcus Garvey's Universal Negro Improvement Association (UNIA) drew tens of thousands of members. Garvey capitalized on symbolic expression that upended social norms:

> Parading through Harlem on August 2, 1920, the UNIA's massed ranks took three hours to pass by. A chauffeured automobile, preceded by four mounted policemen, conveyed Marcus Garvey, the Provisional President of Africa, in the manner befitting a head of state. Resplendent in brocaded uniform and cocked hat, Garvey acknowledged the cheering onlookers with a regal wave of the hand. More cars trailed behind him, carrying regalia-attired lesser officials, including the Knight Commanders of the Distinguished Order of the Nile.

> Then came thousands of walking rank-and-file. Uniformed contingents marched in proud lockstep: the Black Star Line Choir, the Philadelphia Legion, the Black Cross Nurses, the Black Eagle Flying Corps, the African Motor Corps. Swaying bands from Norfolk and New York City "whooped it up." Then a forest of banners, each emblazoned with a slogan— variations on "Africa for the Africans!"—snaked its way down Lenox Avenue. They were borne aloft by UNIA members who came from Liberia, Canada, Panama, British Guiana, the Caribbean islands, and a dozen states of the Union. Hundreds of cars and more mounted policemen ended "the greatest parade ever staged anywhere in the world by Negroes."

Fairclough cautions against dismissing "Garveyism" as mere showmanship; for one thing, it "reflected a popular fad of a type all too common in the 1920s—when millions of Americans, whites and blacks, donned exotic hats and robes to become Masons, Elks, Oddfellows, and Shriners." Garvey's contemporaries took him seriously, and he became "the first black nationalist—the only one before or since—to create a mass movement." The movement proved short-lived, due in part to Garvey's contentious positions and unconventional alliances (among other views, Garvey espoused racial separatism and "racial purity" that earned him the support of white segregationists). But unlike the NAACP, Garvey's UNIA "was entirely led, controlled, and financed by black people," and it "fostered racial pride in ways the NAACP simply could not."[56]

As Garvey's displays embodied one form of assembly, a less flamboyant kind of assembly emerged in Harlem: "Caught up in the controversies of which Garvey was the center, or brooding over the conditions in American life to which he pointed, many blacks began to write about them, as though reacting to Garvey's harangues, even if they seldom agreed with him." The writers that were part of the Harlem Renaissance drew upon "a body of common experiences that in turn helped to promote the idea of a distinct and authentic cultural community." John Hope Franklin and Alfred Moss Jr. stress the interconnectedness between message and group that these writers experienced: "It was only natural that leaders of the Harlem Renaissance in New York would tend to move in the same social circles. There was a community of spirit and point of view that found its expression not only in the cooperative ventures of a professional nature but also in the intimate social relationships that developed. Perhaps these Harlemites felt that form and substance could be given to their efforts through the interchange of ideas in moments of informality." These "moments of informality" spread across mixed race clubs, literary parties, and other events that created "a cohesive force in the efforts of the group."[57]

While both suffragists and African Americans built on ideas of assembly in the Progressive Era, the most frequent articulations of the right came from an increasingly vocal labor movement. Widespread labor unrest had emerged with the increase in industrialization and immigration at the end of the nineteenth century. The Great Strike of 1877 had involved more than one hundred thousand workers throughout the country and brought to a halt most of the nation's transportation system. By the early 1880s, the Knights of Labor had organized hundreds of thousands of workers. The Haymarket Riot of 1886 and the Pullman Strike of 1894 sandwiched "almost a decade of labor unrest punctuated by episodes of spectacular violence" that included "the strike of the Homestead Steel workers against the Carnegie Corporation, the miners' strikes in the coal mining regions of the East and hardrock states in the West, a longshoremen's strike in New Orleans that united black and white workers, and numerous railroad strikes." But these labor efforts remained largely unorganized, and direct appeals to the freedom of assembly did not begin in earnest until the Industrial Workers of the World (IWW) formed in 1905.[58]

The IWW (nicknamed the "Wobblies") emerged out of a conglomeration of labor interests dissatisfied with the reform efforts of the American Federation of Labor. Led by William Haywood, Daniel De Leon, and Eugene Debs, the Wobblies employed provocative words and actions. The preamble to their constitution declared that "the working class and the employing class have nothing in common," and the IWW advocated this message in gatherings and demonstrations throughout the country. The freedom of assembly figured prominently in their appeals to constitutional protections during organized strikes in major industries, including steel, textile, rubber, and automobile, from 1909 to 1913. In 1910, Wobblies highlighted the denial of the right to assemble at a demonstration in Spokane. When members of the IWW invoked the rights of speech and assembly during the Paterson Silk Strike of 1913, Paterson mayor H. G. McBride responded that these protections extended to the striking silk workers but not to the Wobblies: "I cannot stand for seeing Paterson flooded with persons who have no interest in Paterson, who can only give us a bad name, who can despoil in a few hours a good name we have been years in building up, and I propose to continue my policy of locking these outside agitators up on sight." True to his word, McBride arrested a number of IWW leaders, including Elizabeth Gurley Flynn. Later that year, the IWW publication *Solidarity* protested that "America today has abandoned her heroic traditions of the Revolution and the War of 1812 and has turned to hoodlumism and a denial of free speech and assembly to a large and growing body of citizens."[59]

The Interwar Years and the Rise of Assembly

Progressives' reliance on the right of assembly confronted a roadblock in the emerging anticommunist hysteria. As Irwin Marcus has observed, "Unrest associated with the assertiveness of women, African Americans, and immigrant workers could be ascribed to the influence of the Communists and inoculating Americans with a vaccine of 100 percent Americanism was offered as a cure for national problems." The rising Americanism verged on claiming the freedom of assembly as one of its casualties. On the eve of America's entry into the First World War, President Wilson predicted to *New York World* editor Frank Cobb that "the Constitution would not survive" the war and "free speech and the right of assembly would go." Seven months later, Wilson's words seemed ominously prescient when the Bolshevik Revolution in Russia triggered the first Red Scare. Over the next few years, the federal government constrained the freedom of assembly through shortsighted legislation like the Espionage Act of 1917 (and its 1918 amendments) and the Immigration Act of 1918, and the Justice Department's infamous Palmer Raids in 1920.[60]

Despite the Red Scare, and probably because of some of the flagrant abuses of civil liberties that occurred during it, libertarian interpretations of the First Amendment that had surfaced prior to the First World War took shape in the interwar period. Harvard law professor Zechariah Chafee led the doctrinal charge and "provided intellectual cover for Justices Holmes and Brandeis when they began to dissent in First Amendment cases in the fall of 1919."[61]

References to free speech and assembly also increased in political rhetoric. In 1920, Senator Warren Harding's acceptance speech as the Republican presidential nominee warned that "we must not abridge the freedom of speech, the freedom of press, or the freedom of assembly." In 1921, the Intercollegiate Liberal League organized at Harvard and asserted that it would "espouse no creed or principle other than the complete freedom of assembly and discussion in the college." Meanwhile, Samuel Gompers repeatedly invoked the freedoms of speech and assembly in his battle against labor injunctions.[62]

The importance of assembly—broadly construed not only as a right to attend a meeting but also as a right to form and participate in groups—is strikingly evident in Brandeis's famous concurrence in *Whitney v. California*. Anita Whitney's appeal stemmed from her conviction under California's Criminal Syndicalism Act for having served as a delegate to the 1919 organizing convention of the Communist Labor Party of California. The Court rejected her argument that the California law violated her rights under the First Amendment, expressing particular concern that her actions had been undertaken in concert with others, which "involve[d] even greater threat to the public peace and security than the isolated utterances and acts of individuals."[63]

Rejecting this rationale, Brandeis penned some of the most well-known words in American jurisprudence: "Those who won our independence ... believed that freedom to think as you will and to speak as you think are means indispensable to the discovery and spread of political truth; that without free speech and assembly discussion would be futile; that with them, discussion affords ordinarily adequate protection against the dissemination of noxious doctrine; that the greatest menace to freedom is an inert people; that public discussion is a political duty; and that this should be a fundamental principle of the American government." The connection between "free speech and assembly" lies at the heart of Brandeis's argument—the phrase appears eleven times in his brief concurrence. The Court had linked these two freedoms only once before; after *Whitney*, the nexus occurs in more than one hundred of its opinions.[64]

Brandeis's link between speech and assembly suggests two important connections. First, it recognizes that a group's expression includes not only the spoken words of those assembled but also the expressive message inherent in their very act of gathering. Second, it emphasizes that the rights of speech and assembly extend across time, preceding the expressive moment to guard against prior restraints that would prevent that moment from ever occurring. Just as actual speech is not a necessary condition for the protections of speech, physical presence is not a necessary condition for the protections of assembly.[65]

There was, however, one group that even Brandeis considered beyond the constitutional protections of free assembly: the Ku Klux Klan. The year after *Whitney*, Brandeis joined an 8–1 majority in *Bryant v. Zimmerman* that rejected the Klan's challenge to New York's Walker Law, which mandated that associations requiring a membership oath and having twenty or more members file documents including a membership roster and a list of officers. Under the law, members of an association with knowledge that the association had failed to register were guilty of a misdemeanor. George Bryant, who had been imprisoned after the Klan failed to register, argued that the New York statute deprived him of "liberty" and prevented him "from exercising his right of membership in the organization," in violation of the Due Process Clause of the Fourteenth Amendment. The Court concluded that liberty "must yield to the rightful exertion of the police power" and there "can be no doubt that under that power the State may prescribe and apply to associations having an oath-bound membership any reasonable regulation calculated to confine their purposes and activities within limits which are consistent with the rights of others and the public welfare."[66]

Thirty years later, the State of Alabama leaned heavily on *Bryant* in arguing for disclosure of the NAACP's membership list in *NAACP v. Alabama*. The Court rejected the comparison, noting that the Klan's violent nature was a far cry from the NAACP. The Klan's prominence at the time the Court decided *Bryant* also likely played a role. Following World War I, the Klan had garnered millions of recruits with its appeals to "traditional American values." During the 1920s, Klan members rose to political power in states across the union, and Klan rallies drew tens of thousands of supporters. The frenzy proved short-lived—by the Depression, the Klan had fewer than a hundred thousand members, and its continued decline likely explains the Court's willingness to tolerate the Klan's expressive antics in its landmark 1969 decision, *Brandenburg v. Ohio*. But when the Court decided *Bryant* in 1928, the Klan's prominence—and its propensity for violence—was alive and well.[67]

Around this time, appeals to assembly increased in the rhetoric of labor activists. In the early 1920s, the conservative wing of the Supreme Court issued a series of antilabor decisions aimed at stopping picketing and union organizing. But by 1933, workers had successfully obtained legislative relief through the National Industrial Recovery Act, which provided the first guarantee to workers of the right to organize in associations. Two years later, the Wagner Act added additional protections for associational rights of workers. These initial statutory protections set in motion a byzantine legislative structure whose intricacies far exceed the scope of this book. It is nevertheless useful to highlight some of the invocations of assembly advanced in the context of these statutory developments.[68]

On April 10, 1936, Congress initiated hearings on legislation to authorize the Committee on Education and Labor to investigate "violations of the rights of free speech and assembly and undue interference with the right of labor to organize and bargain collectively." National Labor Relations Board chairman J. Warren Madden testified that "the right of workmen to organize themselves into unions has become an important civil liberty" and that workers could not organize without exercising the rights of free speech and assembly. Following the hearings and subsequent approval of the Senate measure, the committee's chairman Hugo Black named Senator Robert La Follette Jr. of Wisconsin to chair a subcommittee to investigate these concerns. The La Follette Committee embarked with "the zeal of missionaries" in an exhaustive investigation that spanned five years.[69] When it concluded, La Follette reported to Congress that "the most spectacular violations of civil liberty . . . [have] their roots in economic conflicts of interest" and emphasized that "association and self-organization are simply the result of the exercise of the fundamental rights of free speech and assembly."[70]

Rhetoric across the political spectrum during the mid-1930s echoed the increased appeals to assembly in the labor context. In a 1935 speech on Constitution Day, former president Herbert Hoover listed assembly among the core freedoms that guarded liberty. That same year, President Roosevelt's interior secretary Harold Ickes referred to the freedoms of speech, press, and assembly as "the three musketeers of our constitutional forces" during an address before an annual luncheon of the Associated Press. Ickes asserted that "we might give up all the rest of our Constitution, if occasion required it, and yet have sure anchorage for the mooring of our good ship America, if these rights remained to us unimpaired."[71]

In 1937, the Supreme Court incorporated the freedom of assembly against the states in *De Jonge v. Oregon*. Dirk De Jonge had spoken before a group of 150 people at a Portland meeting that occurred under the auspices of the Communist Party. During his speech, De Jonge protested the conditions at the county jail and the actions of the police in response to an ongoing maritime strike. The orderly meeting was open to the public, and only a fraction of the attendees were communists. De Jonge was convicted under Oregon's criminal syndicalism statute, which prohibited "the organization of a society or assemblage" that "advocate[d] crime, physical violence, sabotage or any unlawful acts or methods as a means of accomplishing or effecting industrial or political change or revolution."[72]

A unanimous Supreme Court reversed the conviction. Chief Justice Hughes emphasized that the broad statute meant: "However innocuous the object of the meeting, however lawful the subjects and tenor of the addresses, however reasonable and timely the discussion, all those assisting in the conduct of the meeting would be subject to imprisonment as felons if the meeting were held by the Communist Party." Hughes rejected this outcome: "The First Amendment of the Federal Constitution expressly guarantees that right [of assembly] against abridgment by Congress. But explicit mention there does not argue exclusion elsewhere. For the right is one that cannot be denied without violating those fundamental principles of liberty and justice which lie at the base of all civil and political institutions,—principles which the Fourteenth Amendment embodies in the general terms of its due process clause." Hughes underscored the significance of applying the right of assembly to state action by observing that "the right of peaceable assembly is a right cognate to those of free speech and free press and is equally fundamental." In words strikingly similar to Brandeis's *Whitney* concurrence, Hughes emphasized the need "to preserve inviolate the constitutional rights of free speech, free press and free assembly in order to maintain the opportunity for free political discussion, to the end that government may be responsive to the will of the people and that changes, if desired, may be obtained by peaceful means. Therein lies the security of the Republic, the very foundation of constitutional government."[73]

Months later, the Court underscored in *Herndon v. Lowry* that "the power of a state to abridge freedom of speech and of assembly is the exception rather than the rule." The case involved the appeal of Angelo Herndon, a young black man affiliated with the Communist Party in Georgia who had attempted to organize black industrial workers. In 1933, Georgia had convicted Herndon of attempting to incite an insurrection under a Reconstruction era law and sentenced him to eighteen to twenty years' imprisonment (the insurrection conviction was a capital offense, but the jury had recommended mercy). The state had argued that Herndon was "attempting to organize a Negro Republic in Georgia." The trial court emphasized that Herndon "was an organizer and induced a number of persons to become members of the Communist Party," an "attempt to induce others to combine in [violent] resistance to the lawful authority of the state." The Communist Party's International Labor Defense pursued his appeals, and within two years, "white liberals, labor leaders, and other citizens joined blacks and radicals in viewing the conviction as a serious threat to basic civil liberties, especially the rights of free speech and free assembly." After Herndon had spent years languishing in a Georgia prison while his appeals went up and down the courts, the Supreme Court concluded that the statute under which he had been convicted was "merely a dragnet which may enmesh anyone who agitates for a change of government." Herndon's efforts to solicit members and hold meetings fell squarely within the boundaries of the right of peaceable assembly.[74]

In 1938, Dewey's essay "Creative Democracy: The Task Before Us" asserted that "the free play of facts and ideas" is "secured by effective guarantees of free inquiry, free assembly and free communication" and cautioned that "merely legal guarantees of the civil liberties of free belief, free expression, free assembly are of little avail if in daily life freedom of communication, the give and take of ideas, facts, experiences, is choked by mutual suspicion, by abuse, by fear and hatred." Later that year, the American Bar Association's Committee on the Bill of Rights hailed the importance of the right of assembly in an amicus brief to the Third Circuit in *Hague v. Committee for Industrial Organization*. The appeal involved Mayor Frank Hague's repeated denials of a permit to the Committee for Industrial Organization (CIO) to hold a public meeting in Jersey City. Hague's permit denials had gained such notoriety that when a CIO delegation met with congressional representatives, Representative Knute Hill "inquired whether Mayor Hague would prevent a group of Congressmen from hiring a hall in Jersey City to speak on the Bill of Rights." The committee's lengthy amicus brief emphasized that "the integrity of the right 'peaceably to assemble' is an essential element of the American democratic system," involving "the citizen's right to meet face to face with others for the discussion of their ideas and problems—religious, political, economic or social," that "assemblies face to face perform a function of vital significance in the American system," and that public officials had the "duty to make the right of free assembly prevail over the forces of disorder if by any reasonable effort or means they can possibly do so."[75]

The brief garnered an unusual amount of attention. The American Bar Association wrote: "The filing of the brief was widely hailed as a great step in the defense of liberty and the American traditions of free speech and free assembly as basic institutions of democratic government. The clear and earnest argument of the brief was attested as an admirable exposition of the fundamental American faith. Hardly any action in the name of the American Bar Association in many years, if ever, has attracted as wide and immediate attention and as general acclaim, as the preparation and filing of this brief." The *New York Times* reviewed the brief with similarly effusive language: "This brief ought to stand as a landmark in American legal history. It ought to be multiplied and spread about in all communities in which private citizens, private organizations or public officials dare threaten or suppress the basic guarantees of American liberty. It ought to be on file in every police station. It ought to be in every public library, in every school library, and certainly in the home of every voter in Jersey City." The Third Circuit ruled in favor of the CIO, but Hague appealed to the Supreme Court, setting the stage for an even broader judicial endorsement of the freedom of assembly.[76]

In 1939, assembly joined religion, speech, and press as one of the "Four Freedoms" celebrated at the New York World's Fair. Fair organizers commissioned Leo Friedlander to design a group of statues commemorating each of the four freedoms. Grover Whalen, the president of the fair corporation, credited *New York Times* president and publisher Arthur Sulzberger with the idea: "Mr. Sulzberger pointed out that if we portrayed four of the constitutional guarantees of liberty in the 'freedom group' we could teach the millions of visitors to the fair a lesson in history with a moral. The lesson is that freedom of press, freedom of religion, freedom of assembly and freedom of speech, firmly fixed in the cornerstone of our government since the days of Washington, have enabled us to build the most successful democracy in the world. And the moral is that as long as these freedoms remain a part of our constitutional set-up we can face the problems of tomorrow, a nation of people calm, united and unafraid."[77]

The buildup to the opening of the fair began with New Year's Day speeches broadcast internationally from Radio City Music Hall. Dorothy Thompson, the "First Lady of American journalism," delivered a speech on the freedom of assembly. Calling assembly "the most essential right of the four," Thompson elaborated: "The right to meet together for one purpose or another is actually the guaranty of the three other rights. Because what good is free speech if it impossible to assemble people to listen to it? How are you going to have discussion at all unless you can hire a hall? How are you going to practice your religion, unless you can meet with a community of people who feel the same way? How can you even get out a newspaper, or any publication, without assembling some people to do it?"[78]

Three months later, Columbia University president Nicholas Butler penned a *New York Times* editorial entitled "The Four Freedoms." With the European conflict in mind, Butler warned of the "millions upon millions of human beings living under governments which not only do not accept the Four Freedoms, but frankly and openly deny them all." The following month, the *Times* ran an editorial by Henry Steele Commager, who decried the assaults on the "four fundamental freedoms" and concluded his essay by asserting: "The careful safeguards which our forefathers set up around freedom of religion, speech, press and assembly prove that these freedoms were thought to be basic to the effective functioning of democratic and republican government. The truth of that conviction was never more apparent than it is now."[79]

On April 30, 1939, the opening day of the World's Fair, New York mayor Fiorello La Guardia called the site of Friedlander's four statues the "heart of the fair." A month later, the Supreme Court issued its *Hague* decision. Justice Roberts relied on the Privileges and Immunities Clause to hold the freedom of assembly applicable to Mayor Hague's actions. The *New York Times* coverage of the decision pronounced that "with the right of assembly reasserted, all 'four freedoms' of [the] Constitution are well established." *Hague*'s words on the heels of the tribute to the four freedoms at the World's Fair appeared to have anchored the freedom of assembly in political discourse. Indeed, a poll by Elmo Roper's organization at the end of 1940 reported that 89.9 percent of respondents thought their personal liberties would be decreased by restrictions on freedom of assembly (compared to 81.5 percent who expressed concern over restrictions on "freedom of speech by press and radio"). Americans appeared resolute in their belief in the indispensability of free assembly to democracy.[80]

Politics and history decided otherwise. On January 6, 1941, President Roosevelt proclaimed "four essential human freedoms" in his State of the Union Address. Rather than refer to the freedoms of speech, religion, assembly, and press that had formed the centerpiece of the World's Fair, Roosevelt's "Four Freedoms Speech" called for freedom of speech and expression, freedom of religion, freedom from want, and freedom from fear. The new formulation—absent assembly—quickly overtook the old. Seven months later, Roosevelt and Churchill incorporated the new four freedoms into the Atlantic Charter. In 1943, Norman Rockwell created four paintings inspired by Roosevelt's four freedoms. The *Saturday Evening Post* printed the paintings in successive editions, accompanied by matching essays expounding upon each of the freedoms. And like the earlier four freedoms, the new ones were also set to stone. Roosevelt commissioned Walter Russell to create the Four Freedoms Monument, which was dedicated at Madison Square Garden. Today, the Franklin and Eleanor Roosevelt Institute honors well-known individuals with the Four Freedoms Award.[81]

Although Roosevelt's four freedoms omitted assembly, the right did not immediately disappear from political and legal discourse. In 1941, an illustrious group called the Free Company penned a series of radio dramas about the First Amendment. Attorney General Robert Jackson and Solicitor General Francis Biddle helped shape the group, which included Robert Sherwood (then Roosevelt's speechwriter), William Saroyan, Maxwell Anderson, Ernest Hemingway, and James Boyd. The group operated under what was "virtually a Government charter" to spread a message of democracy.[82]

Orson Welles wrote the Free Company's play on the freedom of assembly. "His Honor, the Mayor" portrayed the dilemma of Bill

Knaggs, a fictional mayor confronted with an impending rally of a group called the "White Crusaders." After deciding to allow the rally, the mayor addressed the crowd that had gathered in protest: "Don't start forbiddin' anybody the right to assemble. Democracy's a rare and precious thing and once you start that—you've finished democracy! Democracy guarantees freedom of assembly unconditionally to the worst lice that want it. . . . All of you've read the history books. You know what the right to assemble and worship God meant to most of those folks that first came here, the ones that couldn't pray the way they wanted to in the old country?" The play concluded with music followed by the solemn voice of the narrator: "Like his honor, the Mayor, then, let us stand fast by the right of lawful assembly. Let us say with that great fighter for freedom, Voltaire, 'I disapprove of what you say but I will defend to the death your right to say it.' Thus one of our ancient, hard-won liberties will be made secure and we, differing though we may at times among ourselves, will stand together on a principle to make sure that government of the people, by the people, for the people shall not perish from the earth." Not everyone shared these sentiments. Following the broadcast of "His Honor, the Mayor," the Hearst newspaper chain and the American Legion attacked it as "un-American and tending to encourage communism and other subversive groups" and "cleverly designed to poison the minds of young Americans." The next week, J. Edgar Hoover drafted a Justice Department memorandum "concerning the alleged Communist activities and connections of Orson Welles."[83]

Later in 1941, festivities around the country marked the sesquicentennial anniversary of the Bill of Rights. In Washington D.C.'s Post Square, organizers of a celebration displayed an oversized copy of the Bill of Rights next to the four phrases: "Freedom of Speech, Freedom of Assembly, Freedom of Religion, Freedom of the Press." The Sesquicentennial Committee, with President Roosevelt as its chair, issued a proclamation describing the original four freedoms as "the pillars which sustain the temple of liberty under law." Days before the attack on Pearl Harbor, Roosevelt declared that December 15, 1941, would be Bill of Rights Day. Roosevelt heralded the "immeasurable privileges" of the First Amendment and signed the proclamation for Bill of Rights Day against the backdrop of a mural listing the original four freedoms.[84]

The photo op was not without irony; less than three months later, Roosevelt signed Executive Order 9066 authorizing the internment of Japanese Americans. The federal government's pervasive denial of civil liberties to Japanese Americans included the denial of the right of assembly and began almost immediately after Pearl Harbor. Emily Roxworthy reports that "the FBI endorsed the logic that the very gathering of Japanese Americans into a group guaranteed that suspicious activities would take place" and "the supposed political disinterest of religious organizations especially attracted FBI suspicion, as did 'Americanization' campaigns originating within Japanese communities." Greg Robinson notes that Japanese Americans corralled into the (ironically named) "assembly centers" encountered harsh restrictions: "In Santa Anita [one of the preinternment assembly centers], . . . use of the Japanese language—the first language of many inmates, and in some cases their only language—was strictly banned in public meetings without the express consent of the administration. . . . When a group at Santa Anita, led by Shuji Fujii (Kibei editor of the prewar left-wing newspaper *Doho*), circulated petitions demanding that bans on Japanese language and on public assembly be lifted, they were arrested by center police."[85]

Although the Supreme Court infamously endorsed the president's restrictions on the civil liberties of Japanese Americans in *Hirabayashi v. United States* and *Korematsu v. United States,* it elsewhere affirmed a core commitment to the Bill of Rights generally and the freedom of assembly in particular. In 1943, Justice Jackson wrote in *West Virginia v. Barnette:* "The very purpose of a Bill of Rights was to withdraw certain subjects from the vicissitudes of political controversy, to place them beyond the reach of majorities and officials and to establish them as legal principles to be applied by the courts. One's right to life, liberty, and property, to free speech, a free press, freedom of worship and assembly, and other fundamental rights may not be submitted to vote; they depend on the outcome of no elections."[86]

Two years later, the Court emphasized in *Thomas v. Collins* that restrictions of assembly could only be justified under the "clear and present danger" standard that the Court had adopted in its free speech cases. R. J. Thomas, the president of the United Auto Workers, had traveled to Texas with the express purpose of testing the constitutionality of the Manford Act, which required that all union organizers register with the secretary of state and imposed other substantive restrictions. The act represented Texas's first attempt to regulate labor unions, and its provisions infuriated J. Frank Dobie, who argued: "A man can stand up anywhere in Texas, or sit down either, and without interference invite people, either publicly or privately, to join the Republican party, the Holy Rollers, the Liars Club, the Association for Anointing Herbert Hoover as a Prophet, the Texas Folklore Society—almost any organization on earth but one—but it is against the law in Texas for a man unless he pays a license and signs papers to invite any person to join a labor union." The *New York Times* was more circumspect, editorializing that "the layman probably does not see the law as having any far-reaching effects on the rights of the laboring man or the rights of workers to join or to refrain from joining labor unions."[87]

Thomas found himself in contempt after defying a Texas court's temporary restraining order forbidding him to solicit members without the proper license and registration under the Manford Act. The Supreme Court overturned the contempt conviction in a 5–4 decision. Because of the "*preferred place* given in our scheme to the great, the indispensable democratic freedoms secured by the First Amendment," the Court concluded that only "the gravest abuses, endangering paramount interests, give occasion for permissible limitation." Justice Rutledge's opinion noted that the right of assembly guarded "not solely religious or political" causes but also "secular causes," great and small. And Rutledge gestured toward the expressive nature of assembly by noting that the rights of the speaker and the audience were "necessarily correlative."[88]

A further endorsement of assembly came by way of the executive branch in the 1947 Report of the President's Committee on Civil Rights. The report indicated that the "great freedoms" of religion, speech, press, and assembly were "relatively secure" and that citizens were "normally free . . . to assemble for unlimited public discussions." Noting growing concerns about "Communists and Fascists," the committee asserted that it "unqualifiedly opposes any attempt to impose special limitations on the rights of these people to speak and assemble."[89]

The Demise of Assembly

The rhetorical tributes to assembly in Supreme Court opinions and popular discourse overshadowed what was lacking: a clear doctrinal framework for resolving constitutional cases asserting that right. Frequent invocations of Brandeis's "free speech and assembly" usually meant that the Court resolved challenges to the latter within the growing doctrinal framework of the former. By the mid-1960s, the only cases invoking the freedom of assembly were those overturning convictions of African Americans who had participated in peaceful civil rights demonstrations. In political discourse, Martin Luther King Jr. appealed to assembly in his *Letter from a Birmingham Jail* and in his speech *I've Been to the Mountaintop*, which he delivered just prior to his assassination. But by the end of the 1960s, the right of assembly in law and politics was largely confined to protests and demonstrations. Earlier intimations of a broadly construed right—one that encompassed social and other "nonpolitical" gatherings and extended to a group's composition and membership as well as its moment of expression—were largely forgotten.[90]

In 1983, the Court swept the remnants of assembly within the ambit of free speech law in *Perry Education Association v. Perry Local Educators' Association*. Justice White reasoned:

> In places which by long tradition or by government fiat have been devoted to assembly and debate, the rights of the State to limit expressive activity are sharply circumscribed. At one end of the spectrum are streets and parks which have immemorially been held in trust for the use of the public and, time out of mind, have been used for purposes of assembly, communicating thoughts between citizens, and discussing public questions. In these quintessential public forums, the government may not prohibit all communicative activity. For the State to enforce a content-based exclusion it must show that its regulation is necessary to serve a compelling state interest and that it is narrowly drawn to achieve that end. The State may also enforce regulations of the time, place, and manner of expression which are content-neutral, are narrowly tailored to serve a significant government interest, and leave open ample alternative channels of communication.

The doctrinal language came straight out of the Court's free speech cases and made slight mention of the right of assembly (a perilous foreshadowing of the Court's "merging" of the speech and association claims in *Christian Legal Society v. Martinez*). With *Perry*, even cases involving protests or demonstrations could now be resolved without reference to assembly. The Court's 1988 opinion in *Boos v. Barry* exemplifies this change. *Boos* involved a challenge to a District of Columbia law that prohibited, among other things, congregating "within 500 feet of any building or premises within the District of Columbia used or occupied by any foreign government or its representative or representatives as an embassy, legation, consulate, or for other official purposes." The petitioner challenged the "deprivation of First Amendment speech and assembly rights" and argued that "the right to congregate is a component part of the 'right of the people peaceably to assemble' guaranteed by the First Amendment." Justice O'Connor's opinion for the Court cited *Perry* three times and resolved the case under a free speech analysis without mentioning the freedom of assembly. The Court, in fact, has not addressed a freedom of assembly claim in thirty years.[91]

CHAPTER 3

THE EMERGENCE OF ASSOCIATION
IN THE NATIONAL SECURITY ERA

Perry and *Boos* demonstrate how some aspects of assembly have been swept within the Court's free speech doctrine. But at least part of the reason for the forgetting of assembly has been the emergence and entrenchment of a different right: the judicially recognized right of association. The rise of this right of association in many ways depended upon surrounding political and cultural contexts, which I have divided into two eras. The *national security era* began in the late 1940s and lasted until the early 1960s. It formed the background for the initial recognition of the right of association in *NAACP v. Alabama.* The *equality era* began in the early 1960s and included an important reinterpretation of the right of association in *Roberts v. United States Jaycees.* I discuss the national security era in this chapter and the equality era in the next chapter.

Three factors shaped the right of association in the national security era: (1) the conflation of rampant anticommunist sentiment with the rise of the Civil Rights Movement (a political factor); (2) infighting on the Court over the proper way to ground the right of association in the Constitution (a jurisprudential factor); and (3) the pluralist political theory of mid-twentieth-century liberalism that emphasized the importance of consensus, balance, and stability (a theoretical factor).

The primary political factor was the historical coincidence of the Second Red Scare and the Civil Rights Movement. From the late 1940s to the early 1960s, the government's response to the communist threat pitted national security interests against expressive freedoms. Segregationists capitalized on these tensions by analogizing the unrest stirred by the NAACP to the threats posed by communist organizations, and even charged that communist influences had infiltrated the NAACP. The Supreme Court responded unevenly, denying constitutional protections to communist organizations in the name of order and stability but protecting the NAACP.

The jurisprudential factor shaping the right of association involved disagreement on the Court over the constitutional source of association. The issue was most evident when the Court sought to limit state (as opposed to federal) law. Justices Frankfurter and Harlan argued that association constrained state action because it, like other rights, could be derived from the "liberty" of the Due Process Clause of the Fourteenth Amendment (the *liberty argument*). Justices Black, Douglas, Brennan, and Warren insisted that association could be located in some aspect of the First Amendment and argued that it be given the same "preferred position" as other First Amendment rights. On their view, the right of association applied to the states because the Fourteenth Amendment had incorporated the provisions of the First Amendment (the *incorporation argument*). Disagreement between the justices over the liberty argument and the incorporation argument framed the legal discussion that shaped the right of association.

The theoretical factor influencing the shaping of association was the pluralism popularized by David Truman and Robert Dahl in the 1950s and 1960s, which emphasized the balance, stability, and consensus among groups rather than the juxtaposition of groups against the state. Truman and Dahl supported their views by appealing to the two great theorists of association in the American context: James Madison and Alexis de Tocqueville. The pluralist claims and their attendant interpretations of Madison and Tocqueville helped establish a theoretical background that qualified group autonomy with the interests of the democratic state.

These factors contributed to three changes affecting group autonomy in the shift from assembly to association: (1) dissenting and destabilizing groups protected by the right of assembly were weakened by a right of association predicated upon a bounded consensus; (2) social practices that constituted forms of political life in the context of the right of assembly were depoliticized by a right of association that narrowed the scope of what constituted the "political"; and (3) assemblies as forms of expression were supplanted by associations as means of expression. This chapter and the one that follows illustrate the plausibility of these changes and their connection to the shift from assembly to association. Chapter 5 considers the implications of these changes through a theory of assembly.

The Postwar Political Context and the Communist Threat

The political context that shaped the constitutional right of association centered around a growing paranoia over the threat of domestic communism in the late 1940s and early 1950s. The ubiquity of the communist scare across the branches of state and federal government upset the checks and balances that should have guarded against pervasive incursions into civil liberties. It was not the first time that the American experiment faltered under such pressures, and as recent reactions to the threat of domestic terrorism attest, it would not be the last. But peculiar to the emergence of the right of association in the context of what became the Second Red Scare—perhaps in a way paralleled only by the right of assembly asserted by the Democratic-Republican Societies in the 1790s—was the claim by those outside of the political mainstream to an untested constitutional right of group autonomy during a politically tumultuous time.[1]

The federal government had actively pursued the threat of domestic communism since the formation of the House Committee on Un-American Activities (HUAC) in 1938. Concern over "subversive" government employees had prompted the Hatch Act in 1939, the Civil Service Commission's War Service Regulations in 1942, and the formation of the Attorney General's Interdepartmental Committee on Investigations that same year. In 1947, the President's Committee on Civil

Rights reported that while "the government has the obligation to have in its employ only citizens of unquestioned loyalty," our "whole civil liberties history provides us with a clear warning against the possible misuse of loyalty checks to inhibit freedom of opinion and expression." The committee specifically cautioned of the dangers posed by "any standard which permits condemnation of persons or groups because of 'association.'"[2]

With an irony that rivaled President Roosevelt's Bill of Rights Day proclamation, President Truman established the Federal Employee Loyalty Program the same year his civil rights committee issued its report. The program empowered the federal government to deny employment to "disloyal" individuals. Within a year, the FBI had examined more than two million federal employees and conducted more than 6,300 full investigations. The government's loyalty determination considered "activities and associations" that included "membership in, affiliation with or sympathetic association with any foreign or domestic organization, association, movement, group or combination of persons, designated by the Attorney General as totalitarian, fascist, communist, or subversive." Attorney General Tom Clark quickly generated a list of 123 subversive organizations. Clark testified before a HUAC subcommittee that the government intended to "isolate subversive movements in this country from effective interference in the body politic." In a speech delivered shortly before his testimony, he declared that "those who do not believe in the ideology of the United States should not be allowed to stay in the United States."[3]

Thomas Emerson and David Helfeld attacked the loyalty program in a 1947 article in the *Yale Law Journal,* contending that the investigations encompassed "not only membership and activity in organizations, including labor unions, but private beliefs, reading habits, receipts of mail, associations, and personal affairs." They charged that the program relied upon "the legal premise that Federal employees are entitled to no constitutional protection" and ignored "the right to freedom of political expression embodied in the First Amendment." To Emerson and Helfeld, the "concept of the right to freedom of political expression" emerged from "the specific guarantees of freedom of speech, freedom of the press, the right of assembly and the right to petition the government." This right of political expression was "basic, in the deepest sense, for it underlies the whole theory of democracy."[4]

Emerson and Helfeld did not explicitly reference a "freedom of association," but they cited a speech delivered earlier in the year to the State Bar of California by the powerful federal judge, Charles Wyzanski Jr. In that speech, Wyzanski had offered "an inquiry into freedom of association," suggesting that despite the "verbal kinship of the phrases freedom of speech, freedom of assembly and freedom of association[,] . . . the triad represented an ascending order of complexity." The term "association" implied "a body of persons who have assembled not on an *ad hoc,* but on a more or less permanent, basis and who are likely to seek to advance their common purposes not merely by debate but often in the long run by overt action." The "peculiarly complicated" freedom of association "cuts underneath the visible law to the core of our political science and our philosophy." Wyzanski contended that by the time of Gunnar Myrdal's 1944 book, *An American Dilemma,* "freedom of association was considered a deeply rooted characteristic of American society."[5]

But the "deeply rooted characteristic" was not evident in 1947. As the executive branch embarked on its loyalty investigations of government employees, the HUAC subpoenaed movie producers, screenwriters, and directors to examine alleged communist affiliations. Hollywood personalities, including Humphrey Bogart, Lauren Bacall, Groucho Marx, and Frank Sinatra, formed the Committee for the First Amendment and flew to Washington to support those called to testify. In October of 1947, ten Hollywood witnesses refused on First Amendment grounds to answer questions from the HUAC. But the "Hollywood Ten" were largely abandoned after Congress cited them for contempt. Within a month, top Hollywood executives agreed to blacklist them, and the Committee for the First Amendment "folded almost as fast as it had formed."[6]

In their investigative hearings, the HUAC and the Senate Internal Security Subcommittee (SISS) routinely asked witnesses whether they were currently or had ever been a member of the Communist Party. The question posed a catch-22. On the one hand, witnesses who denied any affiliation could be charged with perjury based on circumstantial evidence that suggested otherwise. On the other hand, those who admitted to a communist affiliation usually suffered adverse economic and social consequences. As a result, a growing number of witnesses refused to answer questions. Initially, most of these witnesses invoked the Fifth Amendment right against self-incrimination. But observers increasingly saw this as an admission of guilt by those they labeled "Fifth Amendment Communists." Accordingly, witnesses began turning to the First Amendment. As with the Hollywood Ten, reliance on the First Amendment usually resulted in contempt of Congress citations.[7]

The executive and legislative actions to curtail communist activity took on added urgency in light of global events, including the Berlin blockade, the first Soviet test of an atomic bomb, and Mao Tse-tung's overthrow of Chiang Kai-shek's government in China. Alger Hiss's 1950 perjury conviction and the espionage convictions of Julius and Ethel Rosenberg the following year reinforced fears of an ongoing domestic communist threat. As Lucas Powe has written, "Americans, very much including Supreme Court justices, viewed these trials against the backdrop of communist expansion in Europe and Asia, and an aggressive anticommunism became a staple of American politics and society." In light of the unsettling domestic and global developments, citizens and politicians across the political spectrum welcomed the government's intervention as a necessary defense against the spread of communism. The 1950 McCarran Internal Security Act added to the fervor by authorizing detention camps for subversives and requiring communists to register with the Subversive Activities Control Board. When Truman vetoed the act out of concern that it would lead to "Gestapo witch hunts," Congress overrode his veto.[8]

The first indication of the Supreme Court's complicity in the communist scare came in its 1950 decision *American Communications Association v. Douds. Douds* involved a challenge to the Taft-Hartley amendments to the National Labor Relations Act (NLRA), which required that union officers submit affidavits disavowing membership in or support of the Communist Party before a union could receive the NLRA's protections. The Court upheld the affidavit requirement. Chief Justice Vinson reasoned that the act protected the country from "the so-called 'political strike.'" He referred to "substantial amounts of evidence" presented to Congress "that Communist leaders of labor unions had in the past and would continue in the future to subordinate legitimate trade union objectives to obstructive strikes when dictated by Party leaders, often in support of the policies of a foreign government."[9]

The Court's communist concerns continued in *Dennis v. United States,* a decision that ACLU national chairman Roger Baldwin later called "the worst single blow to civil liberties in all our history." *Dennis* came to the Court after FBI director J. Edgar Hoover initiated Smith Act prosecutions of twelve senior leaders of the Communist Party of the United States of America (CPUSA). The government charged the defendants with violating the act's membership clause, which made it unlawful "to organize any society, group, or assembly of persons who teach, advocate, or encourage the overthrow or destruction of any government in the United States by force or violence, or to be or become a member of, or affiliate with, any such society, group, or assembly of persons, knowing the purposes thereof." The government construed the act so broadly that it "made no effort to prove that this attempted overthrow was in any sense imminent, or even in the concrete planning stages." Following a nine-month trial, the jury convicted all twelve defendants after less than a day of deliberation.[10]

Vinson's plurality opinion in *Dennis* recounted the speech-protective views of Holmes and Brandeis and conceded that "there is little doubt that subsequent opinions have inclined toward the Holmes-Brandeis rationale." But Vinson refashioned Holmes's clear and present danger standard, concluding that with respect to the CPUSA, "it is the existence of the conspiracy which creates the danger." Milton Konvitz quipped that Vinson's interpretation of Holmes and Brandeis was "doctrine reduced to a phrase." Justice Black's dissent lamented, "Public opinion being what it now is, few will protest the conviction of these Communist petitioners. There is hope, however, that in calmer times, when present pressures, passions and fears subside, this or some later Court will restore the First Amendment liberties to the high preferred place where they belong in a free society." As Black anticipated, *Dennis* generated little public outcry, and even liberals like Norman Thomas and Arthur Schlesinger supported the decision. One of the lone openly critical voices was Eleanor Roosevelt, who wrote the day after the decision: "I am not sure our forefathers—so careful to guard our rights of freedom of speech, freedom of thought and freedom of assembly—would not feel that the Supreme Court had perhaps a higher obligation." Roosevelt spent the following two summers criticizing *Dennis* in public forums with Justice Douglas, an endeavor that at times met with hostility.[11]

Dennis opened the floodgates for additional FBI investigations and prosecutions. The Justice Department began pursuing "second-string" CPUSA leadership and over the next few years charged 126 communists with conspiracy under the Smith Act. Paul Robeson, W. E. B. Du Bois, Lewis Mumford, Eleanor Roosevelt, and Henry Steele Commager launched sporadic efforts to halt the prosecutions or obtain amnesty for defendants. Albert Einstein also figured prominently in these efforts. When the SISS subpoenaed a high school English teacher named William Frauenglass to question him about possible communist affiliations in May of 1953, Frauenglass wrote Einstein requesting a letter of support. Einstein's response, which appeared as part of a front-page story in the *New York Times,* counseled that "every intellectual who is called before the committees ought to refuse to testify" despite the inevitable consequences. Six months later, Albert Shadowitz, an electrical engineer, drove to Princeton to see Einstein after receiving a subpoena from the SISS. Einstein supported Shadowitz's intention to rely on the First Amendment rights of speech and association rather than the Fifth Amendment in his refusal to answer the committee's questions. At his public hearing, Shadowitz cited the First Amendment and noted that "Professor Einstein advised me not to answer."[12]

Despite these efforts by Einstein and others, widespread public concern for the accused never materialized, and the government routinely won even its weakest cases. Anticommunist concerns also pervaded state legislation. In 1952, the Court reviewed a speech and assembly challenge to a New York law that denied employment in its public schools to any person who advocated the violent overthrow of the government or who joined a society or group of persons knowing that it advanced such advocacy. The law took aim at "members of subversive groups, particularly of the Communist Party and its affiliated organizations," who had been "infiltrating into public employment in the public schools of the State." In passing the restrictive statute, the New York legislature had found that "the members of such groups use their positions to advocate and teach their doctrines . . . without regard to truth or free inquiry" in ways "sufficiently subtle to escape detection in the classroom." In *Adler v. Board of*

Education, a 6–3 majority concluded that New York had acted "in the exercise of its police power to protect the schools from pollution and thereby to defend its own existence."[13]

Nine months after *Adler,* the Court finally set limits on anticommunist legislation. Justice Clark's majority opinion in *Wieman v. Updegraff* struck down an Oklahoma statute that required state employees to affirm, among other things, that they had not within the preceding five years "been a member of . . . any agency, party, organization, association, or group whatever which has been officially determined by the United States Attorney General or other authorized public agency of the United States to be a communist front or subversive organization." Clark distinguished *Adler* by emphasizing that the New York law had required a person to have *known* the purposes of the society or group that he or she had joined. In contrast, Oklahoma's law mandated that "the fact of association alone determines disloyalty and disqualification; it matters not whether association existed innocently or knowingly."[14]

Frankfurter's concurrence in *Wieman* referred to "a right of association peculiarly characteristic of our people." That same year, Thomas Emerson and David Haber's treatise *Political and Civil Rights in the United States* contended that the "right of association is basic to a democratic society." Emerson and Haber asserted that association "embraces not only the right to form political associations but also the right to organize business, labor, agricultural, cultural, recreational and numerous other groups that represent the manifold activities and interests of a democratic people."[15]

In the midst of the Second Red Scare and early hints of a right of association, two men who would deeply influence the development of that right joined the Supreme Court: John Harlan and William Brennan. Brennan, who succeeded Sherman Minton in 1956, became the chief intellectual architect of the Warren Court and arguably "the most important jurist of the second half of the century." His tenure on the Court included the first official recognition of the right of association in *NAACP v. Alabama* and its transformation in the opinion he wrote twenty-six years later in *Roberts v. United States Jaycees.* Harlan, who replaced Robert Jackson in 1955, wrote the Court's opinion in *NAACP v. Alabama.* His role on the Court is often cast as "conservative" based on his close relationship with Felix Frankfurter, his deference to national security decisions by government officials, and his constant sparring with the Warren Court liberals. But this label obscures the complexity of his thought. Within his first few months on the Court, Harlan expressed discomfort over Smith Act prosecutions and associational restrictions on communists and let slip that he had little patience for "McCarthyite garbage."[16]

Harlan's constitutional hermeneutic also proved important in shaping the right of association. He believed that the "full scope" of the liberty of the Due Process Clause of the Fourteenth Amendment could not be "found in or limited by the precise terms of the specific guarantees else-where provided in the Constitution." For Harlan, the meaning of consti-tutional law was "one not of words, but of history and purposes." This required an appropriate balancing of past tradition with present reform: "The balance of which I speak is the balance struck by this country, having regard to what history teaches are the traditions from which it developed as well as the traditions from which it broke. That tradition is a living thing. A decision of this Court which radically departs from it could not long survive, while a decision which builds on what has survived is likely to be sound." These views about liberty and tradition opened Harlan to the kind of arguments that would later be advanced to ground the right of association in the Constitution.[17]

On Monday, June 17, 1957, with Brennan and Harlan now in place, the Court released a quartet of decisions curtailing the government's anti-communist efforts in what became known as "Red Monday." Three of the decisions checked actions by the federal government. *Service v. Dulles* ordered the reinstatement of a federal government employee who had been dismissed based on loyalty concerns. *Watkins v. United States* reversed John Watkins's contempt conviction following his refusal on First Amendment grounds to respond to questions from the HUAC about his alleged communist affiliations. *Yates v. United States*, the most important of the three decisions against the federal government, involved the appeal of fourteen leaders of the Communist Party in California convicted under the Smith Act. Harlan's majority opinion distinguished between advocacy of forcible overthrow of the government as an "abstract principle" on the one hand and "advocacy or teaching of action" on the other. Based on this standard, the Court directed that five of the convictions be over-turned outright and the other nine remanded for retrial. More important,

Harlan's statutory interpretation effectively constrained future Smith Act prosecutions.[18]

The fourth Red Monday decision, *Sweezy v. New Hampshire,* involved state rather than federal action. The New Hampshire attorney general had subpoenaed Paul Sweezy, the well-known Marxist economist and founder of the *Monthly Review,* to testify about alleged communist affiliations. Like Watkins, Sweezy refused to answer certain questions on First Amendment grounds. The Superior Court of Merrimack County, New Hampshire, found him in contempt and ordered his imprisonment. The New Hampshire Supreme Court upheld his conviction despite its assertion that "the right to associate with others for a common purpose, be it political or otherwise," was one of the "individual liberties guaranteed to every citizen by the State and Federal Constitutions." Chief Justice Warren's plurality opinion reversed the conviction, concluding that New Hampshire's statute impermissibly extended to "conduct which is only remotely related to actual subversion."[19]

Sweezy brought to the foreground an important legal question about the right of association: its constitutional source. Thomas Emerson, who represented Sweezy before the Court, noted that the New Hampshire Supreme Court had referred to "speech and association" rights in its review of Sweezy's conviction. But Emerson also recognized that the New Hampshire court had cited only "the Federal Constitution" as its basis for these rights. Emerson offered two more specific possibilities. First, he argued that New Hampshire's law deprived Sweezy "of liberty and property without due process of law, contrary to the Fourteenth Amendment of the Constitution of the United States." Second, he wrote that "it can hardly be doubted that the requirements of the First Amendment, made applicable to the states through the Fourteenth Amendment, impose comparable or identical limits on state power."[20]

The differences between these arguments may seem like hairsplitting to nonlawyers, but they reflect a doctrinal divide that complicated the Court's efforts to settle on a jurisprudential framework for the right of association. The disagreement centered on how rights located in the federal Constitution could limit *state* action. The Supreme Court had initially concluded that the substantive provisions of the Bill of Rights limited only the federal government and did not apply to the states. But the Fourteenth

Amendment's Due Process Clause had subsequently established—in language similar to the Fifth Amendment—that states could not "deprive any person of life, liberty, or property, without due process of law."[21]

Whether the liberty of the Fourteenth Amendment encompassed specific provisions in the Bill of Rights remained unclear at the time of *Sweezy*. In 1922, Justice Pitney had written for a majority of the Court that "neither the Fourteenth Amendment nor any other provision of the Constitution of the United States imposes upon the States any restriction about the freedom of speech." But three years later, Justice Sanford concluded in *Gitlow v. New York* that "we may and do assume that freedom of speech and of the press which are protected by the First Amendment from abridgment by Congress are among the fundamental personal rights and 'liberties' protected by the due process clause of the Fourteenth Amendment from impairment by the States." Chief Justice Hughes reached a similar conclusion about assembly in *De Jonge v. Oregon:* because "the right of peaceable assembly is a right cognate to those of free speech and free press, and is equally fundamental," it fell within "those fundamental principles of liberty and justice which lie at the base of all civil and political institutions—principles which the Fourteenth Amendment embodies in the general terms of its due process clause."[22]

Gitlow and *De Jonge* made clear that states, like the federal government, could not "impair" the freedoms of speech, press and assembly, but the decisions didn't identify the source of those restrictions. Justice Cardozo suggested two possibilities in *Palko v. Connecticut:* (1) that certain provisions from the Bill of Rights had been "brought within the Fourteenth Amendment by a process of absorption"; and (2) that restrictions against the federal government from "the specific pledges of particular amendments" were "implicit in the concept of ordered liberty" and thereby valid against the states through the Fourteenth Amendment. Restating Cardozo's alternatives suggests the following two possibilities:

(1) The *incorporation argument,* which holds that the due process clause of the Fourteenth Amendment incorporated the specific rights enumerated in the First Amendment, thereby making those rights applicable to the states; and

(2) ·The *liberty argument,* which holds that rights similar to those in the First Amendment were implicit in the liberty protected by the due process clause of the Fourteenth Amendment.[23]

Douglas, Black, and Frankfurter had previously sparred over the differences between the incorporation and liberty arguments. In 1943, Douglas's majority opinion in *Murdock v. Pennsylvania* referred without elaboration to "the First Amendment, which the Fourteenth makes applicable to the states." Four years later, Black's majority opinion in *Everson v. Board of Education* echoed the same language. Frankfurter dissented in both cases. He didn't see anything in the text of the Fourteenth Amendment that applied the Bill of Rights to the states. Two years later, he rebuffed Douglas and Black in his majority opinion in *Wolf v. Colorado:* "The notion that the 'due process of law' guaranteed by the Fourteenth Amendment is shorthand for the first eight amendments of the Constitution, and thereby incorporates them, has been rejected by this Court again and again, after impressive consideration.... The issue is closed."[24]

Black and Douglas disagreed with Frankfurter not only about the *source* of the constitutional limits on state action but also about the *extent* of those limits. For Black, the rights in the First Amendment were "absolute" and could not be restricted by state action. Douglas did not always go that far, but he argued in *Murdock* that the freedoms of the First Amendment held a "preferred position." Frankfurter considered the preferred position language a "mischievous phrase" which "expresse[d] a complicated process of constitutional adjudication by a deceptive formula" and which implied "that any law touching communication is infected with presumptive invalidity." He argued instead for a "balancing" that weighed the interests of the government against the liberty of the Fourteenth Amendment. On this view, Frankfurter would defer to a legislative judgment if a restriction of speech or assembly had a "rational basis." Justice Jackson described the tension between the two positions in *West Virginia v. Barnette:*

> In weighing arguments of the parties, it is important to distinguish between the due process clause of the Fourteenth Amendment as an instrument for transmitting the principles of the First Amendment and

those cases in which it is applied for its own sake. The test of legislation which collides with the Fourteenth Amendment, because it also collides with the principles of the First, is much more definite than the test when only the Fourteenth is involved. Much of the vagueness of the due process clause disappears when the specific prohibitions of the First become its standard. The right of a State to regulate, for example, a public utility may well include, so far as the due process test is concerned, power to impose all of the restrictions which a legislature may have a "rational basis" for adopting. But freedoms of speech and of press, of assembly, and of worship may not be infringed on such slender grounds. They are susceptible of restriction only to prevent grave and immediate danger to interests which the State may lawfully protect.

The upshot of these two perspectives was that the Court would be more likely to uphold a state law restricting expressive freedom if it followed the liberty argument and more likely to strike down the law if it followed the incorporation argument.[25]

Sweezy added a new wrinkle: unlike the rights of speech, press, assembly, and religion at issue in earlier cases, the right of association appeared nowhere in the text of the Constitution. Under the liberty argument, association (like any other right enforced against the states) was implicit in the liberty of the Fourteenth Amendment. The incorporation argument faced a greater hurdle because it claimed that the Fourteenth Amendment relied upon provisions found in the First Amendment. The only possible explanation to support the incorporation argument was that a right implicit in the First Amendment implicitly applied to states through the Fourteenth Amendment. That was one more degree of inference than the liberty argument. Penumbras formed by emanations, as Douglas would later characterize it.[26]

Chief Justice Warren's plurality opinion, joined by Douglas, Black, and Brennan, relied on the incorporation argument: "The right to engage in political expression and association ... was enshrined in the First Amendment." Frankfurter, joined by Harlan, concurred only in the result. In Frankfurter's view, the justices were confined to "the limited power to review the action of the States conferred upon the Court by the Fourteenth Amendment." The Court had to undertake "the narrowly circumscribed but exceedingly difficult task of making the final judicial accommodation between the competing weighty claims that underlie all such questions of due process." Frankfurter made no reference to the First Amendment but relied instead upon "'the concept of ordered liberty' implicit in the Due Process Clause of the Fourteenth Amendment." His concurrence rested upon "a judicial judgment in balancing two contending principles—the right of a citizen to political privacy, as protected by the Fourteenth Amendment, and the right of the State to self-protection."[27]

Civil Rights and the Right of Association

The divide between the liberty argument and the incorporation argument persisted when the Court formally recognized a constitutional right of association the following year in *NAACP v. Alabama*. The proximity between a waning but still active concern over domestic communism and the expanding Civil Rights Movement led to widely divergent claims about the relationship between the two. On the one hand, the federal government increasingly viewed segregation as undercutting its stance against communist ideology. Its amicus brief in *Brown v. Board of Education* argued that "the United States is trying to prove to the people of the world, of every nationality, race, and color, that a free democracy is the most civilized and most secure form of government yet devised by man," and that segregation jeopardized "the effective maintenance of our moral leadership of the free and democratic nations of the world." This view prevailed in the northern media as well. The *New York Times* described *Brown* as a "blow to communism." The *Washington Post* added that with *Brown*, "America is rid of an incubus which impeded and embarrassed it in all of its relations with the world."[28]

In contrast to these attempts to link integration with democracy, southern conservatives argued that integration advocates were controlled by communists. The charges were not entirely surprising: segregationists had associated communism and black activism since the turn of the century and the early days of the NAACP. In the 1930s, this link between "red" and "black" solidified in the minds of many southerners when the Communist Party's legal arm, the International Labor Defense, undertook the celebrated defenses of Angelo Herndon and the "Scottsboro Boys." But the "southern red scare" of the 1950s pressed the connections between these two "radical" movements beyond the realm of plausibility. And while segregationists "never found any good evidence that Communists had a perceptible influence in the NAACP," they nevertheless perpetuated a link "to discredit the civil rights movement by associating it with the nation's greatest enemy."[29]

Chief Justice Warren's *Brown* opinion fueled efforts to steer anticommunist sentiment toward civil rights activists. His famous footnote 11 cited four nonlegal sources—including Gunnar Myrdal and two other authors who had "what passed for communist leanings during that era." In response to the decision, Georgia's lieutenant governor denounced the "meddlers, demagogues, race baiters, and communists [who] are determined to destroy every vestige of states' rights." Mississippi senator James Eastland, who at the time chaired both the Senate Judiciary Committee and the SISS, argued that the Court in *Brown* had "responded to a radical, pro-Communist political movement in this country." Eastland, Arkansas senator John McClellan, and Louisiana representative Edwin Willis used their positions on the SISS, HUAC, and other investigative subcommittees to hold public hearings on "Communist influence in civil rights protests." One of the most forceful advocates of the link between communism and civil rights in the South was Mississippi Circuit Court judge Tom P. Brady. Lucas Powe writes that "Brady saw *Brown* as a virtual communist plot to mandate the amalgamation of the races." The summer after the Court's decision, Brady spearheaded the creation of the Citizens' Councils, which purported to be a "nonviolent alternative to the Ku Klux Klan" that would ensure economic ruin to anyone supporting integration. According to Neil McMillen, "the nexus between the NAACP and the international Communist apparatus was the central motif of literally hundreds of Council speeches and publications."[30]

In late 1954 and early 1955, Citizens' Councils sprang up across Alabama. From October to December 1955 alone, membership in the Alabama Councils grew from "a few hundred to twenty thousand." The councils made clear their intentions to bury civil rights advocates in Alabama under economic and social pressures: "The white population in this country controls the money, and this is an advantage that the council will use in a fight to legally maintain complete segregation of the races. We intend to make it difficult, if not impossible, for any Negro who advocates desegregation to find and hold a job, get credit or renew a mortgage." This background highlights the importance of the membership lists at issue in *NAACP v. Alabama:* once the names of NAACP members became public, the Citizens' Councils would ensure dire consequences.[31]

The controversy leading to *NAACP v. Alabama* began in June of 1956, when Alabama attorney general John Patterson initiated an action to enjoin the NAACP from operating within the state, arguing that the group was a "business" that had failed to register under applicable state law. The state court trial judge issued the injunction ex parte, explaining that he intended "to deal the NAACP a mortal blow from which they shall never recover." The judge also ordered the NAACP to produce its membership list, which Patterson had requested as part of a records review. When the NAACP refused to comply, the judge responded with a $10,000 contempt fine, which he increased to $100,000 five days later. After the Alabama Supreme Court rejected the NAACP's appeal of the judge's order through a series of disingenuous procedural rulings, the NAACP appealed to the United States Supreme Court.[32]

In its petition for certiorari, the NAACP contended that the actions of Patterson and the Alabama courts amounted to "a serious interference with essential freedom of speech, freedom of assembly, freedom of association, and the right to petition" and "an unlawful restraint by the State of Alabama of First Amendment rights." Despite the mention of association, the NAACP's substantive legal arguments relied on the rights of speech and assembly. In contrast to its cert petition, which implicitly made the incorporation argument, the NAACP's brief endorsed the liberty argument: the organization and its members were "merely invoking their constitutionally protected rights of free speech and free association guaranteed under the due process clause of the Fourteenth Amendment." The brief elaborated that "the unimpaired maintenance of freedom of association and free speech is considered essential to our political integrity" and quoted from Frankfurter's *Wieman* concurrence that the right of association was "peculiarly characteristic of our people." In its reply brief, the state of Alabama conceded the existence of a right of association. Using "association" and "assembly" interchangeably, the state contended that "like the other basic First Amendment freedoms, freedom of assembly is protected by the Fourteenth Amendment against unreasonable impairment by the states." The Court, according to the state, had "recently reaffirmed" the "constitutional status of association" in *Sweezy*.[33]

First Amendment scholar Leo Pfeffer submitted an amicus brief on behalf of a number of organizations, including the American Jewish Congress, the American Baptist Convention, the Commission on Christian Social Progress, the American Civil Liberties Union (ACLU), and the American Veterans Committee. The Court refused to consider the brief, but Pfeffer's arguments are preserved in the record and illuminate the conflation of the constitutional and doctrinal concepts in the case. Pfeffer was best known for his work on the First Amendment's religion clauses, but his 1956 book *The Liberties of an American* had included a section on assembly and association in which he had asserted that despite the absence of any mention of association in the Bill of Rights, "there can be little doubt that [the founding fathers] recognized the right to associate as a liberty of Americans." He elaborated by drawing a distinction between association and assembly: "When men band together for a single public demonstration of feeling or expression of a grievance they exercise their right of assembly; when they continue banding and acting together until the grievance is redressed they exercise their right of association. Freedom of indefinite or permanent association is as fundamental to democracy and as much a liberty of Americans as freedom of temporary assembly, and no less entitled to constitutional protection." But a few sentences later, Pfeffer collapsed the distinction, referring to "the right of assembly (i.e., association)."[34]

In his amicus brief, Pfeffer opened by appealing both to the liberty argument and to the incorporation argument: "Freedom of association is a liberty guaranteed against Federal infringement by the Fifth Amendment to the United States Constitution and against state infringement by the Fourteenth. In addition it is one of the co-equal guarantees of the First Amendment applied to the states by the Fourteenth." In support of the liberty argument, Pfeffer contended that "a constitutional provision protecting liberty against arbitrary governmental deprivation would have little meaning if it did not encompass the freedom of men to associate with each other." Turning to the incorporation argument, he revealed the same confusion between association and assembly that he had exhibited in *The Liberties of an American*. He argued on the one hand that association was broader than assembly: "'Freedom of association' may be viewed as a right to conduct indefinitely continuing assemblies." But he also asserted that assembly, not association, offered the key framework: "Freedom of assembly is not limited to occasional meetings but includes the organization of associations on a permanent basis." This kind of confusion over the relationship of association to assembly would extend well beyond Pfeffer.[35]

Oral argument in *NAACP v. Alabama* focused almost entirely on procedural and jurisdictional questions related to Alabama state law. The justices showed little interest in the freedom of association and asked no questions about its constitutional basis. NAACP attorney Robert L. Carter, who had advanced the incorporation argument in his cert petition and the liberty argument in his brief, now reverted back to the incorporation argument: the denial of "free speech and freedom of association" infringed upon a right "protected by the First Amendment." Alabama assistant attorney general Edmon Rinehart made no argument regarding the constitutional source of association but conceded its status as an individual right.[36]

The justices agreed that Alabama had infringed upon the associational rights of the members of the NAACP. After they had met in conference, Warren assigned the opinion to Harlan with the understanding that it would be unsigned or per curiam, in keeping with the Court's practice in post-*Brown* race cases. But Harlan soon realized that "it would reflect adversely on the Court were we to dispose of the case without a fully reasoned opinion" and convinced his colleagues that he should write a full opinion.[37]

Harlan's opinion for a unanimous Court framed the constitutional question in terms of the "fundamental freedoms protected by the Due Process Clause of the Fourteenth Amendment." He began his constitutional analysis by citing *De Jonge v. Oregon* and *Thomas v. Collins* for the principle that: "Effective advocacy of both public and private points of view, particularly controversial ones, is undeniably enhanced by group association, as this Court has more than once recognized by remarking upon the close nexus between the freedoms of speech and assembly." *De Jonge* and *Thomas* had established that the freedom of assembly applied to the states through the Fourteenth Amendment, that it covered political, economic, religious, and secular matters, and that it could only be restricted "to prevent grave and immediate danger to interests which the State may lawfully protect." Moreover, after observing that the Court in *American Communications Association v. Douds* had referred to "the varied forms of governmental action which might interfere with freedom of assembly," Harlan concluded that "compelled disclosure of membership in an organization engaged in advocacy of particular beliefs is of the same order."[38]

Based on these precedents, Harlan could have resolved the case under the freedom of assembly. But he instead shifted away from assembly, finding it "beyond debate that freedom to engage in association for the advancement of beliefs and ideas is an inseparable aspect of the 'liberty' assured by the Due Process Clause of the Fourteenth Amendment, which embraces freedom of speech." The Alabama courts had constrained the "right to freedom of association" of members of the NAACP. These members had a "constitutionally protected right of association" that meant they could "pursue their lawful private interests privately" and "associate freely with others in doing so." Writing a few years after *NAACP v. Alabama*, Thomas Emerson suggested that Harlan "initially treated freedom of association as derivative from the first amendment rights to freedom of speech and assembly, and as ancillary to them," and then "elevated freedom of association to an independent right, possessing an equal status with the other rights specifically enumerated in the first amendment." But Harlan's opinion is more ambiguous than Emerson suggests: it is not clear that Harlan relied at all on the First Amendment to ground association—the opinion, in fact, never mentions the First Amendment. A related question was whether Harlan's opinion tied the new right of association more closely to the right of speech or to the right of assembly. Harlan's reference to "the close nexus between speech and assembly" highlighted both rights, but the two decisions that he cited for this view were assembly cases, not speech cases. It is more likely that, as George Smith has argued, "the broad concept of a right of association . . . developed largely out of the right of assembly and in part out of due process concepts."[39]

Harlan's vagueness about the source of the right of association may explain how he marshaled a unanimous opinion. In an earlier draft that he circulated to his colleagues, Harlan had written: "It is of course firmly established that the protection given by the First Amendment against federal invasion of such rights is afforded by the Due Process Clause of the Fourteenth Amendment against state action." Douglas and Frankfurter were both troubled by the draft language, but for opposite reasons. Frankfurter pushed Harlan to rely expressly on the liberty argument and avoid any mention of the First Amendment: "Why in heaven's name must we, whenever some discussion under the Due Process Clause is involved, get off speeches about the First Amendment? Why can't you . . . state in two or three sentences that to ask disclosure of membership . . . is, in the light of prior decisions, merely citing them, an invasion of the free area of activity under the Fourteenth Amendment not overcome by any solid, as against a very tenuous, interest of the state in prying into such freedom of action by individuals[?]"[40]

Douglas, on the other hand, feared that Harlan's due process analysis diluted the First Amendment as it applied to the states: "If the right of free speech is watered down by the Due Process clause of the Fourteenth Amendment and made subject to state regulation, then the police power of the state has a pretty broad area for application. If we are dealing here with something that can be regulated then I think we are in very deep water in this case, as for the life of me I do not see why a state could not have a rational judgment for believing that an organization like the NAACP was a source of a lot of trouble, friction, and unrest." Douglas expressed particular concern over Frankfurter's proposed balancing approach, which Harlan had endorsed in earlier opinions: "I thought that when we dealt with these racial problems and with free speech and free assembly and religious problems we were dealing with something that is right close to the absolute."[41]

Harlan had no affinity for Douglas's argument, but he also expressed "the most serious misgivings" about Frankfurter's advice. Nonetheless, his revised draft eliminated any reference to the First Amendment. This concerned Black, who thought that the opinion now read "as though the First Amendment did not exist." Black notified Harlan that he planned on submitting a brief concurrence to specify "that the state has here violated the basic freedoms of press, speech and assembly, immunized from federal abridgement by the First Amendment, and made applica[ble] as a prohibition against the states by the Fourteenth Amendment." But he relented six days later, writing to Harlan that while he "would prefer our holding be supported by different reasoning," he realized that doing so would prevent the unanimous decision so important to the Court in cases involving questions of race.[42]

In the midst of satisfying Frankfurter, Douglas, and Black, Harlan had one other hurdle to clear with his opinion. The state of Alabama had argued that the Court was bound by *Bryant v. Zimmerman,* the 1928 case in which an 8–1 majority had upheld New York's Manford Act against Ku Klux Klan member George Bryant's challenge. The Court had dismissed Bryant's assertion of a Fourteenth Amendment due process liberty right "of membership in the association," concluding that this right "must yield to the rightful exertion of the police power." Justice Van Devanter's opinion had noted: "There can be no doubt that under that power the State may prescribe and apply to associations having an oath-bound membership any reasonable regulation calculated to confine their purposes and activities within limits which are consistent with the rights of others and the public welfare. . . . Requiring [membership lists] to be supplied for the public files will operate as an effective or substantial deterrent from the violations of public and private right to which the association might be tempted if such a disclosure were not required." This broad deference to police power, with explicit approval of the public disclosure of the Klan's membership list, may have prompted Douglas's concern that resolving *NAACP v. Alabama* under the liberty argument would make it difficult to distinguish *Bryant.* Harlan concluded that *Bryant* "was based on the particular character of the Klan's activities, involving acts of unlawful intimidation and violence," and emphasized the "markedly different considerations in terms of the interest of the State in obtaining disclosure." That was a plausible distinction, but Harlan's efforts to appease the concerns raised by Frankfurter, Douglas, and Black left uncertain both the constitutional source of the right of association and its applicability in other contexts.[43]

Association after *NAACP v. Alabama*

It was clear that *NAACP v. Alabama* had broken new constitutional ground, but specifying exactly what had taken place proved elusive. The

Washington Post editorialized that the Court had "cut through the flum-mery of Alabama's treatment of the NAACP and dealt with it as an outright violation of the freedom of *assembly*." The *New York Times* suggested that the Court had relied on the liberty argument, writing that the decision rested upon "one of the 'fundamental freedoms' guaranteed by the due process clauses [*sic*] of the Fourteenth Amendment." Meanwhile, the first round of commentary in the law reviews endorsed the incorporation argument, contending that Harlan's opinion had located the freedom of association in the First Amendment. The only thing clear from these initial reactions was that nobody was clear about the source or scope of the new right of association.[44]

The Court's first opportunities to apply *NAACP v. Alabama* came the following term in *Uphaus v. Wyman* and *Barenblatt v. United States*, two cases involving inquiries into alleged communist affiliations. The new freedom of association could have muted the overzealous investigations of the waning days of the McCarthy era. But while Anthony Lewis had charac-terized *NAACP v. Alabama* as "an illustration of the court's concern for the Constitutional right to express beliefs and ideas, however unpopular, through effective means," when the Court turned from the NAACP to the Communist Party, it became clear that not all associations were created equal.[45]

Uphaus involved another inquiry by New Hampshire's attorney general, Louis Wyman, who had been on the losing end of the Court's *Sweezy* decision two years earlier. Without mentioning the freedom of associa-tion, Justice Clark suggested that the case turned on "the single question of whether New Hampshire, under the facts here, is precluded from compelling the production of the documents by the Due Process Clause of the Fourteenth Amendment." Clark concluded that the "governmental interest in self-preservation is sufficiently compelling to subordinate the interest in associational privacy." Brennan filed a lengthy dissent premised on "the constitutionally protected rights of speech and assembly." Because he saw "no valid legislative interest" behind Wyman's inquiry, Brennan didn't see the need for any balancing of interests. He thought that the "Court's approach to a very similar problem in *NAACP v. Alabama* should furnish a guide to the proper course of decision here."[46]

Barenblatt, which unlike *NAACP v. Alabama* and *Uphaus* involved a congressional action, gave the Court its first opportunity to explain how the new right of association applied to the *federal* government. There were two possibilities. If association were a First Amendment right, then it would apply directly to actions of Congress. If, on the other hand, association were rooted in liberty, it presumably would apply to the federal government through the Due Process Clause of the Fifth Amendment. Harlan's opinion for the Court endorsed the former view: "The precise constitutional issue confronting us is whether the Subcommittee's inquiry into [Barenblatt's] past or present membership in the Communist Party transgressed the provisions of the First Amendment."[47]

Barenblatt presented facts similar to those in *Watkins,* one of the Court's 1957 Red Monday decisions. The HUAC had summoned Lloyd Barenblatt, who had taught psychology at Vassar, to ask him questions about an alleged affiliation with the Communist Party while he had been a graduate student at the University of Michigan. Like Watkins, Barenblatt had refused on First Amendment grounds to answer questions. In the earlier case, Chief Justice Warren had skirted the First Amendment challenge and instead concluded in general due process terms that Watkins could not reasonably have been expected to know which questions from the HUAC were pertinent to its legitimate inquiry. (Frankfurter later referred to Warren's efforts as that "god-awful *Watkins* opinion.") Harlan, writing for the Court in *Barenblatt,* distinguished *Watkins* on the basis that the HUAC questions to Barenblatt were relevant to the inquiry.[48]

Like Clark in *Uphaus,* Harlan largely eschewed the right of association and instead used a "balancing of interests" analysis. Frankfurter had been pushing for this approach for some time, first in his *Dennis* concurrence and more recently in his *Sweezy* concurrence. When Harlan circulated a draft of his *Barenblatt* opinion, Frankfurter responded with the suggestion that Harlan include "a few pungent paragraphs putting the case in its setting." This should happen "before the reader gets involved in the details of balancing." Harlan's revised opinion incorporated Frankfurter's suggestions and emphasized "the close nexus between the Communist Party and violent overthrow of government."[49]

As Lucas Powe notes, Harlan never explained how the government's "right of self preservation" related to "asking a former psychology instructor at Vassar about meetings when he was a graduate student." Moreover, Harlan failed to articulate a single interest of Barenblatt's against which the government's interests could be balanced, noting only that "the record is barren of other factors which, in themselves, might sometimes lead to the conclusion that the individual interests at stake were not subordinate to those of the state." Black's dissent quipped that Harlan had rewritten the First Amendment to read, "Congress shall pass no law abridging the freedom of speech, press, assembly and petition, unless Congress and the Supreme Court reach the joint conclusion that on balance the interest of the Government in stifling these freedoms is greater than the interest of the people in having them exercised." In a poignant passage, Black wrote:

> The fact is that, once we allow any group which has some political aims or ideas to be driven from the ballot and from the battle for men's minds because some of its members are bad and some of its tenets are illegal, no group is safe. . . . History should teach us [that] in times of high emotional excitement, minority parties and groups which advocate extremely unpopular social or governmental innovations will always be typed as criminal gangs, and attempts will always be made to drive them out. It was knowledge of this fact, and of its great dangers, that caused the Founders of our land to enact the First Amendment as a guarantee that neither Congress nor the people would do anything to hinder or destroy the capacity of individuals and groups to seek converts and votes for any cause, however radical or unpalatable their principles might seem under the accepted notions of the time.[50]

Neither Clark in *Uphaus* nor Harlan in *Barenblatt* had elaborated upon the constitutional right of association that the Court had recognized in its previous term. Harlan referred only once to "rights of association assured by the Due Process Clause of the Fourteenth Amendment." Clark mentioned "associational privacy" made applicable through "the Due Process Clause of the Fourteenth Amendment." But both decisions avoided a direct application of the new right, which would come not in a communist case but in one with facts remarkably similar to those in *NAACP v. Alabama.*[51]

In *Bates v. City of Little Rock,* the Court reviewed the convictions of two NAACP records custodians who had refused to produce local membership lists as required by ordinances in two Arkansas cities. Like the disclosure order that had led to the Alabama litigation, the Arkansas ordinances were designed to cripple the NAACP. Relying on the freedom of association, Justice Stewart's majority opinion cited *De Jonge* and *NAACP v. Alabama* to link association with assembly: "Like freedom of speech and a free press, the right of peaceable assembly was considered by the Framers of our Constitution to lie at the foundation of a government based upon the consent of an informed citizenry—a government dedicated to the establishment of justice and the preservation of liberty [citing the First Amendment]. And it is now beyond dispute that freedom of association for the purpose of advancing ideas and airing grievances is protected by the Due Process Clause of the Fourteenth Amendment from invasion by the States." As with Harlan's wording in *NAACP v. Alabama*, Stewart's language could be read to support either the incorporation argument or the liberty argument. To confuse matters further, Black and Douglas argued in a joint concurrence: "The ordinances as here applied violate freedom of speech and assembly guaranteed by the First Amendment which this Court has many times held was made applicable to the States by the Fourteenth Amendment. . . . One of those rights, *freedom of assembly, includes of course freedom of association;* and it is entitled to no less protection than any other First Amendment right."[52]

Ten months after *Bates,* Stewart again wrote for the majority, in *Shelton v. Tucker.* The case involved a challenge to an Arkansas statute requiring every teacher at a state-supported school or college to file an annual affidavit disclosing all organizations to which he or she had belonged or regularly contributed in the previous five years. Although the affidavit requirement wasn't overtly aimed at the NAACP, the Arkansas statute clearly targeted the organization. In *Bates,* Stewart had cited *De Jonge* to link association and assembly. In *Shelton,* he again cited *De Jonge* but now omitted any reference to assembly, referring instead to a "right of free association, a right closely allied to freedom of speech and a right which, like free speech, lies at the foundation of a free society." Unlike the unanimous decisions in *NAACP v. Alabama* and *Bates,* the Court split 5–4 in *Shelton,* with Frankfurter and Harlan joined by Clark and Whittaker in dissent. Harlan's dissent asserted that "the rights of free speech and association embodied in the 'liberty' assured against state action by the

Fourteenth Amendment are not absolute," reiterating both his liberty argument and his endorsement of a kind of balancing.[53]

In 1961, a year after *Shelton*, Douglas wrote the majority opinion in *Louisiana v. NAACP.* The case had arisen in 1956, after Louisiana sought to enjoin the NAACP from doing business in the state. The state asserted that the NAACP had violated two statutes, the first of which prohibited associations from doing business with out-of-state communist or subversive organizations, and the second of which required "benevolent" associations to disclose the names and addresses of all officers and members regulating associations. The Court struck down both statutes. Douglas dispensed with the first provision on vagueness grounds without referring to the right of association. Turning to the second provision, Douglas wrote that "freedom of association is included in the bundle of First Amendment rights made applicable to the States by the Due Process Clause of the Fourteenth Amendment." He interpreted *Shelton* to have emphasized that "any regulation must be highly selective in order to survive challenge under the First Amendment" and peppered his opinion with other references to the First Amendment. The four dissenting justices in *Shelton* concurred in the judgment but not in Douglas's opinion.[54]

The first four cases in which a majority of the Court had explicitly relied on the constitutional right of association (*NAACP v. Alabama, Bates, Shelton,* and *Louisiana v. NAACP*) had all invalidated regulations aimed at the NAACP. These decisions were vital to the Civil Rights Movement. As Samuel Walker has argued, "the NAACP could not have survived in the South, and the civil rights movement would have been set back for years, without the new freedom of association protections." But if upholding a right of association for members of the NAACP sustained that organization's existence, the failure to enforce that same right on behalf of members of the CPUSA almost certainly contributed to its demise.[55]

While a majority of the Court had already shown a reluctance to apply or even acknowledge a right of association for communists in *Uphaus* and *Barenblatt,* the trend intensified in 1961. In *Communist Party v. Subversive Activities Control Board (SACB),* the Court reviewed the Subversive Activities Control Act, which imposed registration and disclosure requirements on "subversive" organizations. Harry Kalven has suggested that *SACB* "should have been the architectonic case for freedom of association" because the statute at issue "aimed at sanctioning association and thus openly posed the issue that had been disguised as a speech problem in *Dennis.*" Instead, the Court upheld the entire act in the same 5–4 split as *Uphaus* and *Barenblatt.* Frankfurter wrote the lengthy majority opinion, distinguishing the case from *NAACP v. Alabama, Bates,* and *Shelton* based on "the magnitude of the public interests which the registration and disclosure provisions are designed to protect" and "the pertinence which registration and disclosure bear to the protection of those interests." Although the justices disagreed on the outcome, they all agreed that the right of association applied to the federal government through the First Amendment.[56]

On the same day that it decided *SACB,* the Court issued its 5–4 decision in *Scales v. United States.* Harlan wrote the opinion upholding a conviction under the Smith Act's membership clause, which he construed as requiring proof of "active" rather than merely "passive" membership in the Communist Party. Harlan insisted that a conviction under the act required the government to establish more than mere membership, but "active and purposive membership, purposive that is as to the organization's criminal ends."[57]

All nine justices had backed the right of association for the NAACP in *NAACP v. Alabama, Bates,* and *Louisiana v. NAACP.* Stewart's vote had ensured a similar outcome in *Shelton.* But in *Uphaus, Barenblatt, SACB,* and *Scales,* Stewart joined Frankfurter, Harlan, Whittaker, and Clark to deny these same associational protections to the CPUSA. In the words of ACLU legal director Mel Wulf, there were "red cases and black cases." Kalven phrased it more bluntly: "The Communists cannot win, the NAACP cannot lose."[58]

There was certainly a kind of double standard at work, but it was more complicated than Wulf and Kalven suggested. For one thing, the conservative justices were largely convinced by the severity of the communist threat they perceived. We can now see clear instances of overreaching on and off the Court, but it remains the case that communist organizers generally raised national security concerns different from those that civil rights activists raised.

Harlan's judicial restraint and deference to government officials on national security matters made him less than eager to join the Warren Court's curtailment of government inquiries in the name of civil liberties. *NAACP v. Alabama* had been an easy case for him because he believed that Alabama hadn't shown *any* legitimate interest in the NAACP's membership list. *Bates* differed from *NAACP v. Alabama* and required a balancing of interests. Although the decision ended up unanimous, Harlan had originally drafted a dissent. According to Brennan's conference notes, Harlan believed that while "there can be little doubt that much of the association information called for by the statute will be of little or no use whatever to the school authorities," he could "not understand how those authorities can be expected to fix in advance the terms of their inquiry so that it will yield only relevant information." *Shelton* had been even closer than *Bates* and hinged on Stewart's vote. The four dissenters (Frankfurter, Harlan, Whittaker, and Clark) believed that the government had shown a rational relationship between its articulated interest and the nature of the regulation. And while Stewart disagreed in *Shelton*, his position in the communist cases left open the possibility that a better articulated government interest would prevail over an NAACP claim to the right of association.[59]

The fracture over communism and civil rights meant that a Supreme Court case connecting communism and the NAACP "was every segregationist's dream" and offered "the South the chance to take out the NAACP by painting the organization red." That case began in 1956, when the Florida legislature started to investigate an alleged communist influence on the NAACP. As part of its inquiry, the legislative investigation committee subpoenaed the membership list of the organization's Miami branch. Theodore Gibson, the custodian of the list, refused to produce it, asserting that doing so would violate the associational rights of members of the NAACP. He did, however, volunteer to answer questions based on his personal knowledge, and when the committee provided him with the names and pictures of fourteen individuals, he testified that they were not to his knowledge members of the NAACP. The committee nonetheless cited Gibson for contempt for his failure to produce the records, and he was fined $1,200 and sentenced to six months' imprisonment. The Florida Supreme Court upheld his conviction, and Gibson appealed to the United States Supreme Court.[60]

At the conference following oral argument, Warren protested that affirming *Gibson* would mean overruling *NAACP v. Alabama* because even under a balancing theory the state had shown "no adequate interest." But Harlan viewed the investigation as "a bona fide inquiry into Communism" rather than "a plot to destroy [the] NAACP." The justices voted to uphold the conviction, and it appeared that the government's national security interests would prevail over the NAACP's right of association. Frankfurter, the senior justice in the majority, assigned the opinion to Harlan.[61]

Five months later, before Harlan had circulated a draft of his opinion, Whittaker retired from the Court, and the case (now deadlocked at 4–4) was held over for reargument. Then Frankfurter suffered a stroke and left the Court. When *Gibson* was reargued the following term, Byron White had replaced Whittaker, and Arthur Goldberg had succeeded Frankfurter. Goldberg provided the fifth vote for the NAACP. He wrote the majority opinion, distinguishing the case from earlier legislative investigation cases because Gibson had not been asked about his own associations with the Communist Party. Samuel Walker suggests that "*Gibson* was the clearest indication of the extent to which the Court granted to the NAACP the protections it had refused to extend to the Communists."[62]

Black and Douglas wrote separate concurrences. In Black's view, "the constitutional right of association includes the privilege of any person to associate with Communists or anti-Communists, Socialists or anti-Socialists, or, for that matter, with people of all kinds of beliefs, popular or unpopular." Douglas's concurrence posited three arguments for rooting association in the First Amendment. He first advanced the incorporation argument, describing "the authority of a State to investigate people, their ideas, their activities," and asserted that "by virtue of the Fourteenth Amendment the State is now subject to the same restrictions in making the investigation as the First Amendment places on the Federal Government." Douglas took direct aim at Harlan in a footnote: "Some have believed that these restraints as applied to the States through the Due Process Clause of the Fourteenth Amendment are less restrictive on them than they are on the Federal Government. That is the view of my Brother Harlan. . . . But that view has not prevailed. The Court has indeed applied the same First Amendment requirements to the States as to the Federal Government." Douglas then highlighted the right of assembly:

> Joining a lawful organization, like attending a church, is an associational activity that comes within the purview of the First Amendment, which provides in relevant part: "Congress shall make no law . . . abridging the freedom of speech, or of the press; or the right of the people, peaceably to assemble, and to petition the government for a redress of grievances." "Peaceably to assemble" as used in the First Amendment necessarily involves a coming together, whether regularly or spasmodically. Historically the right to assemble was secondary to the right to petition, the latter being the primary right. But today, as the Court stated in *De Jonge v. Oregon,* "The right of peaceable assembly is a right cognate to those of free speech and free press and is equally fundamental." Assembly, like speech, is indeed essential in order to maintain the opportunity for free political discussion, to the end that government may be responsive to the will of the people and that changes, if desired, may be obtained by peaceful means. The holding of meetings for peaceable political action cannot be proscribed. A Free Society is made up of almost innumerable institutions through which views and opinions are expressed, opinion is mobilized, and social, economic, religious, educational, and political programs are formulated.

Finally, Douglas revisited the "bundle of rights" language that had appeared in his *Louisiana v. NAACP* opinion and his *SACB* dissent. He connected this bundle to a "right of privacy": "The right of association has become a part of the bundle of rights protected by the First Amendment, and the need for a pervasive right of privacy against government intrusion has been recognized, though not always given the recognition it deserves. Unpopular groups like popular ones are protected. Unpopular groups if forced to disclose their membership lists may suffer reprisals or other forms of public hostility. But whether a group is popular or unpopular, the right of privacy implicit in the First Amendment creates an area into which the Government may not enter." According to Douglas, then, the right of association was: (1) derivative of the First Amendment right of assembly; (2) "part of the bundle of rights protected by the First Amendment"; and (3) related to "the right of privacy implicit in the First Amendment."[63]

As the Court proceeded in its attempts to ground the new right of association, scholars produced a stream of historical and doctrinal analyses. Book-length treatments included Glenn Abernathy's *Right of Assembly and Association*, Charles Rice's *Freedom of Association,* and David Fellman's *Constitutional Right of Association.* These works attempted to narrate a history of association absent from nearly two centuries of American constitutional law. Fellman, for example, suggested that "however ill-defined they may be, the rights of association have a definite place in American constitutional law." Rice argued that "the right to associate for the advancement of ideas ha[d] been recognized implicitly in the past, and it ha[d] underlain important decisions which have been formally ascribed to the application of other freedoms." Carl Beck's *Contempt of Congress* took the most creative route, referring to a nonexistent "freedom of political affiliation [clause] of the First Amendment."[64]

Abernathy provided the most comprehensive account of association. He had first speculated about a right of association in a 1953 article published in the *South Carolina Law Quarterly.* Quoting extensively from Tocqueville and Arthur Schlesinger, Abernathy had suggested that the importance of freedom of association in a democratic society "cannot be overestimated." Noting that the Supreme Court had at that time yet to recognize a right of association, he argued that it was nonetheless "a right cognate to those of free speech and free assembly." Abernathy expressed concern that Congress's anticommunist legislation and the Court's *Adler* decision hindered Americans from joining all but the most "ultra-acceptable" associations. He decried "shotgun legislation which endangers the whole institution of voluntary association" and argued for a "broad freedom to associate." But Abernathy's principal concern for group autonomy had little to do with protecting unpopular or dissenting groups like the Communist Party. Rather, in his instrumental view, "[associations] serve as a training ground for group participation, organization and management of people and programs, and for democratic acceptance of the majority will. They can also serve as a potential influence for improvement of communication between the individual and the government. Concerted demands for action by associations of people have a better chance for accomplishing the desired governmental action than do scattered individual requests. And the information furnished to administrators and legislators by private associations of various kinds is in many instances vital to the intelligent treatment of particular problems."[65]

Abernathy's book-length treatment eight years later underscored the themes of his earlier article: "Experience in various associations is virtually a guarantee of respect for the majority view. It does not necessarily lead to complete acceptance of the majority will, but it does lead usually to a sufficient respect for that will to enable the group to act in concert once a decision has been made. This acquiescence in the decisions of the majority, based in large part on experience in associations of various types, is an important explanation of the fact that Americans can close ranks and function as a strongly united nation after an election which is preceded by almost violent contests between the two major political parties." This characterization contained two implicit assumptions, neither of which is inherent in the nature of groups. The first was that a kind of bounded consensus across groups ensured stability in the midst of disagreement. The second was that the internal practices of associations mirrored majoritarian democratic practices.[66]

Abernathy intimated that *NAACP v. Alabama* had relied expressly on the right of assembly. He argued that the decision had placed the right of association within an "expanded meaning" of the right of assembly, and that association was "clearly a right cognate to the right of assembly." The right of assembly "need not be artificially narrowed to encompass only the physical assemblage in a park or meeting hall. It can justifiably be extended to include as well those persons who are joined together through organizational affiliation." Abernathy also noted an additional constraint imposed by the right of association:

> It must be noted that [*NAACP v. Alabama*] does not clearly extend the First Amendment protection to *all* lawful affiliations or organizations. What Justice Harlan discusses is the association "for the advancement of beliefs and ideas." Clearly a vast number of existing associations would fall within this description, but it is questionable whether the characterization would fit the purely social club, the garden club, or perhaps even some kinds of trade or professional unions. *No such distinction has been drawn in the cases squarely involving freedom of assembly questions.* The latter cases emphasize that the right extends to any lawful assembly, without a specific requirement that there be an intention to advance beliefs and ideas.

In observing the limitation in scope, Abernathy had detected an important distinction in Harlan's opinion between assembly and association. He quickly brushed it aside: "The practical effect, of course, may be unimportant, since fairly obviously the Court would be inclined to scrutinize restrictions on social clubs less closely than those on organizations identifying themselves more intimately with the political process." But the real danger is greater than Abernathy surmised; it becomes apparent when we consider who decides whether an organization exists "for the advancement of beliefs or ideas" or is involved "intimately with the political process." The Court would reveal the extent of this danger a generation later in its creation of intimate association and expressive association and the subjective interpretations that they required. As Abernathy noted, these constraints are absent in the right of assembly.[67]

It is not entirely surprising that scholarly treatment of the right of association reflected the Court's own lack of clarity. Writing in 1964, Thomas Emerson observed that "the constitutional source of 'the right of association,' the principles which underlie it, the extent of its reach, and the standards by which it is to be applied have never been clearly set forth," and that "the various justices have differed among themselves on all these matters." Emerson warned that "a general 'right of association' does not carry us very far in the solution of concrete issues" and "current problems involving associational rights must be framed and answered in terms of more traditional constitutional doctrines." But because the right of association was in large part a right without a constitutional history, its contours were more likely to be shaped by the intellectual context in which it emerged than by "traditional constitutional doctrines."[68]

Pluralist Political Theory

The preceding sections of this chapter addressed two contextual factors that contributed to the constitutional framework for the right of association: (1) a political factor (the conflation of anticommunist sentiment and the rise of the Civil Rights Movement); and (2) a jurisprudential factor (the infighting on the Court over the proper way to ground the right of association and the relationship between association and assembly). This section introduces a theoretical factor: the pluralist political theory of the mid-twentieth century. Pluralist assumptions popularized by David Truman and Robert Dahl exacerbated the political and jurisprudential factors affecting the right of association and helped the new right gain traction in legal and political discourse.

The pluralist tradition that began in the early twentieth century changed the way in which American political thought conceived of the relationship between groups and the state. Unlike some of its British antecedents, American pluralism advanced its own insistent claim that politics relocated among groups achieved a harmonious *balance* within a broad *consensus* that supported American democracy. The balance assumption sprang from the pluralist need to attribute the relative stability in democratic society to something other than centralized state power. The consensus assumption perpetuated an exaggerated claim of homogeneity in American history and culture that downplayed funda-mental differences between groups. These two assumptions were present in early American pluralists like Arthur Bentley, and they became even more pronounced in postwar pluralists like Truman and Dahl.[69]

Truman and Dahl invoked familiar authorities to support their assump-tions of balance and consensus: Tocqueville's *Democracy in America* and Madison's *Federalist* No. 10. But their interpretive efforts misread Madison and decontextualized Tocqueville. With Madison, they converted a nega-tively construed "faction" into an inherently valuable and implicitly benign "interest." With Tocqueville, they extrapolated a theory derived from the harmony of interests observed in a homogenous segment of the population in preindustrial America to the diversity of interests existing in an increasingly fractured industrialized society. Perhaps most ironically, the pluralist adaptations of Madison and Tocqueville jettisoned both theorists' warnings about the tyranny of the majority. By presupposing conformity to basic majoritarian conceptions of democracy as a predicate to associa-tional autonomy, pluralists reopened the door to state control and endorsed the very danger against which Madison and Tocqueville had hedged. These pluralist views—and their consequences—set the theoret-ical context for the constitutional right of association that emerged in the 1950s and 1960s.[70]

The pluralist thought that captured American political science in the mid-twentieth century began with theorists who challenged the modern state's claim to sovereignty, which had gained prominence in German idealism and entered American political thought through Francis Lieber. While Lieber and others had placed the locus of power and politics in the state, early pluralists looked instead at the groups that constituted society. The pluralist argument ran contrary not only to German idealism but also to classical liberalism, which in its own way assumed the primacy of the state. The critique of state-centered theory meant that the state "began to lose ground as an account of political reality." But pluralists weren't anarchists, and without Leviathan, they needed something else to account for the relative peace that they observed in American society. They concluded that in the absence of state coercion (the existence of which they downplayed), stability came from a balancing of interests and power among the various groups that made up the political life of society.[71]

The pluralist view of balanced power began with Arthur Bentley's *Process of Government,* which provided one of the earliest systematic attempts to challenge state-centered theory. Bentley's "group basis of politics" focused on interests expressed through group activity. He described "the push and resistance between groups" as "pressure" and suggested that "the balance of the group pressures *is* the existing state of society." For Bentley, groups formed the fundamental ontology of politics: "When the groups are adequately stated, everything is stated." Despite its frontal attack on state sovereignty, *The Process of Government* received scant attention in its first printing in 1908. It would, in fact, take a generation before political scientists embraced it for its theory and methodology. But in the intervening years, the monist account of state sovereignty suffered a further setback when German idealism fell out of favor after the First World War.[72]

The alternative theory of politics that emerged in American political thought arrived through the British pluralist Harold Laski. Laski challenged the assumption that the state absorbed all individual loyalties within a community. In Herbert Deane's words, Laski's early political writings were a "constant polemic" against "the conception that the state is to political theory what the Absolute is to metaphysics, that it is mysteriously One above all other human groupings, and that, because of its superior position and higher purpose, it is entitled to the undivided allegiance of each of its citizens." Laski asserted that "the state is only one among many forms of human associations," and he advocated decentralized power in which individuals increasingly turned to private groups to meet their interests and needs. He believed the transfer of governmental functions to private entities divided political power. During the early 1920s, Laski repeatedly "turned to pluralism as both a 'realistic' account of politics and as the basis of a new democratic theory."[73]

While Laski and other British pluralists posited a polarized relationship between groups and the state, American pluralism took a more benevolent form that gained wide acceptance in the 1930s through "mutually reinforcing empirical studies of group activity and accounts of the new image of democracy which were contrasted with totalitarianism." By the end of the 1930s, "liberalism in political science largely meant pluralism, and pluralism was both a descriptive and a normative thesis." Pendleton Herring's 1940 book *The Politics of Democracy* claimed that "along with party integration and governmental accountability, political rationality was to be found in the conflict and adjustment between interest groups." This meant that "democracy was not a matter of theology and creeds, but the practice of tolerance and compromise." The pluralist notion of balance extended from political to economic descriptions with John Kenneth Galbraith's ideas of "countervailing power" and "counterpressures." Meanwhile, David Riesman argued that power was distributed among "veto groups" that displayed a "necessary mutual tolerance" and "mirror[ed] each other in their style of political action, including their interest in public relations and their emphasis on internal harmony of feelings." Godfrey Hodgson later recalled the fusion of balance and stability that permeated the pluralist era, observing that "the businessman and the unskilled laborer, the writer and the housewife, Harvard University and the Strategic Air Command, International Business Machines and the labor movement, all had their parts to play in one harmonious political, intellectual, and economic system."[74]

In 1951, David Truman's *Governmental Process* described "the vast multiplication of interests and organized groups in recent decades" whose activities "imply controversy and conflict, the essence of politics." Truman asserted that "the behaviors that constitute the process of government cannot be adequately understood apart from the groups."

These interests balanced each other: multiple memberships in "potential groups" collectively formed a "balance wheel" in politics. Truman argued that "without the notion of multiple memberships in potential groups it is literally impossible to account for the existence of a viable polity such as that in the United States or to develop a coherent conception of the political process."[75]

The most important theorist of postwar pluralism was Robert Dahl. Although he drew upon early pluralists like Laski, his outlook was defined by the "behavioral approach" that manifested "a strong sense of dissatisfaction with the achievements of conventional political science, particularly through historical, philosophical, and the descriptive-institutional approaches." With Dahl's influence, "the mid-1960s marked the apotheosis of pluralism as the substance of the vision of both domestic and comparative politics accepted by behavioralism, and it was embedded in most of the conceptual schemes for political analysis." Over time, Dahl muted some of his more strident assertions, but his initial claims shaped a generation of political science scholarship.[76]

Dahl sought to describe how power was exercised in political decision making. He started with the premise that the United States was a "polyarchy," by which he meant a "mixture of elite rule and democracy." Against the "ruling-elite model" advanced by sociologists like C. Wright Mills, Dahl argued that power was diffused among a wide range of groups. Democracy was a "government by minorities." Avigail Eisenberg explains the conclusions that flow from this premise: "The direction that public policy follows depends on the nature of the coalition of minorities that dominates the policy-making scene at any given instant. The groups' reliance on each other creates an informal system of checks and balances in which no group is able to dominate the others. There is no chance for a minority to dominate a coalition because other minorities within the coalition will defect. Similarly, majorities are unable to pose a threat, since they are comprised of small groups, any of which may defect from the coalition if the policy direction changes." Paradoxically, then, the lack of widespread agreement produced a stability that prevented discord. For Dahl, the American political system reflected "a relatively efficient system for reinforcing agreement, encouraging moderation, and maintaining social peace."[77]

Dahl's most explicit endorsement of pluralism is found in his 1967 text *Pluralist Democracy in the United States:* "Multiple centers of power, none of which is or can be wholly sovereign," represented "the fundamental axiom in the theory and practice of American pluralism," which meant that "because one center of power is set against another, power itself will be tamed, civilized, controlled, and limited to decent human purposes, while coercion, the most evil form of power, will be reduced to a minimum." Dahl recognized that in polyarchies "a great many questions of policy are placed in the hands of private, semipublic, and local governmental organizations such as churches, families, business firms, trade unions, towns, cities, provinces, and the like." But his list left curiously ambiguous which entities were "private" and which were "semipublic." Further, Dahl seemed unduly sanguine in his assessment that "whenever a group of people believe that they are adversely affected by national policies or are about to be, they generally have extensive opportunities for presenting their case and for negotiations that may produce a more acceptable alternative." Like earlier pluralists, Dahl generally failed to account for the kinds of public power now dissipated among private groups. Thus, for example, he contended that most conflict between groups would be resolved not by coercion but by "peaceful adjustment."[78]

Some of Dahl's claims about the "extensive opportunities" for negotiations and prospects for "peaceful adjustment" seemed terribly at odds with events unfolding in American society, like civil rights sit-ins, campus activism, and antiwar protests. But as John Gunnell writes, the behavioralism popularized by Dahl meant that "at the very historical moment that events such as [these] were taking place, political science research seemed to ignore these matters in favor of the study of such things as voting." The pluralist narrative that power dispersed among groups led to a balanced equilibrium resonated with the statistically driven methods that had entered the discipline of political science. Pluralists, like some of their quantitative heirs in political science today, believed that by identifying the proper data and methodology, politics could be reduced to a system of solvable equations. Because equations balanced and followed logical patterns, then so must the forms of power that pluralists observed in groups.[79]

Even more pronounced than the pluralist gloss on balance was its assumed consensus of democratic beliefs and values. The beginnings of this consensus narrative emerged in the era of industrialization. The economic focus of progressive reforms of the early twentieth century had led to "a belief in the capacity of American abundance to smooth over questions of class and power by creating a nation of consumers." In Alan Brinkley's assessment, liberal reformers were confident "that their new consumer-oriented approach to political economy had freed them at last from the need to reform capitalist institutions and from the pressure to redistribute wealth and economic power."[80]

The pluralist consensus can be traced to Bentley, who asserted that all struggles between groups proceeded within a "habit background." These constraints limited "the technique of the struggle" employed by groups such that "when the struggle proceeds too harshly at any point there will become insistent in the society a group more powerful than either of those involved which tends to suppress the extreme and annoying methods of the groups in the primary struggle." These background assumptions had a tremendous normalizing effect: "It is within the embrace of these great lines of activity that the smaller struggles proceed, and the very word struggle has meaning only with reference to its limitations." As Myron Hale concluded: "Bentley's science of politics ended in a science of control within a closed system."[81]

Although Bentley's early hints at a consensus narrative were only later adopted by postwar pluralists, the idea of consensus was in the air elsewhere in American political thought. Writing in 1939, John Dewey concluded that American culture had produced "a basic consensus and community of beliefs." Fourteen years later, Daniel Boorstin echoed Dewey in heralding the national consensus of liberal values as part of the "genius of American politics." The growing consensus was also buttressed by historians like Louis Hartz, whose 1955 book *The Liberal Tradition in America* argued that the "moral unanimity" of Americans stemmed from a "nationalist articulation of Locke" that had been the only significant intellectual influence upon the American founders. While earlier historians like Charles Beard had focused on tensions arising from class distinctions, mid-twentieth-century scholarship heralded "the consensus, rather than the conflict, between Americans." By the late 1950s, the liberal endorsement of a welfare and labor system predicated on a fundamental belief in the capitalist state prompted Daniel Bell to declare the "end of ideology."[82]

Against this background, Truman's *Governmental Process* called attention to "potential" groups that reflected "those interests or expectations that are so widely held in the society and are so reflected in the behavior of almost all citizens that they are, so to speak, taken for granted." These "widely held but unorganized interests" constituted the "rules of the game." And the rules of the game enforced by unorganized interests constrained the practices of organized interests. In other words, a sufficiently homogenous background consensus shared by all citizens not only sustained the public order—which, for Truman, included "reinforcing widely accepted norms of 'public morality'"—but also bounded the extent to which groups diverged from that shared consensus. Broad compliance was critical because "the existence of the state, of the polity, depends on widespread, frequent recognition and conformity to the claims of these unorganized interests and on activity condemning marked deviations from them." The rules of the game give politics a "sense of justice," and violating them "normally will weaken a group's cohesion, reduce its status in the community, and expose it to the claims of other groups."[83]

But Truman also recognized that his balance wheel would encounter friction based on differences in group experiences, frames of reference, and "rationalizations." To illustrate how the normative effects of a group on its members could lead to beliefs outside the mainstream, Truman posited the example of military training: "A group of professional military officers, recruited at an early age, trained outside of civilian institutions, and practising the profession of arms in comparative isolation from other segments of the society, easily may develop the characteristics of a caste. Such a group not only will generate its own peculiar interests but also may arrive at interpretations of the 'rules of the game' that are at great variance with those held by most of the civilian population. In such a case multiple membership in other organized groups is slight and that in potential widespread groups is unlikely." For Truman, this unattended divergence from the rules of the game threatened the health of democracy, and he saw it advancing within groups far less innocuous than the United States military. Communist organizations provided one example of worrisome groups falling outside the consensus. The rising Civil Rights Movement in the South provided another example: "The emergence in the disadvantaged classes of groups that reflect materially different interpretations of the widespread interests may encourage conflict and at the same time provide an inadequate basis for peaceful settlement. The appearance of groups representing Negroes, especially in the South, groups whose interpretations of the 'rules of the game' are divergent from those of the previously organized and privileged segments of the community, are a case in point."[84]

Truman believed that widespread divergence could be mitigated because the rules of the game could be "acquired by most individuals in their early experiences in the family, in the public schools (probably less effectively in the private and parochial schools), and in similar institutionalized groups that are also expected to conform in some measure to the 'democratic mold.'" He didn't expressly acknowledge it, but the imposition of a "democratic mold" collapsed pluralism into a position similar to the state-centered idealism that pluralism had originally challenged: lurking behind a seemingly benign agreement of values was the normative (and coercive) association of the state. As Earl Latham suggested in 1952, the state is the "custodian of the consensus" and "helps to formulate and to promote normative goals, as well as to police the agreed rules." Reflecting the degree to which pluralism had diverged from its initial antistatist claims, Latham added that "in the exercise of its normative functions," the state "may even require the abolition of groups or a radical revision of their internal structure."[85]

Dahl, like Hartz, Bell, and Truman, located American politics within a broad consensus: "Prior to politics, beneath it, enveloping it, restricting it, conditioning it, is the underlying consensus on policy that usually exists in the society among a predominant portion of the politically active members. Without such a consensus no democratic system would long survive the endless irritations and frustrations of elections and party competition. With such a consensus the disputes over policy alternatives are nearly always disputes over a set of alternatives that have already been winnowed down to those within the broad area of basic agreement." For Dahl, this consensus was not a normative aspiration but an empirical fact. Under his influence, methodological assumptions set the rules of debate over what counted as politics and scholarship on politics, and in this way behavioralists enforced their own normative consensus on political thought. The dominance of research paradigms buttressed normative claims, and consensus about methodology uncritically reinforced consensus about substance.[86]

Dahl argued that the pluralist consensus included "a belief in democracy as the best form of government, in the desirability of rights and procedures insuring a goodly measure of majority rule and minority freedom, and in a wide but not necessarily comprehensive electorate." Writing in 1961, he asserted: "To reject the democratic creed is in effect to refuse to be an American. As a nation we have taken great pains to insure that few citizens will ever want to do anything so rash, so preposterous—in fact, so wholly un-American." Dahl also believed that the "ideological convergence reflecting a wide acceptance by Americans of their institutions" made it "extraordinarily difficult (and, up to now, impossible) to gain a big public following for a movement that openly seeks comprehensive, radical, or revolutionary changes in a large number of American institutions." As a result, Dahl argued that "radical movements" had been wholly ineffective in American politics: "Throughout the history of the United States, political life has been almost completely blanketed by parties, movements, programs, proposals, opinions, ideas, and an ideology directed toward a large mass of convergent 'moderate' voters. The history of radical movements, whether of right or left, and of antisystem parties, as they are sometimes called, is a record of unrelieved failure to win control over the government." But as long as groups operated within the boundaries of consensus, Dahl believed that the American political system provided "a high probability that any active and legitimate group will make itself heard effectively at some stage in the process of decision."[87]

The consensus assumption of pluralism laid the foundation for the freedom of association in two ways. First, it established an implicit expectation that groups were valuable to democracy only to the extent that they reinforced and guaranteed democratic premises and, conversely, that groups antithetical to these premises were neither valuable to democracy nor worthy of its protections. Second, because the consensus excluded groups beyond the margins of acceptability, the pluralist gloss on the groups that remained within its boundaries was unqualifiedly positive. Groups were not only fundamental to American politics, they created harmony and balance through reasoned and appropriately constrained disagreement.

The idea that groups were valuable to democracy only to the extent that they supported democracy was bereft of either authority or tradition in American political thought. And because pluralists were attempting to define themselves in opposition to the oppressive tendencies they observed in European politics, they needed to appeal to the American context to substantiate their views. On the subject of groups and associations, Madison and Tocqueville were the obvious candidates. Madison had argued in *Federalist* No. 10 that one of the most important advantages of "a well constructed union" was its "tendency to break and control the violence of faction." The "latent causes of faction" were "sown in the nature of man." As Madison elaborated: "A zeal for different opinions concerning religion, concerning government, and many other points, as well of speculation as of practice; an attachment to different leaders ambitiously contending for preeminence and power; or to persons of other descriptions whose fortunes have been interesting to the human passions, have, in turn, divided mankind into parties, inflamed them with mutual animosity, and rendered them much more disposed to vex and oppress each other than to cooperate for their common good." Factions, by Madison's definition, were adverse "to the permanent and aggregate interests of the community."[88]

Pluralists looking back at Madison through the lens of the presumed consensus of mid-twentieth-century America read his negative connotations out of the *Federalist*. Truman suggested that Madison's factions "carry with them none of the overtones of corruption and selfishness associated with modern political groups." Theodore Lowi charged that Truman's reasoning turned Madison on his head:

> Note, for example, the contrast between the traditional and the modern definition of the group: Madison in *Federalist 10* defined the group ("faction") as "a number of citizens, whether amounting to a majority or minority of the whole who are united and actuated by some common impulse of passion, or of interest, *adverse to the right of other citizens, or to the*

permanent and aggregate interests of the community." Modern political science usage took that definition and cut the quotation just before the emphasized part. In such a manner, pluralist theory became the handmaiden of interest-group liberalism, and interest-group liberalism became the hand-maiden of modern American positive national statehood.[89]

Unlike Truman, Dahl recognized Madison's belief "that a faction will produce tyranny if unrestrained by external checks." But Dahl misread Madison's apprehension to pertain solely to "majority factions." Although nothing in Madison's account assigned an inherently positive value to divided interests, Dahl contended that "no political group has ever admitted to being hostile to" the "permanent and aggregate interests of the community." Rather, the "numerous, extended, and diverse" minority interests were part of "the restraints on the effectiveness of majorities imposed by the facts of a pluralistic society." These varied interests operated within a broad consensus and posed no inherent danger to democracy. Dahl thought that Madison had underestimated "the importance of the inherent social checks and balances existing in every pluralistic society" that came through these interests and had not appreciated "the role of social indoctrination and habituation in creating attitudes, habits, and even personality types requisite to a given political system."[90]

Lance Banning has argued that the "pluralist misreading" of *Federalist* No. 10 attained its "widest influence" through Dahl. The "cruder forms" of this misreading suggested "that Madison delighted in the clash of special interests and identified the outcome of such clashes with the public good." Quoting Daniel Walker Howe, Banning notes that "'faction' was not a value-free concept for Publius; a faction was by defi-nition evil." Madison biographer Ralph Ketcham also dissents "from the view that sees Madison, especially in his tenth *Federalist Paper,* as validating modern conflict-of-interest politics." By disregarding the dangers inherent in minority factions, pluralism transformed Madison's faction into a domesticated group whose interests were broadly aligned with those of the modern liberal state.[91]

Unlike Madison, Tocqueville drew no negative conclusions about "voluntary associations." He instead "subverted" Madison's analysis of factions and "regarded associations as a valuable way of connecting people by overcoming some effects of individualism." Tocqueville's optimism stemmed in part from his idealized view of associations in America: "In America the citizens who form the minority associate, in order, in the first place, to show their numerical strength, and so to diminish the moral authority of the majority; and, in the second place, to stimulate competition, and to discover those arguments which are most fitted to act upon the majority; for they always entertain hopes of drawing over their opponents to their own side, and of afterward disposing of the supreme power in their name. Political associations in the United States are therefore peaceable in their intentions, and strictly legal in the means which they employ; and they assert with perfect truth that they only aim at success by lawful expedients." In other words, Tocqueville presupposed that associations in America would never seriously threaten the stability of government in America. He elaborated, tellingly, that "in a country like the United States, in which the differences of opinion are mere differences of hue, the right of association may remain unrestrained without evil consequences."[92]

Dahl believed that Tocqueville was "struck by the degree of political, social, and economic equality among Americans" and had "made this observation the very kernel of his famous analysis of American democracy." Dahl maintained, based on his reading of Tocqueville, that "Americans almost unanimously agree on a number of general propositions about democracy." Writing in 1961, he contended: "Throughout the country then the political stratum has seen to it that new citizens, young and old, have been properly trained in 'American' principles and beliefs. Everywhere, too, the pupils have been highly motivated to talk, look and believe as Americans should. The result was as astonishing an act of voluntary political and cultural assimilation and speedy elimination of regional, ethnic, and cultural dissimilarities as history can provide. The extent to which Americans agree today on key propositions about democracy is a measure of the almost unbelievable success of this deliberate attempt to create a seemingly uncoerced nation-wide consensus." Importantly, Dahl recognized that Tocqueville had written in a preindustrial era different from the current landscape: "The America that Tocqueville saw . . . was the America of Andrew Jackson. It was an agrarian democracy, remarkably close to the ideal often articulated by Jefferson. Commerce, finance, and industry erupted into this agrarian society in a gigantic explosion. By the time the [nineteenth] century approached its last decade, . . . the America of Tocqueville had already passed away." But Dahl insisted that despite the growing inequality of resources following these changes, a "universal creed of democracy and equality" persisted in mid-twentieth-century America.[93]

The pluralist appropriation of Tocqueville's account of associations overlooked two complications. The first was that Tocqueville's case study of America in the 1830s had focused on an extraordinarily homogenous population, thus giving him an excessively sanguine view of harmony amidst difference. Rogers Smith has noted that Tocqueville and later accounts that draw upon him

> center on relationships among a minority of Americans—white men, largely of northern European ancestry—analyzed in terms of categories derived from the hierarchy of political and economic status such men held in Europe: monarchs and aristocrats, financial and commercial burghers, farmers, industrial and rural laborers, indigents. Because most European observers and most white American men regarded these categories as politically basic, it is understandable that from America's inception they thought that the most striking fact about the new nation was the absence of one specific type of fixed, ascriptive hierarchy. There was no hereditary monarchy or nobility native to British America itself, and the Revolution rejected both the authority of the British king and aristocracy and the creation of any new American substitutes. Those genuinely momentous features of American political life made the United States appear remarkably egalitarian in comparison to Europe.

But as Smith observes, the "relative egalitarianism that prevailed among white men" left unaddressed immense inequities pertaining to gender, race, culture, religion, and sexual orientation. When associations expanded to these interests—as they increasingly did by the mid-twentieth century—differences of opinion were no longer merely differences of hue, and Tocqueville's theory lost its descriptive purchase. Pluralists to a large degree failed to recognize Tocqueville's limits and as a result adopted an understanding of balance and consensus that excluded significant classes of people from their description of the political process. As Grant McConnell argued in 1966, "farm migrant workers, Negroes, and the urban poor have not been included in the system of 'pluralist' representation so celebrated in recent years." He insisted that "however much these groups may be regarded as 'potential interest groups,' the important fact is that political organization for their protection within the pluralist framework can scarcely be said to exist."[94]

The second problem with relying on Tocqueville to buttress pluralist accounts of mid-twentieth-century America was the shifting boundary between public and private in the years since *Democracy in America*. Tocqueville had assumed a political order bifurcated between a relatively limited government—which exercised law, authority, and coercion—and a larger private sphere that consisted of nongovernmental social and economic relations. The theoretical impetus for this split came from a Lockean liberalism whose "most distinctive feature" was "its insistence that government should be limited so as to free individuals to undertake private as well as public pursuits of happiness, even if this option erodes public spiritedness in practice." Locke's separation of public and private created a sphere autonomous from government control. But it also tacitly granted greater political legitimacy to the public realm, a realm that soon became synonymous with the state.[95]

This conceptual framework was not especially problematic when the right of assembly had entered the American constitutional scheme through the First Amendment. In 1791, the state was relatively limited in scope and left a broad nonpublic realm free from coercive regulation. Although the extent to which early American citizens viewed this nonpublic domain as "private" is difficult to pinpoint, they clearly believed it fell outside of the relatively limited realm controlled by government. Yet groups that assembled outside the sanction of government were nonetheless "public" in the sense of being visible to others and "political" in the sense of demonstrating and advocating an alternative way of life. The Democratic-Republican Societies gathered and feasted and paraded, suffragist groups held conventions and marches, and abolitionists rallied citizens to awareness and action.[96]

This early American understanding of public and private for the most part endured at the time of Tocqueville's visit to the United States.

Tocqueville believed that citizens in a Jacksonian democracy conceived of a narrow public realm confined to governmental functions: "In the American republics the activity of the central Government never as yet has been extended beyond a limited number of objects sufficiently prominent to call forth its attention." Tocqueville saw associations as necessary to maintaining democratic order through civic virtue because he viewed the nongovernmental sphere as more determinative in shaping the lives and values of citizens than the more narrowly defined "government."[97]

The difficulty in the pluralist adaptation of Tocqueville's framework was that the reach of "government" or "public" in mid-twentieth-century America was far greater than Tocqueville had ever conceived. The growth of the market economy had initially reinforced Lockean understandings of public and private. But unprecedented advances in industrialization and bureaucracy that produced quasi-public corporations eventually rendered simplistic dualisms obsolete. Early twentieth-century legal thinkers began to question the assumption that "private law could be neutral and apolitical" amid "a widespread perception that so-called private institutions were acquiring coercive power that had formerly been reserved to governments." Legal realists characterized "the distinction in classical liberalism between private and public law as arbitrary, demonstrating that all private transactions involved the state and that all law was, in an important sense, public law." Following these realist premises, New Deal reformers invaded the private realm with an expanded administrative state. The New Deal assumed that "the instruments of government provided the means for conscious inducement of social change" and established "an indeterminable but expanding political sphere." The Supreme Court mounted a short-lived resistance to this ideology in the mid-1930s, and a decade later the Court embraced the new liberalism.[98]

At the same time that the government was expanding its reach into previously private domains, corporations, universities, and unions grew in number and size and increasingly assumed quasi-governmental functions. In Henry Kariel's description, "organizational giants such as General Motors, the Teamsters Union, the Farm Bureau, and the American Medical Association ... emerged as full-fledged political regimes" and blurred "the formerly useful distinction between the public and the private." Even as the pluralist critique of state-centered theory redirected the study of politics toward the group, "the discovery that precious little in human life is immune to bureaucratization . . . dispelled some of the magic of the group." The giant private bureaucracies were not akin to "that wonderful and wholly legitimate conglomeration of little groups which visitors from abroad [had] traditionally identified with Americanism." They were rather "a newer set of large-scale organizational power blocs" that had come to "comprise most of the public order and occupy much of the public mind." Dewey suggested an "eclipse of the public" had created "many publics."[99]

Tocqueville had seen only one public, and its normative influence had been overshadowed by the private groups that he observed. By the middle of the twentieth century, that was no longer the case. The conception of "public" had moved in two directions. First, the increased role of government as welfare provider and the emergence of the modern administrative state had expanded the government's public realm into previously private domains. Second, the power of large private organizations increasingly extended beyond the boundaries of those organizations. Lost in this mix was a subtle transformation in the understanding of the "political," which pluralist thought confined to those "interests" and "pressure groups" directly engaged with governmental processes. That characterization was doubly problematic: it kept hidden private groups that exerted economic coercion but at the same time depoliticized private groups that were neither governmental nor economic. Truman and Dahl recognized the changing roles of public and private, but they largely embraced the New Deal expansion as a favorable dissipation of public power without fully recognizing its consequences.

Critics soon exposed the pluralist oversights. In 1966, Grant McConnell's *Private Power and American Democracy* challenged the "comfortable assumption that interest groups will balance each other in their struggles and produce policies of moderation." McConnell questioned the pluralist assumption that "private associations" were, in fact, private. He argued that the facile distinction between "public" and "private" had "been seriously blurred in recent years." McConnell suggested that the infusion of quasi-public authority into private associations could not be ignored: "When, under the guise of serving an ideal of democracy as the self-government of small units, the coercive power of public authority is given to these groups, their internal government becomes a matter of serious concern."[100]

McConnell also challenged the pluralist balance assumption "that private associations are mutually countervailing," which he viewed as "a modern gloss on the argument of Madison and his colleagues in the Federalist Papers." The pluralist account suggested that "by opposing each other, private associations supposedly check any overly greedy attempts by particular associations to extend their power," such that "in the large community democracy is insured." McConnell responded that in practice, "private associations tend to be jealous of rivals." These associations "seek to prevent the rise of competitors in the fields they have marked as their own" and "often, when such rivals do exist, there is bitter conflict between them, conflict that has as its object the destruction of one or the other."[101]

Other challenges to pluralist arguments came from Michael Rogin, Theodore Lowi, and William Connolly. Rogin argued that the pluralist theory of group politics had reintroduced "social cohesion in a constitutional, industrial society." This underlying "social consensus plays an overwhelming role in the pluralist vision" and had "define[d] out of existence any conflict between groups and the public interest." Lowi contended that Dahl's conception "relie[d] on an extremely narrow definition of coercion, giving one to believe that coercion is not involved if physical force is absent" and "depend[ed] on an incredibly broad and idealized notion of what is peaceful about peaceful adjustment." Lowi charged that ignoring these complexities meant that "interest group liberalism" helped create "the sense that power need not be power at all, control need not be control, and government need not be coercive." Connolly similarly asserted that pluralists like Dahl had disregarded "notable discontinuities" between the conditions of postwar American society and the "basic preconditions to the successful operation of pluralist politics" that Tocqueville had stipulated. For example, Connolly suggested that "the emergence of the large-scale, hierarchical organization has significantly altered the character of the voluntary association" since the time of Tocqueville's writing.[102]

As the critics intimated, because pluralist theory of the 1950s assumed the status quo of an enlarged public sphere, its endorsement of group sovereignty was really epiphenomenal to a further legitimization of the public welfare function of the state and the increasingly bureaucratized corporations and universities that mimicked state functions and organization. The blending and overlap of public and private fundamentally altered the political arrangements about which Tocqueville and Madison had theorized. Contrary to some pluralist beliefs, power didn't disappear or dissipate; it just became less visible.[103]

The Tyranny of the Majority

Madison and Tocqueville held different views about the inherent goodness of groups, but both theorists turned to groups as a check against majority rule. Madison thought that majorities could be "unjust and interested" and sacrifice to their "ruling passion or interest both the public good and the rights of other citizens." He relied on factions to ensure that a majority would be "unable to concert and carry into effect schemes of oppression." Tocqueville warned similarly of the "tyranny of the majority." He contended that the majority "often has despotic tastes and instincts," and he called the "omnipotence of the majority" the "greatest danger for American Republics." As Sheldon Wolin suggests, by the second volume of *Democracy in America,* Tocqueville had moved away from concern over an explicitly legislative imposition of majority will to a more nuanced form of cultural hegemony. Wolin surmises that for Tocqueville "the danger was not that a legislative majority might ride roughshod over minority rights but a strange lack of opposition to the dominant set of values—and this despite an unprecedented degree of liberty and fully guaranteed rights of expression. He insisted that there was no country in which there was less intellectual independence and freedom of discussion than in America. His explanation was that in a democracy the majority combined physical, moral, and legal authority. Democracy's vaunted inclusiveness did not extend to the critic who espoused unorthodox views; he would eventually feel the whole weight of the community against him." Madison and Tocqueville implicitly recognized that the capacity for groups to exist detached from and even antithetical to the will of the majority in some ways reflected a destabilizing freedom. Mid-twentieth-century pluralism never acquiesced in this description, but it is exactly right: group autonomy presupposes the risk of volatile disagreement rather than stability to the democratic experiment.[104]

The risks that Madison and Toqueville identified went largely unacknowledged by the pluralist political thought that pervaded the background in which the constitutional freedom of association emerged. The pluralist consensus assumption established boundaries within which measured disagreement could unfold but through which dissenting voices were marginalized or silenced. The pluralist balance assumption asserted a harmonious stability between those associations that remained within the consensus boundaries. Together, consensus and balance depoliticized political dissidents and disguised political power. The result provided an explanation for a stable democratic polity, but it was a skewed explanation. Pluralists exalted associational autonomy largely because the associations accepted by the consensus neither threatened democratic stability nor diverged from democratic values.

The influences of pluralism weren't confined to academic political science—its currents were also reflected in the larger social milieu of the lawyers and judges who shaped the right of association. As Ronald Kahn has argued, "legal theory and education in the 1950s had within them a deep program of social control whose objective was supporting the consensus about polity and law that they believed existed." Certain dimensions of the "legal process" school also drew upon "an assumed social consensus about the acceptability of the American legal system" and upon "pluralism's emphasis on the importance of interest-group jostling." More broadly, as Richard Posner has emphasized, "the remarkable political consensus of the late 1950s and early 1960s" meant that "it was natural to think of law not in political but in technical terms."[105]

Nor were Supreme Court justices immune from these influences. Goldberg referred to the "stabilizing influence of the law" and law as "a balance wheel." Frankfurter and Harlan both had strong ties to the legal process theorists, and Frankfurter and the pluralist Laski were close friends. In a 1948 concurrence, Frankfurter quoted from one of Laski's articles, noting that "the right of association, like any other right carried to its extreme, encounters limiting principles." Harlan's 1963 address to the American Bar Association revealed pluralist assumptions of balance and consensus lurking beneath his federalism: "What other political system could have afforded so much scope to the varied interests and aspirations of a dynamic people representing such divergencies of ethnic and cultural backgrounds, and at the same time unified them into a nation blessed with material and spiritual resources unparalleled in history?" Brennan, at odds with Harlan on so many issues, seemed to converge with his pluralist assumptions. In a 1964 address to the Conference of Chief Justices, Brennan stressed "the basic consensus we share, rather than our superficial disagreements." He elaborated: "In but two decades, since the end of World War II, the world and this Nation have witnessed a remarkable transformation. The unity of the human family is becoming more distinct on the horizon of human events. . . . Our political, industrial, agricultural and cultural differences cannot stop the process which is making us a more united nation." The justices who shaped the right of association may not have often cited the pluralists, but at the very time the Court was developing the right of association, the intellectual influence lurked nearby.[106]

The next chapter explores the transformation of the right of association during the equality era, including the Court's important decision in *Roberts v. United States Jaycees.* That transformation further weakened group autonomy and deepened the chasm between the contemporary freedom of association and the historical right of assembly. But what has not been fully recognized about the current vulnerability of group autonomy is that it traces back in part to the factors influencing the original recognition of the right of association—and the Court's departure from the freedom of assembly—just over fifty years ago. The three factors that shaped the right of association in *NAACP v. Alabama* and subsequent cases in the 1960s in many ways paved the way for the transformation that occurred in *Roberts.* First, the largely unquestioned pluralist consensus that gave the Court its baseline for acceptable forms of association in the late 1950s and early 1960s opened the door for the egalitarianism that emerged in the 1970s and placed certain discriminatory associations beyond its contours. Second, the Court's disparate treatment of communist and civil rights associations in the 1950s and 1960s carved a path for later cases like *Roberts* to deny associational protections to certain kinds of groups even in the absence of any imminent threat to democratic security or stability. And finally, the early jurisprudential arguments over the constitutional source of association facilitated Brennan's later distinction between a right of expressive association connected to the First Amendment and a right of intimate association tied to personal liberty. These developments have left group autonomy—and liberty—more vulnerable to the tyranny of the majority.

CHAPTER 4

THE TRANSFORMATION OF ASSOCIATION IN THE EQUALITY ERA

The second constitutional era of the right of association is the equality era, which began in the mid-1960s. It includes the transformation of the right of association into intimate and expressive components in *Roberts v. United States Jaycees*. As I suggested at the end of the previous chapter, this transformation in some ways took its cues from the foundations established during the national security era. But the equality era also introduced its own political, jurisprudential, and theoretical factors that influenced associational freedom. This chapter focuses on three of these factors, each of which further contributed to the decline of the protections for group autonomy.

The primary political factor affecting the right of association in the equality era involved ongoing efforts to attain meaningful civil rights for African Americans. As the Civil Rights Movement gained traction, civil rights activists shifted from protecting their own associational freedom (as represented in the NAACP cases chronicled in the previous chapter) to challenging segregationists' arguments for group autonomy. Questions about the limits of exclusion became increasingly complex as these challenges extended to private groups.

The jurisprudential factor affecting the right of association in the equality era was the development of another constitutional right that appeared nowhere in the text of the Constitution: the right to privacy. Privacy and association had been linked in some of the Court's earliest cases on the freedom of association, but new connections emerged in the 1965 decision of *Griswold v. Connecticut*. *Griswold*'s framework eventually led to the right of intimate association recognized in *Roberts*.

The theoretical factor dominating the equality era was the rise of Rawlsian liberalism. Rawlsian questions about the relationship between liberty and equality, the limits of public reason, and the contours of individual autonomy dominated scholarly discussions about associational freedom during the equality era. Rawlsian premises also permeated the legal academy during this time, and they are implicit in *Roberts* and the scholarly commentary that followed the Court's decision.

Unlike the emergence of association in the national security era, the transformation of association in the equality era was already a few decades removed from the disappearance of the right of assembly in legal and political discourse. But retracing the transformation of association in this later era highlights how the new version of association further departed from the deference to group autonomy once encompassed by the right of assembly: (1) rejecting dissenting and destabilizing groups in the interests of consensus norms; (2) depoliticizing social practices that once counted as part of political life; and (3) construing groups once seen as forms of expression as merely means of expression. Like the previous chapter, this chapter highlights the historical context in which these changes unfolded. The next chapter explores the implications of these changes by developing a theory of assembly.

Civil Rights in Public and Private

The right of association that emerged in the national security era introduced crucial protections to the NAACP and its efforts to promote equality and civil rights for African Americans. During the equality era, freedom of association claims arose from a much different corner: segregationists who wished to curb the march of integration. The segregationist challenge raised complicated questions about the line between public and private groups. Herbert Wechsler had infamously argued the year after *NAACP v. Alabama* that the freedom of association was implicated in *any* effort at integration, arguing that "integration force[d] an association upon those for whom it [was] unpleasant or repugnant."[1]

Although Wechsler had directed part of his critique against *Brown v. Board of Education,* his argument lacked plausibility in public settings like the schools at issue in *Brown*—it made little sense to argue that segregationists had a freedom to associate (or a right to exclude) in situations where the government provided a public good or service. Within a decade of *Brown,* forced integration in public education, public transportation, public buildings, and public recreational facilities had been widely accepted. Integration also extended to private entities doing business on public property. By 1961, integration applied "to virtually any private concern operating on public property," and three years later, segregation in "most forms of public life" had come to an end. As Gerald Rosenberg suggests, "by the late 1960s and early 1970s there was not as large-scale or as deep-seated a social and cultural aversion to desegregation as there had been in the pre-1964 years."[2]

The critical question for the right of association during the civil rights era was the extent to which it could justify *private* discrimination by whites against African Americans. Three important legal developments answered that question: (1) the Civil Rights Act of 1964; (2) the Court's 1968 decision in *Jones v. Alfred H. Mayer;* and (3) the Court's 1976 decision in *Runyon v. McCrary.*

Title II of the Civil Rights Act of 1964 prohibited racial discrimination in places of "public accommodation." The legislation encompassed inns, restaurants, gas stations, and places of entertainment but exempted private clubs and other establishments "not in fact open to the public." The act's broad scope brought to the forefront an underlying tension between the clash of public and private interests. As Justice Goldberg recognized in his concurrence in *Bell v. Maryland,* a decision issued ten days prior to the enactment of the act, "a claim of equal access to public accommodations" against a restaurant "inevitably involves the liberties and freedoms both of the restaurant proprietor and of the Negro citizen." But despite significant resistance from segregationists, the Civil Rights Act left no doubt in which direction that tension would be resolved. Five years later, the Court made clear in *Daniel v. Paul* that sham attempts to meet the private club exception would not prevail.[3]

The second important development defining the scope of the right of association in the civil rights era was the Court's 1968 decision in *Jones v. Alfred H. Mayer,* which interpreted a Reconstruction era statute, the Civil Rights Act of 1866, to bar racial discrimination in the sale or lease of private property. The Court reasoned that the 1866 act reached even private discrimination because "the exclusion of Negroes from white communities" reflected "the badges and incidents of slavery" that the Thirteenth Amendment sought to remedy. It extended the reach of *Jones* to membership in a community park and playground in *Sullivan v. Little Hunting Park* and a private swimming pool in *Tillman v. Wheaton-Haven Recreation Association. Jones, Sullivan,* and *Tillman* all involved sales or leases related to real property covered under the Fair Housing Act of 1968. The Court's reliance on a somewhat strained interpretation of the Civil Rights Act of 1866 rather than a straightforward application of the Fair Housing Act prompted Justice Harlan (joined by Justice White and Chief Justice Burger) to dissent in *Sullivan,* noting that the "vague and open-ended" construction of the 1866 act risked "grave constitutional issues should [that authority] be extended too far into some types of private discrimination."[4]

These two developments—the Civil Rights Act of 1964 and the Court's decision in *Jones*—both represented major steps toward ending segregation. Both also constrained group autonomy. But few people today object to these constraints along racial or any other lines—the idea that owners of businesses open to the public or sellers of private homes should have a constitutional right to discriminate finds few defenders. In other words, if the constraints on group autonomy ended with these applications, contemporary debates would be virtually nonexistent.

More complicated questions arose from the Court's line of cases addressing private school segregation that culminated in its 1976 decision in *Runyon v. McCrary.* Preliminary challenges to private school segregation focused on government financial support, and in the late 1960s, the Court affirmed a number of decisions enjoining state tuition grants to students attending racially discriminatory private schools. In 1973, the Court concluded in *Norwood v. Harrison* that state-funded textbook loans to students attending these schools were "not legally distinguishable" from tuition grants.[5]

Norwood was the Court's first explicit consideration of the conflict between antidiscrimination norms and the right of association. Summarizing recent legislative and judicial developments, Chief Justice Burger reasoned: "Invidious private discrimination may be characterized as a form of exercising freedom of association protected by the First Amendment, but it has never been accorded affirmative constitutional protections. And even some private discrimination is subject to special remedial legislation in certain circumstances." Burger also noted that "although the Constitution does not proscribe private bias, it places no value on discrimination," and simply because "the Constitution may compel toleration of private discrimination in some circumstances does not mean that it requires state support for such discrimination."[6]

Shortly after *Norwood*, the justices addressed the use of public recreational facilities by private segregated schools in *Gilmore v. City of Montgomery*. Justice Blackmun's majority opinion noted that, in contrast to the relatively easy question about integrating public facilities and programs, "the problem of private group use is much more complex." The dispositive question was whether the use of public facilities made the government "a joint participant in the challenged activities." The Court concluded that municipal recreational facilities, including parks, playgrounds, athletic facilities, amphitheaters, museums, and zoos, were sufficiently akin to "generalized governmental services" like traditional state monopolies such as electricity, water, and police and fire protection. Accordingly, the government's acquiescence in the use of these facilities by private groups that discriminated on the basis of race did not rise to the level of government endorsement of discriminatory practices. But Blackmun went even further, noting that the exclusion of a discriminatory group from public facilities would violate the freedom of association. He asserted: "The freedom to associate applies to the beliefs we share, and to those we consider reprehensible," and "tends to produce the diversity of opinion that oils the machinery of democratic government and insures peaceful orderly change." At the same time, he cautioned that "the very exercise of the freedom to associate by some may serve to infringe that freedom for others. Invidious discrimination takes its own toll on the freedom to associate, and it is not subject to affirmative consti-tutional protection when it involves state action."[7]

Two years later, in *Runyon*, the Court retreated from both its defense of the right of association and its state action requirement when it construed another provision of the Civil Rights Act of 1866 to bar racial discrimina-tion by "private, commercially operated, nonsectarian schools." Rejecting the suggestion that the legislation "[did] not reach private acts of racial discrimination," Justice Stewart wrote: "From [the principle of the freedom of association] it may be assumed that parents have a First Amendment right to send their children to educational institutions that promote the belief that racial segregation is desirable, and that the children have an equal right to attend such institutions. But it does not follow that the prac-tice of excluding racial minorities from such institutions is also protected by the same principle." Stewart buttressed his argument with a truncated quotation from *Norwood*. Burger had written in *Norwood* that "*although the Constitution does not proscribe private bias,* it places no value on discrimination." Stewart's quotation omitted Burger's prefatory clause and asserted: "As the Court stated in [*Norwood*], 'the Constitution . . . places no value on discrimi-nation.'" The abbreviated language stood for a broader legal principle. *Norwood* had prevented government subsidization of a disfavored social practice. *Runyon* precluded the practice itself and marked the first time that the Court had denied the right of existence to a private group neither with ties to state action nor meeting the definition of a public accommodation.[8]

Runyon's symbolic importance is beyond challenge. The decision made clear that the Court understood the Civil Rights Act of 1866 "to reach all intentional racial discrimination, public and private, that interfered with the right to contract," and that it trumped the right of association. That core holding has been undisturbed—it was, in fact, codified in the Civil Rights Act of 1991. Few people today believe that private schools ought to have a constitutional right to exclude African Americans.[9]

Runyon's doctrinal significance is less clear, and it is on this doctrinal level that the case maintains its greatest significance for contested questions of group autonomy today. Two moves in particular are open to question, both of which the Court adopted eight years later in the much different context of *Roberts*. The first is Stewart's argument that forced inclusion of unwanted members would not change the core expression of a discriminatory group: "there is no showing that discontinuance of [the] discriminatory admission practices would inhibit in any way the teaching in these schools of any ideas or dogma." Setting aside the political and moral context of *Runyon,* the claim is not persuasive.[10]

Stewart's second questionable doctrinal move is his artificial distinction between the *act* of discrimination and the *message* of discrimination. In Stewart's view, the right of association protected only the latter, and the exclusion of African Americans counted only as the former. In other words, the right of association extended only to the expression of ideas, and exclusion wasn't expression. But that argument makes an arbitrary distinction between act and message that could be applied to any form of expression—burning a flag or a draft card, for example. It tells us nothing about the value or harm of the expression itself.[11]

Association and Privacy

The clash between integration and the right to exclude paralleled a line of cases that emphasized a wholly different aspect of associational freedom: privacy. Frankfurter and Douglas had linked association and privacy in cases during the national security era. And Harlan had referred to "the vital relationship between freedom to associate and privacy in one's associations" in *NAACP v. Alabama.* But the connection deepened after the Court recognized a constitutional right to privacy in *Griswold v. Connecticut.* Because privacy, like association, appeared nowhere in the text of the Constitution, the Court's earlier recognition of the right of association in *NAACP v. Alabama* became an important example of the kind of "penumbral" reasoning that justified the right of privacy in *Griswold.*[12]

There was, however, a definitional problem with the meaning of privacy in the context of association. Brandeis and Warren's classic definition of the right "to be let alone" in their 1890 law review article conveyed a sense of individual autonomy. But references to privacy in the association cases during the national security era had more to do with protecting group autonomy than with endorsing individual autonomy. As Harlan had argued in *NAACP v. Alabama,* "Inviolability of privacy in group association may in many circumstances be indispensable to preservation of freedom of association, particularly where a group espouses dissident beliefs." The kind of privacy envisioned by the Court in *NAACP v. Alabama* did not mean not public; to the contrary, groups like the NAACP and the Communist Party had actively sought public visibility and recognition. Before *Griswold,* privacy in the context of association existed largely to facilitate public and political actions rather than to protect secret or intimate actions.[13]

Griswold struck down a Connecticut law that prohibited the use of contraceptives and the giving of medical advice about their use, specifically the application of this law to the use of contraceptives by married persons. Warren assigned the opinion to Douglas. In a draft that he shared only with Brennan, Douglas made scant reference to a right of privacy and rested his argument almost entirely on the First Amendment freedom of association. Douglas argued that while marriage did "not fit precisely any of the categories of First Amendment rights," it was "a form of association as vital in the life of a man or woman as any other, and perhaps more so." He reasoned that "we would, indeed, have difficulty protecting the intimacies of one's relations to [the] NAACP and not the intimacies of one's marriage relation."[14]

After reviewing the draft, Brennan urged Douglas to abandon his exclusive reliance on the right of association. Brennan argued that marriage did not fall within the kind of association that the Court had recognized for purposes of political advocacy. He suggested that Douglas instead analogize the Court's recognition of the right of association to a similar broadening of privacy into a constitutional right. Because neither privacy nor association could be found in the text of the Constitution, if association could be recognized as a freestanding constitutional right, then so could privacy. Douglas followed Brennan's suggestions and wrote that the "specific guarantees in the Bill of Rights have penumbras, formed by emanations from those guarantees that help give them life and substance."[15]

In addition to its recognition of privacy, Douglas's final opinion also contained some extended language about the constitutional source of the freedom of association. In locating one of the penumbras of privacy in the First Amendment, Douglas wrote:

In *NAACP v. Alabama*, we protected the "freedom to associate and privacy in one's associations," noting that freedom of association was a peripheral First Amendment right. Disclosure of membership lists of a constitutionally valid association, we held, was invalid "as entailing the likelihood of a substantial restraint upon the exercise by [the NAACP's] members of their right to freedom of association." In other words, the First Amendment has a penumbra where privacy is protected from governmental intrusion. In like context, we have protected forms of "association" that are not political in the customary sense but pertain to the social, legal, and economic benefit of the members [citing *NAACP v. Button*].

In a dissenting opinion issued just a month prior to *Griswold*, Douglas had referred to a singular "right of assembly and association." But now he argued that *NAACP v. Alabama* and *Button* "involved more than the 'right of assembly.'" Instead: "The right of 'association,' like the right of belief, is more than the right to attend a meeting; it includes the right to express one's attitudes or philosophies by membership in a group or by affiliation with it or by other lawful means. Association in that context is a form of expression of opinion; and while it is not expressly included in the First Amendment its existence is necessary in making the express guarantees fully meaningful."[16]

Douglas's conception of the right of assembly as no more than "the right to attend a meeting" in *Griswold* departed from his past descriptions of that right. Having thus confined assembly, Douglas suggested that the right of association was "necessary in making the express guarantees [of the First Amendment] fully meaningful." But there was no reason that meaningful protections of assembly required a separate right of association. The Court had long since set forth the broad contours of the rights of speech and assembly in *Thomas v. Collins*: "If the exercise of the rights of free speech and free assembly cannot be made a crime, we do not think this can be accomplished by the device of requiring previous registration as a condition for exercising them and making such a condition the foundation for restraining in advance their exercise and for imposing a penalty for violating such a restraining order. So long as no more is involved than exercise of the rights of free speech and free assembly, it is immune to such a restriction." Douglas, in fact, had quoted this language in his 1961 dissent in *Communist Party v. Subversive Activities Control Board*, adding that "the vices of registration [of an organization] may be not unlike those of licensing." Yet despite his repeated arguments against this kind of prior restraint in the area of free speech, he failed to make the same connection with assembly.[17]

Douglas nevertheless maintained an important understanding of association in *Griswold* that would be lost a decade later in Stewart's instrumental characterization in *Runyon*. He argued that the right of association "includes the right to express one's attitudes or philosophies by membership in a group or by affiliation with it or by other lawful means." In other words, as he had argued in a dissent four years earlier, "joining is one method of expression." For Douglas, the act of association was itself an intrinsically valuable form of expression. For Stewart, it became merely an instrumental means of facilitating expression.[18]

Douglas's reasoning in *Griswold* failed to convince all of his colleagues. Harlan "fully agree[d] with the judgment of reversal" but rejected the incorporation argument that he saw as implicit in Douglas's insistence that "the Due Process Clause of the Fourteenth Amendment does not touch this Connecticut statute unless the enactment is found to violate some right assured by the letter or penumbra of the Bill of Rights." Harlan based his objection on the now familiar liberty argument: "The proper constitutional inquiry in this case is whether this Connecticut statute infringes the Due Process Clause of the Fourteenth Amendment because the enactment violates basic values 'implicit in the concept of ordered liberty.'" Black also disagreed with Douglas's penumbral argument. His dissent lamented:

> One of the most effective ways of diluting or expanding a constitutionally guaranteed right is to substitute for the crucial word or words of a constitutional guarantee another word or words, more or less flexible and more or less restricted in meaning. This fact is well illustrated by the use of the term "right of privacy" as a comprehensive substitute for the Fourth Amendment's guarantee against "unreasonable searches and seizures." "Privacy" is a broad, abstract and ambiguous concept which can easily be shrunken in meaning but which can also, on the other hand, easily be interpreted as a constitutional ban against many things other than searches and seizures. I have expressed the view many times that First Amendment freedoms, for example, have suffered from a failure of the courts to stick to the simple language of the First Amendment in construing it, instead of invoking multitudes of words substituted for those the Framers used.

Black's words were odd in light of his repeated endorsement of the right of association, which had certainly been a failure "to stick to the simple language of the First Amendment in construing it." Moreover, as the Court's association cases in the national security era had shown, substituting a new right of association for the right of assembly had proven "one of the most effective ways of diluting or expanding" the constitutional protections for communists and civil rights activists, respectively.[19]

In 1972, the Court extended *Griswold*'s holding to unmarried persons desiring access to contraception. Brennan's majority opinion in *Eisenstadt v. Baird* relied heavily on *Griswold* but not on Douglas's reasoning. In *Griswold*, Douglas had maintained that part of the right to privacy rested on the "association" of marriage: "We deal with a right of privacy older than the Bill of Rights—older than our political parties, older than our school system. Marriage is a coming together for better or for worse, hopefully enduring, and intimate to the degree of being sacred. It is an association that promotes a way of life, not causes; a harmony in living, not political faiths; a bilateral loyalty, not commercial or social projects. Yet it is an association for as noble a purpose as any involved in our prior decisions." This relational focus may have drawn an unlikely connection between a married couple and the NAACP, but it resisted the kind of individualism that equated associational privacy with "the privacy of private life." In *Eisenstadt*, Brennan shifted the focus away from Douglas's emphasis on the marriage relationship: "It is true that, in *Griswold*, the right of privacy in question inhered in the marital relationship. Yet the marital couple is not an independent entity, with a mind and heart of its own, but an association of two individuals, each with a separate intellectual and emotional makeup. If the right of privacy means anything, it is the right of the individual, married or single, to be free from unwarranted governmental intrusion into matters so fundamentally affecting a person as the decision whether to bear or beget a child." Brennan's language thus converted an understanding of associational freedom rooted in relationships between people to a right of individual autonomy. As H. Jefferson Powell argues, "Brennan's reading of *Griswold* turned Douglas's reasoning on its head" and signaled "the identification of a radically individualistic liberalism as the moral content of American constitutionalism." Ironically, Brennan's reasoning drew upon the liberty argument that Harlan had advanced in *NAACP v. Alabama* and other cases (including his *Griswold* concurrence). The right of privacy utterly detached from the right of association had no First Amendment basis; it came rather from the "liberty" of the Due Process Clause of the Fourteenth Amendment—exactly where Harlan had argued against Brennan that the right of association was itself located.[20]

The Rise of Rawlsian Liberalism

As the Court and commentators applied the new right of association in civil rights and privacy decisions, John Rawls introduced to political and legal discourse a theoretical resource with important implications for these developments. The appearance of Rawls's *Theory of Justice* in 1971 breathed new life into the discipline of political theory, which had increasingly been exiled from political science by the behavioralism of postwar pluralists. But while Rawls came to be viewed as a kind of normative antidote to the ostensibly descriptive pluralist claims that had ruled political science in the 1950s and 1960s, his basic framework echoed many pluralist assumptions. As John Gunnell has written, "the new pluralism is, in many respects, not the same as the old pluralism . . . but it is, at bottom, the same theory." The continuity is particularly evident with respect to questions about group autonomy. Pluralist political thought insisted on a consensus bounded by shared democratic values; Rawlsian liberalism presumed an "overlapping consensus" in which egalitarianism rooted in an individualist ontology trumped and thus bounded difference. Pluralists attributed harmony and balance to group interaction to explain the relative stability that they perceived; Rawls feared a loss of stability and made the preservation of peaceful interactions a cornerstone of his normative theory. Like the pluralist assumptions that preceded them, the Rawlsian premises of consensus and stability pervaded political discourse and influenced the ways in which the equality era reshaped the right of association.[21]

Rawls's theory was self-avowedly motivated by a concern for political stability that could avoid the kind of sectarian religious violence that followed the European Reformation in the sixteenth and seventeenth centuries. Rawls believed that this stability could be attained through the "well-ordered society," that is, "a society effectively regulated by a public political conception of justice." In this society, "everyone accepts, and knows that everyone else accepts, the very same principles of justice." This agreement could be reached without "the oppressive use of state power." Rawls initially asserted that citizens, in spite of their differences, could pursue a common understanding of justice from an "Archimedean point . . . by assuming certain general desires, such as the desire for primary social goods, and by taking as a basis the agreements that would be made in a suitably defined initial situation." He later came to believe that liberal society could never overcome the interminable disagreement that flowed from what he called "conflicting and incommensurable doctrines." But he insisted that we might nonetheless attain political stability that was more than a mere modus vivendi. Rawls believed that while "reasonable pluralism" permitted "a diversity of reasonable comprehensive doctrines," we could discover an "overlapping consensus" about justice from among these comprehensive doctrines by constraining dialogue to "public reason." He thought that the overlapping consensus of reasonable belief would produce agreement over the "basic structure" and the "primary social goods" of society, which include rights, liberties, opportunities, income and wealth, and self-respect.[22]

Rawls included the freedom of association among his "basic liberties." The freedom of association was related to what he called "private society," which "is not held together by a public conviction that its basic arrangements are just and good in themselves." As a result, "there are many types of social union and from the perspective of political justice we are not to try to rank them in value." In fact, "a well-ordered society, and indeed most societies, will presumably contain countless social unions of many different kinds." Importantly, "government has no authority to render associations either legitimate or illegitimate any more than it has this authority in regard to art or science."[23]

Yet at the same time, Rawls's vision for stability depended on consensus, and consensus could only be reached by constraining certain modes of discourse through what Rawls called "public reason." He maintained that the requirement of public reason enabled consensus because political views could be detached from comprehensive doctrines: "We always assume that citizens have two views, a comprehensive and a political view; and that their overall view can be divided into two parts, suitably related." (Years later, in response to numerous critics, Rawls cryptically suggested that the requirement of public reason "still allows us to introduce into political discussion at any time our comprehensive doctrine, religious or nonreligious, provided that, in due course, we give properly public reasons to support the principles and policies our comprehensive doctrine is said to support.")[24]

Rawls may not have been cited in the legal decisions that reshaped the freedom of association in the first part of the equality era, but his influence was close at hand. Legal academics eager to provide intellectual cover to the Warren Court's decisions and its recognition of fundamental rights not found in the text of the Constitution embraced his framework. In 1969, Frank Michelman's foreword in the *Harvard Law Review* adopted a Rawlsian framework for analyzing income and wealth inequality. Eight years later, Kenneth Karst's foreword employed a Rawlsian approach to conclude that the "substantive core" of the Fourteenth Amendment was "a principle of equal citizenship, which presumptively guarantees to each individual the right to be treated by the organized society as a respected, responsible, and participating member." The Rawlsian influence in the legal academy did not go unchallenged, and Laura Kalman suggests that "in the end, Rawls proved helpful only to legal scholars predisposed toward political liberalism who were looking for a way to justify its continuance." But in the first part of the equality era, those scholars held significant sway in the law schools and on the courts.[25]

One of the most important legal scholars shaped by Rawlsian premises was Ronald Dworkin. Dworkin's legal theory made explicit an important assumption underlying Rawls's theory of justice: individual rights prevailed over majoritarian democracy. The "constitutional conception" of democracy held out "rights as trumps" that limited majoritarian preferences when they constrained fundamental values like "equal concern and respect." This meant that "a society in which the majority shows contempt for the needs and prospects of some minority is illegitimate as well as unjust." Dworkin's theory also exposed (and replicated) a tension inherent in Rawls's theory of justice: accepting the "counter-majoritarian difficulty" presupposed an agreement about liberal values. But once illiberal minorities laid claim to fundamental liberal rights, the conflict between competing liberal claims became unavoidable: members of a group engaging in illiberal practices could consistently claim the liberal right to group autonomy.[26]

Unlike Tocqueville and Madison, Rawls and Dworkin never really recognized the value of protecting antimajoritarian groups on nonideological grounds. For Madison and Tocqueville, group autonomy was a boundary marker that didn't engage in a substantive weighing of values. For Rawls and Dworkin, group autonomy and freedom of association were conditioned by equality, self-respect, and other liberal values.

Roberts v. United States Jaycees

The influence of Rawlsian liberalism and the two strands of case law that emerged over the right to exclude and the right to privacy coalesced in *Roberts v. United States Jaycees*, the most important case on the freedom of association in the equality era. In a sweeping decision with significant consequences for associational freedom, the Court simultaneously endorsed the implicit connection between privacy and association and severely curtailed the right to exclude.

The background to *Roberts* began in 1974 and 1975, when the Minneapolis and St. Paul chapters of the Jaycees began admitting women as regular members, in violation of the national organization's bylaws. According to the national organization, women could be "associate individual members" who were ineligible to vote, hold office, or receive certain national awards but could "otherwise participate fully in Jaycee activities." After the national organization threatened to revoke their charters, the two Minnesota chapters filed sex discrimination charges with the Minnesota Department of Human Rights based on the Minnesota Human Rights Act, which declared that it was an unfair discriminatory practice "to deny any person the full and equal enjoyment of the goods, services, facilities, privileges, advantages, and accommodations of a place of public accommodation because of race, color, creed, religion, disability, national origin, or sex." In response, members of the national organization filed suit, alleging that the act violated their rights of speech and association.[27]

The Supreme Court upheld the constitutionality of the act without a dissent. Justice Brennan's majority opinion asserted that previous decisions had identified two separate constitutional sources for the right of association. One line of decisions protected "intimate association" as "a fundamental element of personal liberty." Another set of decisions guarded "expressive association," which was "a right to associate for the purpose of engaging in those activities protected by the First Amendment—speech, assembly, petition for the redress of grievances, and the exercise of religion." Expressive association to pursue "a wide variety of political, social, economic, educational, religious, and cultural ends" was "implicit in the right to engage in activities protected by the First Amendment."[28]

The constitutional hooks for Brennan's categories of intimate and expressive association roughly tracked the liberty argument and the incorporation argument. But in an odd doctrinal twist, the intimate association corresponding to the liberty argument now commanded greater constitutional protection than the expressive association corresponding to the incorporation argument, a reversal of the positions debated on the Court during the national security era. Brennan contended that intimate and expressive association represented, respectively, the "intrinsic and instrumental features of constitutionally protected association." These differences meant that "the nature and degree of constitutional protection afforded freedom of association may vary depending on the extent to which one or the other aspect of the constitutionally protected liberty is at stake in a given case."[29]

Brennan began his analysis by considering whether the Jaycees was an intimate association and announced that "several features of the Jaycees clearly place the organization outside of the category of relationships worthy of this kind of constitutional protection." In the second section of his opinion, Brennan concluded that the Jaycees was an expressive association. He appeared to recognize the significance of the consequences of the Minnesota law to the Jaycees: "There can be no clearer example of an intrusion into the internal structure or affairs of an association than a regulation that forces the group to accept members it does not desire. Such a regulation may impair the ability of the original members to express only those views that brought them together. Freedom of association therefore plainly presupposes a freedom not to associate." And in a critical comment, Brennan noted that "according protection to collective effort on behalf of shared goals is especially important in preserving political and cultural diversity and in shielding dissident expression from suppression by the majority." The sentiment could have come straight from Madison and Tocqueville (absent their pluralist gloss). It reflected the importance of dissenting groups that the freedom of assembly had once recognized.[30]

Brennan quickly downplayed these concerns in light of "Minnesota's compelling interest in eradicating discrimination against its female citizens." He reasoned that Minnesota furthered its compelling interest by assuring women equal access to the leadership skills, business contacts, and employment promotions offered by the Jaycees. Because the Jaycees's willingness to admit women as associate individual members presumably already afforded them most of these opportunities—the associate status precluded voting, holding office, and eligibility for national awards—it is unclear how forced admission of women as full members helped to eradicate gender discrimination in Minnesota. But even more troubling than Brennan's failure to link remedy and harm was his claim that the forced integration of women would have *no effect* on the expressive interests of the Jaycees. There was, according to Brennan, "no basis in the record for concluding that admission of women as full voting members [would] impede the organization's ability to engage in . . . protected activities or to disseminate its preferred views."[31]

Justice O'Connor's oft-cited concurrence is sometimes viewed more favorably than Brennan's majority opinion. Contrary to Brennan, O'Connor viewed expressive association as more than instrumentally valuable. She asserted that "protection of the association's right to define its membership derives from the recognition that the formation of an expressive association is the creation of a voice, and the selection of members is the definition of that voice." If the Jaycees was in fact an expressive association, O'Connor believed it would be entitled to protection from intrusion by the state's antidiscrimination legislation.[32]

Rather than distinguishing between expressive and nonexpressive associations, O'Connor instead proposed drawing a line between predominantly expressive and predominantly commercial organizations. She acknowledged that while the Jaycees was not a political organization, "the advocacy of political and public causes, selected by the membership, is a not insubstantial part of what it does." Nevertheless, she reasoned that the Jaycees's attention to and success in membership drives meant that it was, "first and foremost, an organization that, at both the national and local levels, promotes and practices the art of solicitation and management." Accordingly, "the State of Minnesota ha[d] a legitimate interest in ensuring nondiscriminatory access to the commercial opportunity presented by membership in the Jaycees." For these reasons, the Jaycees presented for O'Connor a "relatively easy case for application of the expressive-commercial dichotomy." Elaborating upon her reasoning, O'Connor explained that "an association should be characterized as commercial, and therefore subject to rationally related state regulation of its membership and other associational activities, when, and only when, the association's activities are not predominantly of the type protected by the First Amendment. It is only when the association is predominantly engaged in protected expression that state regulation of its membership will necessarily affect, change, dilute, or silence one collective voice that would otherwise be heard."[33]

O'Connor's focus on the commercial nature of groups as a boundary line for associational protections holds some promise, but her reasoning is problematic on three counts. First, O'Connor posits a false dichotomy between commercial and expression associations: some commercial associations are expressive and (at least under the Court's understanding of the expressive and nonexpressive divide) some noncommercial organizations are not expressive. Second, her requirement that an association be "predominantly engaged" in protected expression to avoid being classified as commercial leaves vulnerable to regulation some groups that because of their size or unpopularity must devote a substantial portion of their activities to fundraising or other commercial activities. Finally, O'Connor leaves unclear which activities are "of the type protected by the First Amendment."[34]

The Artificiality of Intimate and Expressive Association

The most serious doctrinal shortcoming in *Roberts* was Brennan's creation of the categories of intimate and expressive association. Brennan's arguments implied two corollaries: (1) some associations were "non-intimate," and (2) some associations were "non-expressive." His reasoning thus suggested four possible categories of associations: (1) intimate expressive associations, (2) intimate nonexpressive associations, (3) nonintimate expressive associations, and (4) nonintimate nonexpressive associations. Since *Roberts*, it has become clear that there is no constitutionally significant distinction between these first two categories. Intimate associations receive the highest level of constitutional protection regardless of whether they are also expressive.

The same is not true for the distinctions between the other categories. Brennan's parsing of intrinsic and instrumental value and his reference to the varying "nature and degree of constitutional protection" for intimate and expressive associations signaled a clear privileging of the former over the latter. And the category of expressive association drew a line that left nonintimate nonexpressive associations without any meaningful constitutional protections. The *Roberts* framework thus created the following hierarchically ordered categories of associations:

A)   intimate associations
B)   nonintimate expressive associations
C)   nonintimate nonexpressive associations

It turns out that the groups in B sometimes lose, and the groups in C always lose. Yet despite these consequences, neither intimate nor expressive association represents a constitutionally defensible drawing of lines.[35]

The category of intimate association likely originated in a 1980 article by Kenneth Karst in the *Yale Law Journal*, "The Freedom of Intimate Association." Karst's article sought to recover the relational emphasis in *Griswold* that Brennan had abandoned in *Eisenstadt*. He began by noting that Douglas had focused specifically on the association of marriage. Karst contended that this language had established a freedom of "intimate association," which he suggested was "a close and familiar personal relationship with another that is in some significant way comparable to a marriage or family relationship." The problem with Karst's argument was its implicit corollary that some groups were "non-intimate associations"—and that a constitutionally significant line could be drawn between intimate and nonintimate ones. The argument fails for the simple reason that all of the values, benefits, and attributes that it assigns to intimate associations are equally applicable to many if not most nonintimate associations.[36]

Karst at times recognized the broader applicability of his claims. He noted that "an intimate association, like any group, is more than the sum of its members; it is a new being, a collective identity with a life of its own." And near the end of his article, he wrote that "one of the points of any freedom of association must be to let people make their own definitions of community." Yet despite these occasional concessions, Karst repeatedly placed special value on the relationships that form in intimate associations. For example, he emphasized the importance of "close friendship" in intimate association. For Karst, it was "plain that the values of intimate association may be realized in friendships involving neither sexual intimacy nor family ties," and that "any view of intimate association focused on associational values must therefore include friendship." He also tied intimate association to the kinds of bonds that form through personal interaction: the "chief value in intimate association is the opportunity to satisfy" the "need to love and be loved"; "the opportunity to be cared for by another in an intimate association is normally complemented by the opportunity for caring" that requires a "personal commitment"; "caring for an intimate requires taking the trouble to know him and deal with him as a whole person, not just as the occupant of a role," which "limits the number of intimate associations any one person can have at any one time, or even in a lifetime."[37]

Karst's attention to friendship and personal bonds is eminently reasonable. But the potential for and existence of such close friendships can be found in many kinds of associations. While it may well be that attributes of friendship and personal bonds distinguish small or local groups from large and impersonal groups like behemoth mailing list organizations, surely many small associations that fall outside the bounds of intimacy are capable of producing "close friendships" of the kind that Karst describes. To be sure, some relationships between members of these groups will undoubtedly be superficial and "casual." But this is also true of the relationships that constitute many intimate associations. Karst recognized that protecting the values he saw as inherent in intimate association required offering "some protection to casual associations as well as lasting ones." In fact, "one reason for extending constitutional protection to casual intimate associations is that they may ripen into durable intimate associations." Karst argued that "a doctrinal system extending the freedom of intimate association only to cases of enduring commitment would require intolerable inquiries into subjects that should be kept private, including states of mind." It is hard to understand why these principles wouldn't apply equally to many larger, nonintimate associations.[38]

Karst's other attempts to mark the bounds of intimate association were similarly unavailing:

- "Transient or enduring, chosen or not, our intimate associations profoundly affect our personalities and our senses of self. When they are chosen, they take on expressive dimensions as statements defining ourselves."
- "An intimate association may influence a person's self-definition not only by what it says to him but also by what it says (or what he thinks it says) to others."
- "When two people [voluntarily enter into an intimate association], they express themselves more eloquently, tell us more about who they are and who they hope to be, than they ever could do by wearing armbands or carrying red flags."
- "First Amendment doctrine cautions us to be sensitive to the need to protect intimate associations that are unconventional or that may offend a majority of the community."

Each of these claims applies with equal force if we remove the adjective "intimate." Some associations and associative acts will lack significance for some people, but the extent to which expression, self-definition, and unconventional norms unfold in a group's practices is not contingent upon whether the group is an intimate association.[39]

Some of the conceptual problems with Karst's approach to intimate association likely arose because he wasn't explicitly attempting to distinguish intimate from nonintimate associations. His focus appears to have been on trying to develop a category of intimate association as an alternative to the then-nascent right of privacy and in using the right of intimate association to advance legal protections for homosexual relationships. Today, these particular goals are unlikely to be advanced by the right of intimate association, as evidenced by *Lawrence v. Texas*, the Court's overruling of its decision in *Bowers v. Hardwick*. *Bowers* had drawn two dissents, one from Justice Stevens that emphasized *Griswold*'s liberty arguments, and one from Justice Blackmun that drew upon *Griswold*'s connections between privacy and intimate association (and included two citations to Karst's article). *Lawrence* relied on Stevens's dissent and never mentioned the right of intimate association.[40]

The Court's avoidance of intimate association in *Lawrence* suggests that the doctrinal value of the category may be minimal. But what about the doctrinal harm? The dangers of privileging intimate association become apparent in Brennan's *Roberts* opinion. Brennan began by noting, "Certain kinds of personal bonds have played a critical role in the culture and traditions of the Nation by cultivating and transmitting shared ideals and beliefs; they thereby foster diversity and act as critical buffers between the individual and the power of the State." This language attempts to draw the reader into a kind of Tocquevillean ethos in which intimate associations at once facilitate support for "the Nation" and resistance to "the State."[41]

But Brennan's argument lacks coherence and specificity. What is the difference between nation and state? What are the national culture (singular) and national traditions (plural) brought about by "shared ideals and beliefs"? How do personal bonds "foster diversity" and act as "critical buffers" from state power? More to the point, why are these functions unique to intimate associations? If Brennan's argument is that intimate associations sustain some kind of shared culture ("cultivating and transmitting shared ideals and beliefs"), then why can't nonintimate associations also serve as "schools of democracy"?[42] Conversely, if Brennan means to position intimate associations as "mediating structures" between individuals and the state ("foster[ing] diversity and act[ing] as critical buffers"), then don't some of the largest (and least "intimate") groups have the greatest capacity to resist the state?[43] The passage also belies a more troubling vagueness. It contains an irresolvable tension that doesn't let the reader know whether Brennan is ultimately prioritizing the state, the nonstate group, or the individual, and the answer to that question matters a great deal. From the rest of his opinion and his broader jurisprudence, we might infer that Brennan wants to privilege the individual, then the state, and lastly, the group. But if that is where his argument rests, then some language—"critical buffers," "traditions," "shared ideals"—becomes much harder for him to employ in an unqualified sense.

Brennan next enlisted notions of liberty and autonomy in his defense of intimate association, embracing the individualistic gloss that his *Eisenstadt* opinion cast on *Griswold:* "The constitutional shelter afforded [intimate associations] reflects the realization that individuals draw much of their emotional enrichment from close ties with others. Protecting these relationships from unwarranted state interference therefore safeguards the ability independently to define one's identity that is central to any concept of liberty." These phrases—emotional enrichment, defining one's identity, and the concept of liberty—again call to mind lofty ideals, but their meaning is imprecise. As before, Brennan fails to explain why his reasoning extends only to intimate associations. People form close ties with others through all kinds of associations. Some lifelong friendships emerge from within nonintimate associations; some intimate associations collapse in a matter of months. Self-definition also comes from myriad forms of associations—one's decision to join the ACLU or make a financial contribution to Greenpeace can speak volumes about one's identity.[44]

Like Karst, Brennan fails to offer a convincing rationale for privileging intimate associations over nonintimate ones. His theoretical anchor is the residue of *Eisenstadt* that supplants the inherently relational aspects of association with an individualistic notion of privacy. Intimate association is reduced to intimate individualism.[45]

The second category that Brennan announced in *Roberts* was expressive association. He characterized expressive association as "for the purpose of engaging in those activities protected by the First Amendment—speech, assembly, petition for the redress of grievances, and the exercise of religion." The Court had "long understood as implicit in the right to engage in activities protected by the First Amendment a corresponding right to associate with others in pursuit of a wide variety of political, social, economic, educational, religious, and cultural ends."[46]

Despite his instrumental characterization of expressive association, Brennan proposed an ostensibly protective legal test: "Infringements on [the right of expressive association] may be justified by regulations adopted to serve compelling state interests, unrelated to the suppression of ideas, that cannot be achieved through means significantly less restrictive of associational freedoms." The language of "compelling state interests, unrelated to the suppression of ideas," calls to mind the strict scrutiny standard established in other areas of the Court's First Amendment law. But notice how the reference to "means significantly less restrictive" differs from the usual strict scrutiny language of "least restrictive means." On closer examination, what resembles a strict scrutiny test might actually invert the presumption favoring the protected First Amendment activity to one that favors the government. Brennan's phrasing suggests that a government regulation "to a large extent but not significantly more restrictive of associational freedoms than a less onerous regulation" would survive the test. Although Brennan elsewhere intimated that he was applying strict scrutiny, his only formulation of the legal test proposed a different standard. Unsurprisingly, some courts have construed *Roberts* as intending something less than strict scrutiny.[47]

Brennan's category of expressive association implied that some associations were "nonexpressive." The problems with this line-drawing are not merely doctrinal—they are philosophical. The purported distinction between expressive and nonexpressive association fails to recognize: (1) that all associations have expressive potential; (2) that meaning is dynamic; and (3) that meaning is subject to more than one interpretation. These three claims rely on hermeneutical arguments whose full consideration exceeds the scope of this book, but I will address them briefly in the next chapter.[48]

After *Roberts*

Justice Brennan's reasoning in *Roberts* has been roundly criticized. Nancy Rosenblum observed: "The Jaycees' 'voice' was undeniably altered once it was forced to admit young women as full members along with young men." Aviam Soifer contested: "Surely the Jaycees . . . will be a different organization. Surely that difference will be felt throughout an intricate web of relationships and different voices in immeasurable but nonetheless significant ways." George Kateb suggested: "Brennan's claim that young women may, after their compulsory admission, contribute to the allowable purpose of 'promoting the interests of young men' is absurd." With an eye toward the legal effects of *Roberts,* Andrew Koppelman has noted that "the Court's obliviousness to the obvious burden the antidiscrimination law imposed [on the Jaycees] is not reassuring about future applications of the *Roberts* rule," and Jason Mazzone has cautioned that "the modern notion of 'expression' is a dubious peg on which to hang a constitutional right of free association."[49]

Despite its critical reception in academic circles, *Roberts* opened a large hole in the already attenuated freedom of association, and the Court endorsed its reasoning in two subsequent cases involving private organizations that refused membership to women. In 1987, the Court held in *Board of Directors of Rotary International v. Rotary Club of Duarte* that the Rotary Club had no First Amendment right to exclude women. The following year, in *New York State Club Association v. City of New York,* the Court upheld antidiscrimination laws applied to a consortium of New York City social clubs. Justice White's opinion narrowed the scope of expressive association by announcing that a group must demonstrate that it was "organized for specific expressive purposes" and that "it will not be able to advocate its desired viewpoints nearly as effectively if it cannot confine its membership" to certain classes of people. White emphasized that the right to associate was by no means absolute: it did not mean "that in every setting in which individuals exercise some discrimination in choosing associates, their selective process of inclusion and exclusion is protected by the Constitution."[50]

In 1995, the Court reviewed a challenge from the Irish-American Gay, Lesbian and Bisexual Group of Boston (GLIB) over its exclusion from a Boston parade jointly commemorating St. Patrick's Day and Evacuation Day. Since 1947, the parade had been organized by the South Boston Allied War Veterans Council, a private organization. GLIB challenged its exclusion from the parade under Massachusetts's public accommodations law. Justice Souter's opinion for the Court rejecting GLIB's claim relied on free speech rather than free association. Souter first classified the parade as a form of expression. Because the organizers were private speakers, they were free to select the content of their message. Therefore, they could properly reject GLIB's request to march in the parade. In fact, "whatever the reason" the parade organizers had for excluding GLIB, their decision "boils down to the choice of a speaker not to propound a particular point of view, and that choice is presumed to lie beyond the government's power to control." The free speech analysis seemed fairly straightforward, but it was difficult to reconcile with the Court's approach to association in *Roberts, Duarte,* and *New York State Club Association.*[51]

The Court's most significant case on the right of association after *Roberts* was its 2000 decision in *Boy Scouts of America v. Dale.* A 5–4 majority upheld the right of the Boy Scouts to exclude from their membership a homosexual scoutmaster against a challenge brought under a state anti-discrimination law. Chief Justice Rehnquist's opinion for the Court began by placing the case within the framework of expressive association: "To determine whether a group is protected by the First Amendment's expressive associational right, we must determine whether the group engages in 'expressive association.' The First Amendment's protection of expressive association is not reserved for advocacy groups. But to come within its ambit, a group must engage in some form of expression, whether it be public or private." Rehnquist distanced himself from some of the Court's earlier views on expressive association. Although *New York State Club Association* appeared to have narrowed the right of expressive association to groups that were organized "for specific expressive purposes," Rehnquist argued: "Associations do not have to associate for the 'purpose' of disseminating a certain message in order to be entitled to the protections of the First Amendment. An association must merely engage in expressive activity that could be impaired in order to be entitled to protection." For Rehnquist, the proper inquiry was "whether the forced inclusion of Dale as an assistant scoutmaster would significantly affect the Boy Scouts' ability to advocate public or private viewpoints." And this inquiry required that the Court defer to an organization's purported views: "It is not the role of the courts to reject a group's expressed values because they disagree with those values or find them internally inconsistent. As is true of all expressions of First Amendment freedoms, the courts may not interfere on the ground that they view a particular expression as unwise or irrational."[52]

These strong words hardly seemed credible after *Runyon* and *Roberts.* Justice Stevens's dissent highlighted the doctrinal tension that *Dale* created: "Until today, we have never once found a claimed right to associate in the selection of members to prevail in the face of a State's antidiscrimination law. To the contrary, we have squarely held that a State's antidiscrimination law does not violate a group's right to associate simply because the law conflicts with that group's exclusionary membership policy." Moreover, while *Dale*'s holding favored the Boy Scouts, the Court reaffirmed the fundamental division between intimate and expressive association in *Roberts*.[53]

The Continued Costs of Intimate and Expressive Association

Since *Dale*, two decisions have potently illustrated the dangers of the framework of intimate and expressive association. The first is the Second Circuit's decision in *Chi Iota v. City University of New York*. Alpha Epsilon Pi ("AEPi") is a national social fraternity founded in 1913 "to provide opportunities for the Jewish college man seeking the best possible college and fraternity experience." According to its Supreme Constitution, AEPi seeks "to promote and encourage among its members: Personal perfection, a reverence for God and an honorable life devoted to the ideal of service to all mankind; lasting friendships and the attainment of nobility of action and better understanding among all faiths."[54]

In 2002, the Chi Iota Colony ("Chi Iota") of AEPi formed at the College of Staten Island, a primarily commuter campus of just more than eleven thousand undergraduates. Since its inception, Chi Iota never had more than twenty members. Its past president described the purpose of the fraternity as fostering a "lifelong interpersonal bond termed brotherhood," which "results in deep attachments and commitments to the other members of the Fraternity among whom is shared a community of thoughts, experiences, beliefs and distinctly personal aspects of their lives." In furtherance of those goals, the fraternity limited its membership to males. Chi Iota applied to be chartered and officially recognized by the College of Staten Island in March 2004. The director of the Office of Student Life denied the application on the basis that the fraternity's exclusion of women violated the college's nondiscrimination policy. The denial of official recognition precluded Chi Iota from using the college's facilities, resources, and funding, from using the college's name in conjunction with the organization's name, and from posting events to the college's calendars.[55]

In 2005, the members of Chi Iota filed suit in the United States District Court for the Eastern District of New York, arguing violations of their rights to intimate and expressive association and equal protection. The district court granted the fraternity's motion for a preliminary injunction against the college on its intimate association claim but concluded that Chi Iota had not shown a clear or substantial likelihood of success on its expressive association claim. On appeal, the United States Court of Appeals for the Second Circuit reversed the district court's grant of a preliminary injunction and remanded the case, noting that the fraternity's "interests in intimate association are relatively weak." Although the district court would still have had Chi Iota's intimate and expressive association claims before it on remand, neither looked to have a reasonable chance of success given the posture of the litigation. As the Second Circuit was considering the case, the Chi Iota Colony of the Alpha Epsilon Pi Fraternity at the College of Staten Island disbanded.[56]

Chi Iota is not the most sympathetic plaintiff to bring a freedom of association claim. Although its Jewish roots suggest religious freedom interests, most of its members were nonpracticing Jews. It was a social group, but some of its social activities were coarse and banal, including visits to strip clubs. It may well be that the brothers of Chi Iota were a self-focused, hedonistic group of boys who brought a collective drain on whatever community existed at the mostly commuter campus at the College of Staten Island. But all of this is beside the point. A group's protections shouldn't turn on whether its purposes or activities are sincere or wholesome to an outsider's perspective. Chi Iota's practices and activities meant something to its members. They meant enough for the brothers to pursue membership through an application and rush process, to participate in the group's activities, and to bring a federal lawsuit in an attempt to preserve their associational bonds.[57]

The most recent case to illustrate the dangers of the weakened framework for associational freedom claims is the Supreme Court's decision in *Christian Legal Society v. Martinez*. The Christian Legal Society (CLS) is a "nationwide association of lawyers, law students, law professors, and judges who profess faith in Jesus Christ." Founded in 1961, its purposes include "providing a means of society, fellowship, and nurture among Christian lawyers; encouraging, discipling, and aiding Christian law students; promoting justice, religious liberty, and biblical conflict resolution; and encouraging lawyers to furnish legal services to the poor." The society maintains student chapters at many law schools around the country. These student chapters invite anyone to participate in their events but require members (including officers) to sign a "statement of faith" consistent with the Evangelical Protestant and Catholic traditions. Part of this statement of faith affirms that sexual conduct should be confined to heterosexual marriage. Accordingly, CLS student chapters do not accept as members anyone who engages in or affirms the morality of sex outside heterosexual marriage.[58]

In 2004, the CLS chapter at Hastings College of the Law in San Francisco inquired about becoming a recognized student organization. Hastings officials withheld recognition on the basis that CLS's statement of faith violated the religion and sexual orientation provisions of the school's Nondiscrimination Policy. As a result, the school denied CLS travel funds and funding from student activity fees. It also denied the society the use of the school's logo, use of a Hastings e-mail address, the opportunity to send mass e-mails to the student body, participation in the annual student organizations fair, and reserved meeting spaces on campus. Hastings subsequently asserted that its denial of recognition stemmed from an "accept-all-comers" policy that required all student organizations to accept any student who desired to be a member of the organization.[59]

The society filed suit in federal district court, asserting violations of expressive association, free speech, free exercise of religion, and equal protection. The district court granted summary judgment against CLS on all of its claims. With respect to CLS's expressive association claim, the district court concluded that *Roberts* and *Dale* were inapplicable because "CLS is not being forced, as a private entity, to include certain members or officers" and "the conditioned exclusion of [an] organization from a particular forum [does] not rise to the level of compulsive membership." The district court also asserted that "Hastings has denied CLS official recognition based on CLS's conduct—its refusal to comply with Hastings' Nondiscrimination Policy—not because of CLS's philosophies or beliefs."[60]

Despite resting its holding on the inapplicability of *Roberts* and *Dale*, the court held in the alternative that CLS's claim failed under those authorities as well. It assumed that CLS qualified as an expressive association because Hastings did not dispute that characterization. But the court determined that "CLS has not demonstrated that its ability to express its views would be significantly impaired by complying with [the school's nondiscrimination] requirement." The court concluded: "Unlike the Boy Scouts in *Dale*, CLS has not submitted any evidence demonstrating that teaching certain values to other students is part of the organization's mission or purpose, or that it seeks to do so by example, such that the mere presence of someone who does not fully comply with the prescribed code of conduct would force CLS to send a message contrary to its mission." In fact, there was "no evidence" that "a non-orthodox Christian, gay, lesbian, or bisexual student" who became a member or officer of CLS "by their presence alone, would impair CLS's ability to convey its beliefs."[61]

The society appealed the district court's decision to the United States Court of Appeals for the Ninth Circuit. The appellate court affirmed the district court with a terse two-sentence opinion: "The parties stipulate that Hastings imposes an open membership rule on all student groups—all groups must accept all comers as voting members even if those individuals disagree with the mission of the group. The conditions on recognition are therefore viewpoint neutral and reasonable." CLS petitioned for a writ of certiorari to the United States Supreme Court, arguing, among other things, that the Ninth Circuit's decision created a circuit split with a Seventh Circuit case invalidating the denial of official recognition to a CLS student chapter at the Southern Illinois University School of Law.[62]

A divided Supreme Court rejected CLS's challenge. Justice Ginsburg's majority opinion concluded that Hastings's all-comers policy was "a reasonable, viewpoint-neutral condition on access to the student-organization forum." The majority's free speech analysis is not entirely persuasive—its reasoning obscures a tension between the viewpoint neutrality of the all-comers policy (under a public forum analysis) and Hastings's nonneutral policy preferences expressed through its own speech and subsidies (under something akin to a government speech analysis). But in the context of this book, the majority's failure to take seriously CLS's freedom of association claim is even more disturbing.[63]

From the premise that it "makes little sense to treat CLS's speech and association claims as discrete," Ginsburg concluded that the Court's "limited-public-forum precedents supply the appropriate framework for assessing both CLS's speech and association rights." The problem with this doctrinal move is twofold. First, it essentially elects rational basis scrutiny over strict scrutiny—and therefore all but preordains the outcome. Second, it casts aside the competing constitutional values underlying associational freedom. CLS's associational claim highlights the underlying values conflict in this case: the clash between group autonomy and equality—the same tension at issue in *Runyon* and *Roberts.* Taking this values clash seriously means refusing to make an artificial distinction between expression and conduct and recognizing that, in some cases, they are one and the same. Contrary to Ginsburg's insistence that "CLS's conduct—not its Christian perspective—is, from Hastings' vantage point, what stands between the group and RSO status," CLS's "conduct" is inseparable from its message.[64]

Ginsburg's opinion misses this connection. Quoting from CLS's brief, she writes that "expressive association in this case is 'the functional equivalent of speech itself'" to set up the idea that expressive association is entitled to no more constitutional protection than speech. But CLS had asserted: "Where one of the central purposes of a noncommercial expressive association is the communication of a moral teaching, its choice of who will formulate and articulate that message is treated as the functional equivalent of speech itself." CLS wasn't arguing that association is nothing more than speech but that association is itself a form of expression—who it selects as its members and leaders communicates a message. The society underscored this point elsewhere in its brief, arguing that "because a group's leaders define and shape the group's message, the right to select leaders is an essential element of its right to speak." Ginsburg interpreted this assertion to mean that "CLS suggests that its expressive-association claim plays a part auxiliary to speech's starring role." That interpretation may be consistent with the *Roberts* understanding of expressive association, but as I have argued throughout this book, it misses the more fundamental connection between a group's message and its composition.[65]

Ginsburg distinguished the Court's associational cases like *Dale* and *Roberts* because those cases "involved regulations that *compelled* a group to include unwanted members, with no choice to opt out." But this is really a matter of perspective. Sometimes a group must choose between receiving benefits and adhering to its policies at the cost of those benefits. But withholding some benefits (like access to meeting space or e-mail lists or the opportunity to be part of a public forum) can be akin to stamping out a group's existence. After *Martinez*, the Hastings Christian Group That Accepts All Comers can exist, and the Christian Legal Society for Hastings Law Students That Can Sometimes Meet on Campus as a Matter of University Discretion if Space Is Available but Can't Recruit Members at the Student Activities Fair can exist. But the Hastings Christian Legal Society—whose views and purposes are in no way sanctioned by and able to be explicitly disavowed by Hastings—cannot.[66]

At the close of the equality era, the right of association bore little resemblance to the right of assembly that had existed for almost two hundred years of our nation's history. The confluence of a growing Civil Rights Movement and the dominance of Rawlsian liberalism meant that when principles of equality collided with group autonomy, equality won. An already attenuated right of association established during the national security era now gave way to even more incursions into group autonomy in the equality era. These developments were facilitated by an odd connection between association and privacy that produced a right of intimate association and, in doing so, jettisoned all other groups to a "nonintimate" status. By the end of the equality era, a right of association now quite removed from the right of assembly had fundamentally altered the protections for group autonomy. The next chapter explores these changes and their consequences by sketching a theory of assembly.

CHAPTER 5

A THEORY OF ASSEMBLY

This book has recounted the histories of the rights of assembly and association in American constitutionalism and suggested that the shift from assembly to association has weakened protections for dissenting, political, and expressive groups. The historical narrative closed with two of the most recent casualties of this shift: the Chi Iota fraternity at the College of Staten Island and the Christian Legal Society at Hastings College of the Law. These cases illustrate that we have failed to ground protections for group autonomy in an intellectually honest constitutional framework and have relied instead on artificial distinctions and unexamined premises. Because these shortcomings are unlikely to be remedied by applying the doctrine that has evolved around the right of association in cases like *NAACP v. Alabama, Griswold v. Connecticut,* and *Roberts v. United States Jaycees,* we need to look past association and recover assembly.[1]

We can illustrate the contemporary plausibility of assembly by examining how it fits within our tradition of constitutional interpretation. Philip Bobbitt has suggested that we can evaluate constitutional argument through six "modalities": historical, prudential, textual, structural, precedential, and ethical. Neil Siegel and Robert Cooter have summarized Bobbitt's modalities:

Historical arguments appeal either to preratification history or to postratification history. *Prudential* or *consequentialist* arguments identify the good or bad social consequences of an interpretation. *Textual* arguments rely on the text of the Constitution and the rules for interpreting texts. *Structural* arguments draw inferences from the theory and structure of government created by the Constitution. *Precedential* arguments offer the existence of previous decisions, either past political practice or past judicial rulings, as justifying a certain outcome in a later case. Finally, [*ethical*] arguments tell a story about national identity; they tend to take a narrative or historical form and inquire whether a given interpretation is faithful to the meaning or destiny of the country, its deepest cultural commitments, or its national character.

As Siegel and Cooter have observed, "Interpretations of the Constitution often invoke multiple forms of constitutional authority to support the same conclusions."[2]

The story of the right of assembly recounted thus far in this book enlists each of Bobbitt's modalities in arguing for the place of assembly in our constitutional tradition. The *textual* argument begins with the not irrelevant fact that the right of assembly—unlike association—is actually in the text of the Constitution. It also suggests that assembly was never intended to be limited to the purposes of petition.

The *structural* argument emerges in Chapter 2 but comes more fully to light in the discussion of pluralist interpretations of Madison and Tocqueville in Chapter 3. Assemblies function in our democratic structure to challenge and limit the reach of the state. They extend beyond the formal boundaries of political parties to disrupt the polity with "factions for the rest of us" that offer a check against majoritarian standards and the attempt of government to control dissent.[3]

The *prudential* argument recognizes that assembly, like all rights, is inevitably constrained. Peter de Marneffe's observation about the freedom of association extends as well to the right of assembly: "Some may think of rights as 'absolute,' believing that to say that there is a *right* to some liberty is to say that the government may not interfere with this liberty for *any* reason. But if this is how rights are understood, there are virtually no rights to liberty—because for virtually every liberty there will be *some* morally sufficient reason for the government to interfere with it." But the prudential argument also advocates patience and restraint whenever possible—we don't know what we are destroying or precluding when we stifle the existence of groups, and we often have no way of knowing whether the harms outweigh the benefits.

This latter prudential argument relates closely to the *historical* argument. Every important social movement in this country began as a collection of "unofficial" and "nonpolitical" gatherings. Informal relationships and activities nurtured the nascent groups that eventually produced the greatest political change.[4]

Like the prudential argument, the *precedential* argument cuts in both directions. On the one hand, there is now an established body of case law on the right of association. But I have argued that the doctrinal framework purportedly holding that case law together is highly problematic. A more coherent and equally important body of case law on the right of assembly precedes the relatively new rights of intimate and expressive association.

Finally, the *ethical* argument recognizes that pluralism and dissent are among our nation's deepest cultural commitments. Dissenting practices confront an ever-present challenge by the state to domesticate their destabilizing tendencies. Powerful countervailing visions of stability and consensus from mid-twentieth-century pluralism and Rawlsian liberalism have sought to bind our country together at the cost of silencing the margins of dissent. But the groups that have lived in the shadow of the state have never fully acquiesced.

The story of assembly thus embodies each of Bobbitt's modalities. It reveals four principles that help us see the contours of this right and its contemporary applications:

- Assembly includes dissident groups that act against the common good.
- Assembly extends beyond political groups to religious and social groups of all kinds.
- Just as the freedom of speech guards against restrictions imposed prior to an act of speaking, assembly guards against restrictions imposed prior to an act of assembling—it protects a group's autonomy, composition, and existence.
- Assembly is itself expression—the existence of a group and its selection of members and leaders are themselves forms of expression.

These four principles favor strong protections for the formation, composition, expression, and gathering of groups, especially those groups that dissent from majoritarian standards. But the principles extracted from Chapter 2's historical narrative do not stand alone, for even more can be said about the prudential, historical, and ethical arguments supporting the right of assembly. That is the goal of the first part of this chapter. It situates assembly in the political theory of Sheldon Wolin, whose work can be read as a counternarrative to the consensus arguments of Robert Dahl and John Rawls. Wolin's refusal to accept the state's claims to legitimacy lays a theoretical foundation for the dissenting, political, and expressive assembly.

After developing this political theory, I turn to another dimension of the historical argument. Here I confront Andrew Koppelman's recent book, *A Right to Discriminate?* Koppelman relies heavily on historical argument to support his approach to group autonomy. I argue that the history is more complicated and less dispositive than he suggests. The final two sections of this chapter tease out the implications of constitutional interpretation. I first offer a definition of assembly as a plausible resource for contemporary constitutional argument and explain why a contextual approach to the boundaries of assembly improves upon existing alternatives. I then apply theory to practice by sketching the "missing dissent" in *Roberts v. United States Jaycees.*

A Political Theory of Assembly

Sheldon Wolin first published *Politics and Vision,* his monumental history of political thought, in 1960, at the height of mid-twentieth-century liberalism and only two years after the Supreme Court's initial recognition of the right of association in *NAACP v. Alabama.* He concluded his book with a critique entitled "The Age of Organization and the Sublimation of Politics." In that chapter, he expressed a wariness toward the "group theory of politics" that ignored "the sublimation of the political into forms of association which earlier thought had believed to be non-political." Wolin's prescient critique focused on the migration of power from state to corporation. But writing before the turbulent decades of the 1960s and 1970s and the pluralist critiques of Connelly, Lowi, and

McConnell, he neglected to highlight the *benefits* of decentralizing power and politics: the possibility of reclaiming a form of the "political" by groups that exist apart from both the state and the corporations that came to serve as its proxies.[5]

Wolin's second (expanded) edition of *Politics and Vision* appeared in 2004, after the Civil Rights Movement, the work of John Rawls, and the rise of multiculturalism. In his later work, Wolin recognized not only the dispersion of power to the corporation and the subsequent alliance of corporation and state but also liberalism's continued suppression of difference in an attempt to perpetuate the appearance of stability. Reflecting upon the years following the initial appearance of *Politics and Vision,* Wolin wrote: "The sixties caught liberal theorists by surprise, in part owing to a complacency encouraged by a seemingly wide public consensus based upon liberal beliefs and confirmed in the discourse of consensus popular among social scientists and analytic philosophers." But liberal political thought perpetuated its consensus narrative in spite of the political events that surrounded it, and by the end of the 1970s, the remnants of a New Deal liberalism that once critiqued the status quo were largely engulfed by a liberalism that thrived upon the status quo.[6]

For Wolin, nothing epitomized this change more than Rawls's *Theory of Justice,* which represented "a liberalism being transformed from a critical theory into a legitimizing theory." Part of this legitimization rested on ensuring stability at all costs. In Wolin's assessment, *A Theory of Justice* introduced "proceduralist politics, politics constrained within and firmly constrained by agendas designed beforehand to assure what Rawls regarded as rational outcomes, [which] emerge[d] as the liberal alternative to the threat of destabilization implicitly attributed to participatory politics where structure and agenda are exposed to the vagaries of democratic decision-making." Wolin suggests that "when Rawls submits that *A Theory of Justice* was bound to be challenged by other comprehensive doctrines, he reveals what is really at stake, not the comprehensiveness of doctrines but the threat of conflict." By the time he wrote *Political Liberalism,* Rawls had come to realize that his earlier work had not sufficiently accounted for comprehensive doctrines that would rival the claims of liberalism. Rawls resolved the threat of "unreasonable comprehensive doctrines" with a "political" conception of justice that Wolin aptly surmised "would prove closer in spirit to a Rousseauian regime of public virtue and of a civil religion with reasonableness as its dogma." For Wolin, Rawls's answer means: "The reasonable can fairly be said to be the ideology of a liberal society more haunted by the specter of disagreement than by the conflicts of interest that republican theorists from Harrington to Madison had emphasized. Those who disagree with what is officially pronounced to be reasonable can be dismissed as unreasonable." These "repressive elements in Rawls's liberalism . . . reflect an aversion to social conflict that is in keeping with his elevation of stability, cooperation, and unity as the fundamental values."[7]

Wolin has elsewhere reflected upon the problems of consensus liberalism by distinguishing between "diversity" and "difference." As he argues, "although both 'difference' and 'diversity' refer to dissimilarity and unlikeness, there are some subtle distinctions between them." Liberal pluralism "is more comfortable with diversity than it is with difference," and difference raises "conceptual and practical" tensions with "pluralist democracy." Wolin maintains that difference, unlike diversity, "possesses a certain inner coherence that may indicate the presence of a hard core of nonnegotiability, some element that is too intimately connected with identity to allow for easy compromise." This kind of difference, which I have argued is best protected by the right of assembly, is precisely that which Dahl and Rawls seek to deny. It explains the appeal to consensus theorists of a right of association that depoliticizes and disembodies expression in order to neutralize dissent.[8]

The right of association is in some ways just a bit player in a larger narrative of consensus liberalism that celebrates diversity even as it marginalizes difference. Wolin observes:

> From Roger Williams's *Bloody Tenent* (1644) to John Calhoun's *Disquisition,* Margaret Fuller's *Woman in the Nineteenth Century,* Booker Washington's *Up from Slavery* and the *Autobiography of Malcolm X,* discursive representations of difference have appeared but until recently have had little effect on the main conceptual vocabulary or thematic structure of the theoretical literature of American politics. Instead, from Madison's Tenth *Federalist* to the writings of Mary Follett, Charles Beard, Arthur Bentley, David Truman, and Robert Dahl, those modes of difference mostly disappeared or were reduced to the status of interests. The result: on one side, themes of

separation, dismemberment, disunion, exploitation, exclusion, and revenge and, on the other, themes extolling American pluralism as the distinctive American political achievement and the main reason for the unrivaled stability of American society and its political system.

To Wolin's second list we can add Rawls, who by the time of the second edition of *Politics and Vision* has become for Wolin the paradigmatic thinker of liberalism's suppression of difference. Part of Rawls's genius was his ability to refashion the consensus narrative of mid-twentieth-century pluralism with greater philosophical sophistication. Part of Wolin's genius was to recognize the ways in which Rawls, no less than his pluralist predecessors, masked liberalism's consensus tendencies. Against Rawls and the pluralists, Wolin hints at a way of conceiving politics and difference that is less stable but more democratic. The rest of this section builds on Wolin's insights to give shape to the *dissenting, political,* and *expressive* assembly.[9]

Wolin's challenge to the consensus narratives of pluralism and Rawlsian liberalism points toward the *dissenting assembly.* While not every assembly dissents, the groups that shape the boundaries of autonomy are those that reject consensus norms. We can see why this is the case when we realize that groups conforming to consensus norms have little reason to invoke a claim to group autonomy. Assembly—like speech, or the press, or religion—is most relevant when its exercise is challenged by the state.

The previous two chapters demonstrated how this dissenting characteristic has been marginalized in the bounded consensus accompanying the turn to association. That consensus excluded communist groups during the national security era and segregationist groups during the equality era. Few of us would care if the limits of group autonomy ended with communists and segregationists. But the norms underlying consensus are more pervasive, and they reach deep into the internal practices of many groups. For example, a number of contemporary political theorists support imposing consensus norms on illiberal groups, arguing that the state is justified in reshaping or even eliminating illiberal practices through methods ranging from compulsory education to direct intervention. Nancy Rosenblum has suggested that these kinds of arguments "all aim at congruence between the internal life and practices of voluntary groups and the public culture of liberal democracy." This "logic of congruence" requires "that not only political institutions and public accommodations but also voluntary social groups function as mini-liberal democracies, with a view toward cultivating and sustaining self-respect." Rosenblum recognizes that under the logic of congruence, all associations are vulnerable to "the social preferences of the party in power." The dissenting assembly resists these consensus moves.[10]

The *political assembly* embodies a kind of politics distinct from the politics of the state. In fact, as Stephen Carter has argued, the meanings that groups "discover and assign to the world may be radically distinct from those that are assigned by the political sovereign." Wolin suggests that these kinds of groups represent a "political mode of existence" in which "the political is remembered and recreated." He points to "the recurrent experience of constituting political societies and political practices, beginning with colonial times and extending through the Revolution and beyond to the westward migrations where new settlements and towns were founded by the hundreds; the movement to abolish slavery and the abortive effort at reconstructing American life on the basis of racial equality; the Populist and agrarian revolts of the 19th century; the struggle for autonomous trade unions and for women's rights; the civil rights movement of the '60s and the anti-war, anti-nuclear, and ecological movements of recent decades." These "restorative moments" of the political assembly resist the boundaries that the liberal state would impose. Groups that have resisted the "age of organization" and maintained an existence apart from the structures of the now expanded state rightly claim a form of political existence. Consensus liberalism's denial of that politics reprises monist state theory and claims an exclusive right to pronounce the "real" account of what it means to live together in a shared polity. The political assembly resists this conclusion.[11]

Consensus liberalism's attempt to depoliticize private groups also extends to forms of rationality, most famously in Rawls's concept of public reason. Chapter 4 briefly explored Rawls's influence on legal thought around the time of the changes to the right of association in *Roberts*. One of the fundamental problems with Rawlsian public reason is its imposition of normative constraints on discourse and rationality.

These constraints create a tension between the institutions that compose the "basic structure" of society, on the one hand, and Rawls's purported recognition of the freedom of association in "private society," on the other. Feminist theorists have famously called attention to this ambiguity with respect to the family. It also exists with other kinds of groups. As Rosenblum observes, "One possibility is that associational life is part of the 'basic structure' of a well-ordered society, whose organization and norms must conform to principles of justice because their effects on defining men's rights and duties and influencing their life-prospects 'are so profound and present from the start.'" But "except for serfdom and slavery Rawls does not identify arrangements that must be prohibited as a condition for the morality of association." Accordingly, Rosenblum argues that "we can conclude that associations do not fail in serving their formative moral purposes by being incongruent with the public norms of liberal democracy, or by being insufficiently complex and comprehensive to move members in the direction of appreciation for principles of justice." Rather, "the morality of association provides a pluralist background culture, much of it incongruent with liberal democracy."[12]

Rawls appears to accept the incongruous nature of some associations and allow a certain degree of group autonomy, writing, for example, that "the principles of political justice do not apply to the internal life of a church, nor is it desirable, or consistent with liberty or conscience or freedom of association, that they should." But he maintains an ambiguity that ultimately undermines group autonomy. The problem becomes evident when a court is asked to adjudicate a clash between the right of association and another of the primary goods. Because Rawls requires public reason from "the discourse of judges in their decisions, and especially of the judges of a supreme court," there is every indication that the dispute will have to be resolved on the basis of public reason.[13]

Rawls believes that the "idea of public reason is fully compatible with many forms of nonpublic reason" that "belong to the internal life of the many associations in civil society"—*many* forms of nonpublic reason, but not all, and therein lies the rub. Sometimes the practices underlying a claim to freedom of association cannot be translated into public reason. As Chandran Kukathas observes:

Important though debate may be, it is not always an adequate substitute for demonstration through practice. This is all the more so when the subject of dispute is how one should live. Not all people are capable of articulating their reasons for thinking their way of life is better—or even just better for some. (Nor, for that matter are all capable of articulating their reasons for regarding some influences as malign or corrupting.) Indeed, they may not be aware of many of the advantages (though also, of course, disadvantages) of their practices simply because these are side effects which have not much to do with why they prefer to stick to their ways. Nonetheless, in being able to live a particular way of life they may be quite capable of demonstrating (intentionally or not) its merits. Some need to practise in order to preach.

The political assembly facilitates "practicing in order to preach." It embraces what Robert Cover called the "radical message of the first amendment," which recognizes that "an interdependent system of obligation may be enforced, but the very patterns of meaning that give rise to effective or ineffective social control are to be left to the domain of Babel."[14]

We can illustrate the danger inherent in the kind of public reason that ignores the insights offered by Kukathas and Cover. Suppose that a single-gender private group benefits its members but damages the self-respect of those whom it excludes. Resolving this conflict requires choosing one basic good over another. Rawls may seem agnostic about the outcome of this clash because he recognizes the value of both goods. But suppose the reasons that the men or women have for desiring exclusivity derive from tradition-dependent beliefs and values that neither accord with nor subscribe to Rawlsian public reason. We might consider several such possibilities: an emotive explanation ("we feel better when we gather exclusively as men or women"), an expressive explanation ("we believe that our homogenous gathering best expresses to the world our fundamental beliefs"), or a theological explanation ("we gather exclusively based on our understanding of God's command to us"). By imposing the constraint of public reason, Rawls precludes the judge or judges resolving the dispute from relying on these arguments.

The only remaining arguments that satisfy public reason are tautological claims about the importance of freedom of association for its own sake—or a derivative claim of the importance of emotion, expression, or religion—and these will surely fail against the countervailing claim of damaged self-respect, which is "perhaps the most important primary good," and can easily be articulated in terms of public reason. But the analysis that leads to this conclusion proceeds within an artificially constrained discourse. There is nothing inherent in a procedural scheme of justice that requires either public reason or the outcome it generates. And despite Rawls's aspiration to reach agreement through discussion, decisions based upon public reason will ultimately be enforced by the coercive and violent imposition of the law.[15]

It is important to recognize the implications of Rawls's public reason constraint even when they aren't immediately triggered. For example, a group that is unable to articulate a public reason defense of its practices may nevertheless flourish under a Rawlsian scheme as long as the group is unchallenged. But that group's freedom is contingent on the absence of a public reason challenge. When it encounters a constraint justified in terms acceptable to public reason, the group must either modify its practices or cease to exist unless it can offer a defense grounded in public reason. The political assembly that recognizes competing politics and political vocabularies resists the Rawlsian claim of public reason and the coercive consequences that flow from it.

The *expressive assembly* insists upon the various meanings of a group and its gathering even when they aren't evident to an outsider. Just as "political philosophy constitutes a form of 'seeing' political phenomena" and "the way in which the phenomena will be visualized depends in large measure on where the viewer 'stands,'" so too the meaning assigned to an act or expression is often varied and perspectival. The Supreme Court's category of expressive association obscures these multivalent aspects of expression. The previous chapter claimed that the purported distinction between expressive and nonexpressive association fails to recognize that: (1) all associations have expressive potential; (2) meaning is dynamic; and (3) meaning is subject to more than one interpretation. This chapter elaborates upon these claims.[16]

The first problem with the idea of nonexpressive association is that every association—and every associational act—has expressive potential. Communicative possibility exists in joining, excluding, gathering, proclaiming, engaging, or not engaging. Once a relational association is stipulated between two or more people, any act by those people—when consciously undertaken as members of the association—has expressive potential reflective of that association.[17]

To illustrate why the category of expressive association fails to encompass the broader understanding of meaning suggested here, consider a gay social club. Suppose that the club has twenty members—placing it well outside the currently recognized contours of an intimate association. Suppose further that the club's members engage in no verbal or written expression directed outside their gatherings but make no effort to conceal their membership from their friends, colleagues, and acquaintances who aren't part of the club. There is no way that the members of this club are engaging in "a right to associate for the purpose of engaging in those activities protected by the First Amendment." And yet their act of gathering clearly conveys an expressive message.[18]

The second problem with the reasoning underlying expressive association is that meaning is dynamic. The messages, creeds, practices, and even central purposes of associations change over time. Justice Souter ignores this reality when he argues in his dissent in *Boy Scouts of America v. Dale* that "no group can claim a right of expressive association without identifying a clear position to be advocated over time in an unequivocal way." That standard demands too much. What would it mean for a group to advocate a "clear position" "over time" in "an unequivocal way"?[19]

The final problem with expressive association is that meaning is subject to more than one interpretive gloss. Acknowledging the subjective interpretation of meaning exposes a related problem inherent in the expressive association doctrine: Who decides what counts as the message of the group? Erwin Chemerinsky and Catherine Fisk have criticized the Supreme Court in *Dale* for unduly deferring to a group's leadership for its views about the group's expressive message. But there isn't a readily apparent alternative that more "justly" or more "accurately" captures the group's expressive meaning. For example, it isn't obvious that a majority of the group's members should be recognized as having the authoritative interpretation of the group's meaning, particularly for hierarchically structured groups.[20]

The challenges to determining a group's meaning get even thornier. Consider three different characterizations that Chemerinsky and Fisk offer about the purposes of the Boy Scouts: (I) a "significant number of current and former scouts . . . reasonably believed that scouting was, and should be, about camping"; (2) all members of the Boy Scouts understand that "the Boy Scouts is for boys" and "all presumably believe that same sex experiences offer valuable developmental opportunities for children"; and (3) "[we suspect that the] Boy Scouts of America is understood [by its members] to be about honesty, self-reliance, service, leadership, and camping." These descriptions are not interchangeable. They assign different purposes to the Boy Scouts (camping versus gender-based activities versus camping plus other things), they attribute those purposes to different subsets of the association (a significant number of current and former scouts versus all members versus members), and they attach varying degrees of certainty to the asserted meaning (the belief was "reasonable" versus all members "presumably believed" versus the belief is something that Chemerinsky and Fisk "suspect"). All of these variations and their varying rhetorical emphases spring from the description of a single group in a single law review article. It is not hard to see how the interpretive dilemmas multiply when assertions of purpose and meaning are expanded ever further. The expressive assembly recognizes that multivalent meaning is inherent in a group's expression and cautions that interpretations imposed by outsiders on the group may be epistemologically biased or constrained.[21]

The Neglected History of Assembly

The political theory that I explored in the preceding section gives shape to the dissenting, political, and expressive assembly that resists the state's push for consensus and control. This vision of assembly didn't simply spring forth from the imaginations of political theorists—it is also evident in our nation's history. Yet much of this history has been neglected. Consider, for example, Andrew Koppelman's recent book, *A Right to Discriminate?* In it Koppelman offers one of the most compelling arguments to limit group autonomy for the sake of antidiscrimination law. But he relies upon an incomplete historical account.

Koppelman's opening chapter of *A Right to Discriminate?* is entitled "Origins of the Right to Exclude." Here is a summary of his historical narrative:

(1) Prior to the Civil War, common law recognized that "every business that held itself out as open to serve the public arguably had a legal obligation to serve anyone who sought service."

(2) After "legal rights were for the first time extended to African Americans" following the Civil War, some state courts "held for the first time that most businesses had no common-law duty to serve the public," and some state legislatures "specifically abrogated that duty," both doing so in an effort to allow white businesses to refuse service to black customers.

(3) In the late nineteenth century, many states enacted laws banning racial discrimination in public accommodations.

(4) During the Progressive Era, the Court "created rights to resist the state's power to force private associations to conform to a government-imposed norm."

(5) In the mid-twentieth century, the Court rejected claims that all-white labor unions and political parties could exclude blacks.

(6) The Court's 1953 decision in *Terry v. Adams* rejected a similar claim by a private group that ran a racially exclusive preprimary whose winner "invariably went on to win the general election." The Court "understood that the 'private' nature of the association masked a degree of power that could have an enormous influence on substantive constitutional rights" and "the Court would not deem an association private if it held so much substantive power."

(7) The Court's 1958 decision in *NAACP v. Alabama* recognized a "new understanding of freedom of association" that derived from the freedom of speech.

(8) The Court's 1976 decision in *Runyon v. McCrary* "summarily rejected" the argument that its new freedom of association included a right to exclude.

(9) In revisiting the "right to exclude based on free speech" eight years later in *Roberts v. United States Jaycees*, the Court concluded "much more sympathetically" that the right "sometimes entails a right to exclude unwanted members," but the Court also "imposed doctrinal limits upon the right it had thus created," including a requirement that "the association must establish the nature of its expressive practice and demonstrate just how changes in its

membership will undermine that practice," which the Jaycees failed to do.

(10) Sixteen years later, the Court's decision in *Boy Scouts of America v. Dale* disrupted the "well-settled" law from *Roberts* and "warped the law of free association."[22]

Koppelman's narrative highlights some of the tensions underlying the collision of group autonomy and antidiscrimination law. In my view, he makes several missteps: (1) he links *NAACP v. Alabama* too closely to the right of speech;[23] (2) he neglects the Court's struggle to address segregationist arguments for group autonomy;[24] and (3) he places too much confidence in the "well-settled" nature of the doctrine announced in *Roberts*.[25] Taken in isolation, these challenges to Koppelman's historical narrative might amount to little more than minor quibbles. But their significance grows when we consider another dimension of his narrative: what it leaves out.

Here is a different history to complement Koppelman's account:

(1) Prior to the founding, William Penn and Roger Williams ensured that dissenting religious groups could exercise their freedom in opposition to majoritarian norms in the political antecedents to four of the thirteen colonies: Pennsylvania, Delaware, New Jersey, and Rhode Island.

(2) In 1791, the framers of the Bill of Rights recognized the continued importance of dissenting groups in guaranteeing the rights of assembly and the free exercise of religion in the First Amendment. Every state constitution also included a right of assembly.

(3) Throughout our nation's history, political, religious, and social groups have dissented from majoritarian and consensus standards, often claiming the protections of the right of assembly. State courts have repeatedly enforced state constitutional provisions protecting assembly (with the glaring exception of claims of assembly by free and slave blacks).

(4) The Court's 1937 decision in *De Jonge v. Oregon* incorporated the federal right of assembly against the states. Over the next few years, the vital link between assembly and democracy was reinforced in popular rhetoric (including tributes to assembly as one of the

original "four freedoms") and in decisions like *Herndon v. Lowry* (1937), *Hague v. Committee for Industrial Organization* (1939), and *Thomas v. Collins* (1945).

(5) The Court's 1958 decision in *NAACP v. Alabama* recognized for the first time a constitutional right of association, relying heavily on past decisions pertaining to the right of assembly.

(6) The Court struggled to define the contours of its new right when it extended its protections to the NAACP but denied them to communist groups.

(7) The Civil Rights Act of 1964, the Court's 1968 decision in *Jones v. Alfred H. Mayer*, and other changes to the legal landscape made clear that principles of group autonomy did not justify race-based discrimination in places of public accommodation or in relation to the sale or lease of real property.

(8) The Court struggled to limit a segregationist right to exclude beyond these contexts, eventually concluding in *Runyon v. McCrary* that it did not extend to whites excluding blacks in private schools.

(9) Eight years later in *Roberts v. United States Jaycees*, the Court split the right of association into intimate and expressive components.

(10) Aside from the Court's 2000 decision in *Boy Scouts of America v. Dale*, the freedom of association has offered almost no check against the reach of antidiscrimination law into private groups.

The preceding narrative is, of course, a condensed and oversimplified version of the story that I told in Chapters 2 through 4. But it reveals a more central tension between group autonomy and antidiscrimination norms than Koppelman's account suggests. What are we to make of this tension? Let's first set out two areas of agreement between Koppelman's historical narrative and mine. First, Congress and the Supreme Court have made clear that claims to group autonomy do not permit race-based discrimination in places of public accommodation. Second, *Runyon v. McCrary* is an important decision that addresses the tension between group autonomy and antidiscrimination law and sides decisively against racial discrimination in the context of private schools. These areas of agreement gesture toward some limits on group autonomy. But the narratives also suggest some important differences. For example, while

Koppelman joins most contemporary First Amendment scholars in linking the judicially recognized right of association to the First Amendment's free speech right, the more plausible historical and jurisprudential interpretation locates the antecedents of constitutional association at least as much in the right of assembly as in the right of speech. The link between assembly and association is evident in the Court's opinion in *NAACP v. Alabama*, it is embraced by Justices Black and Douglas in *Bates*, and it is the considered view of First Amendment scholars writing contemporaneously with the appearance of the right of association. Once we complicate Koppelman's history with long-standing notions of assembly that protect dissenting groups from majoritarian norms, resolving the question of a "right to exclude" becomes much more challenging.[26]

A Definition of Assembly

The previous section offered a different history to complement Koppelman's account. It is a history of constitutional text and case law, social movements, and political rhetoric. In many ways, that history displays the theory of the dissenting, public, and expressive assembly that I set forth earlier in this chapter. And I would suggest that it points us toward a definition of assembly that we might embrace today:

> *The right of assembly is a presumptive right of individuals to form and participate in peaceable, noncommercial groups. This right is rebuttable when there is a compelling reason for thinking that the justifications for protecting assembly do not apply (as when the group prospers under monopolistic or near-monopolistic conditions).*

Although I do not mean to suggest that these words or their meaning have existed unchanged throughout our nation's history, the understanding of assembly as a presumptive right to form and participate in peaceable, noncommercial groups has long been ingrained in our constitutionalism. This section describes in greater detail the definitional constraints. The next section addresses the contextual analysis.

The constraint of *peaceability* is found in the text of the First Amendment, which protects "the right of the people peaceably to assemble." The limitation suggests that while the right of assembly protects the formation, composition, expression, and gathering of a group, it does not justify anarchy by group. Indeed, throughout our nation's history, the right of assembly has developed alongside the law of "unlawful assembly." Criminal conspiracies, violent uprisings, and even most forms of civil disobedience have not been sheltered by the right of assembly. In most cases, laws that constrain a group's actions in furthering the state's compelling interest in peaceability will not be inhibited by assembly. Of course, a constraint of peaceability could be manipulated to eliminate any meaningful protections for group autonomy. A similar danger once threatened our free speech jurisprudence and prompted the Court to protect advocacy short of "imminent lawless action" in that area of the law. An understanding of the peaceability constraint on assembly ought to operate with a similar deference.[27]

The second definitional limit on assembly restricts its protections to *noncommercial* groups. Unlike peaceability, that constraint is not found in the text of the First Amendment. But our constitutional, social, and economic history offers broad support for it today—few people endorse a general right of a commercial entity to discriminate in the hiring of its employees or in the customers its serves. Employment law presumes that a commercial entity has no right to discriminate unless it can justify that the discrimination is warranted as a "bona fide occupational qualification." Discrimination on the basis of race, gender, or sexual orientation by commercial groups against customers is even less common. These concessions to antidiscrimination norms in the commercial sector reflect political compromises that reorient but do not eliminate the underlying values clash between equality and autonomy. Their political salience and moral force depends in some ways upon maintaining a workable distinction between commercial and noncommercial.[28]

The general presumption that commercial groups should be given less autonomy than noncommercial groups encompasses historical understandings of the meaning of "public accommodation" but also extends to other commercial entities. Today these limits require some clarification: *groups* like the Jaycees and the Boy Scouts are not *places* of public accommodation. The classification of groups as places of public accommodation is a legal fiction employed by some state courts in recent years, to which the Supreme Court has twice deferred. In *Roberts*, the Supreme

Court endorsed the Minnesota Supreme Court's conclusion that the Jaycees's local chapters were places of public accommodation within the meaning of Minnesota's antidiscrimination statute, noting that "this expansive definition reflects a recognition of the changing nature of the American economy and of the importance, both to the individual and to society, of removing the barriers to economic advancement and political and social integration that have historically plagued certain disadvantaged groups, including women." And in *Dale*, the Court accepted the New Jersey Supreme Court's conclusion that the Boy Scouts was a place of public accommodation under New Jersey's antidiscrimination statute despite noting that the New Jersey court "applied its public accommodations law to a private entity without even attempting to tie the term 'place' to a physical location." The Court's acceptance of these state court contortions collapses any meaningful distinction between public and private and undercuts the moral force behind public accommodations laws.[29]

I do not mean to suggest that recovering a commonsense understanding of "public accommodation" will resolve the difficulty of drawing lines between commercial and noncommercial groups. We will inevitably be left with a distinction that sometimes falls short and sometimes overreaches. The contextual analysis that I propose in the next section offers a partial mitigation of the former by limiting the constitutional protections for certain noncommercial groups. The problem of overreaching (which denies protection to commercial but noncoercive groups) is also troublesome, but few contemporary scholars have attempted to resolve that problem, and I do not do so here. My claim here is only that we can improve upon the current use of "public accommodation," perhaps by moving in the direction of a threshold of "predominantly commercial" or "commercial beyond a reasonable doubt" as a proxy for groups that lie beyond the boundaries of civil society. Neither the Boy Scouts nor the Jaycees approach that threshold.

Toward a Contextual Analysis

The constraints on assembly that I offered in the preceding sections are in some ways quite limiting, excluding from the protections of assembly nonpeaceable and commericial groups. But they also leave unaddressed a diverse set of private groups—cheerful, civic, and orderly groups and contankerous, subversive, and chaotic groups alike. Under the theory of assembly that I am suggesting, the constitutional protections for these groups hinge on whether they satisfy the rebuttable presumption that I have suggested: whether there is a compelling reason for thinking that the justifications for protecting assembly do not apply (as when a group prospers under monopolistic or near-monopolistic conditions). And in almost all cases, the protections of assembly should prevail. In a moment, I will have more to say about this claim. But first I want to explore the shortcomings of two alternatives: (1) the neolibertarian proposal; and (2) the message-based proposal.

Neolibertarian arguments typically posit a bright-line distinction between commercial and noncommercial groups that fully protects the latter, following a path proposed in Justice O'Connor's concurrence in *Roberts v. United States Jaycees*. For example, Michael McConnell, the lead counsel for the Boy Scouts in *Boy Scouts of America v. Dale* and the Christian Legal Society in *Christian Legal Society v. Martinez*, recently argued on behalf of the Christian Legal Society that "all noncommercial expressive associations, regardless of their beliefs, have a constitutionally protected right to control the content of their speech by excluding those who do not share their essential purposes and beliefs from voting and leadership roles."[30]

Koppelman has grouped a diverse group of scholars under the neolibertarian label; in addition to McConnell, he mentions David Bernstein, Dale Carpenter, Richard Epstein, John McGinnis, Michael Paulsen, Nancy Rosenblum, and Seana Shiffrin. He argues that these neolibertarian defenders of group autonomy offer "only slightly modified versions of old, discredited libertarian objections to the existence of any antidiscrimination law at all." Koppelman contends that the neolibertarian argument "overgeneralizes from what is often the case to a claim about what is always the case. Regulation of markets is indeed unnecessary and counterproductive. Except sometimes. The neolibertarians claim that the 'sometimes' does not happen all that often, but this is merely a hunch. It is dangerous for such hunches to become the basis of judge-made law, particularly constitutional law that is immune to legislative reconsideration in light of experience." The neolibertarian hunch would indeed be dangerous to incorporate into a categorical constitutional distinction. It fails to account for the realities of private power. In that regard, Koppelman properly resists a bright-line divide between commercial and noncommercial groups that exempts the latter from any constitutional scrutiny. But resorting to judicial inquiry is not always problematic when a contextual analysis is the best approach that we have.[31]

Koppelman's alternative to the neolibertarian approach is the *message-based* approach established in *Roberts*. In his words, "If an association is organized to express a viewpoint, then constitutional difficulties are raised by a statute that requires it to accept unwanted members if that requirement would impair its ability to convey its message." I have already offered a number of objections to the framework of expressive association that houses this message-based approach. Its categories are unprincipled and its applications arbitrary. What, then, are its benefits? Koppelman recognizes, as have a number of scholars, that the message-based approach of expressive association means that "a group that is stridently prejudiced will receive more protection than one that is quieter about its views" because the overtly prejudiced group can link the attempted enforcement of antidiscrimination law to its core expressive purposes. This explains, for example, why nobody seriously questions the right of the Ku Klux Klan to exclude African Americans from its membership. Koppelman sees this result as "desirable," because "discrimination is not so cheap as it was before, and a group will have to decide whether discrimination is worth the added cost." He believes that "this pressure serves state interests of the highest order and does not prevent groups with strongly held discriminatory ideas from uniting and disseminating them."[32]

There are at least three problems with Koppelman's reasoning. First, it hasn't worked in practice. As *Roberts* itself illustrates, even when courts *have* concluded that a group is an expressive association—in other words, that its purposes are intrinsically tied to its First Amendment expressive rights—antidiscrimination law has generally prevailed. Koppelman acknowledges as much. He notes that while *Roberts* introduced a "balancing test" when "interference with membership . . . demonstrably interferes with expressive practice," as a practical matter "free association claims unrelated to viewpoint discrimination always lost in the Supreme Court under this standard." *Dale* proved to be an exception, but the

Court reconfirmed Koppelman's diagnosis in *Martinez,* a case which assumed that the religious student group was an expressive association.[33]

The second problem with Koppelman's embrace of the message-based approach of expressive association is that it permits the state to decide what belongs at the core of a group's expression. There is an important difference between widespread public perception of a group's discriminatory character and an official pronouncement by the state that discrimination is central to the group's core expression. Koppelman at times seems to recognize this difference. He notes that "it is unseemly, and potentially abusive, for courts to tell organizations—particularly organizations with dissenting political views—what their positions are." Yet imposing an "added cost" on groups that discriminate in their membership to ensure that they are perceived as "stridently prejudiced" is just this kind of move. Moreover, in today's networked and media-saturated world (in which groups with overtly discriminatory policies are readily exposed), it isn't clear that Koppelman's requirement would significantly alter the current landscape.[34]

The third problem with Koppelman's proposal is that every group that challenged antidiscrimination law would presumably meet the threshold of an expressive association once the litigation and attendant media coverage commenced. As Koppelman notes, "In the course of litigation— and certainly once the case was over—the Scouts became so associated with discrimination against gays that they now almost certainly could satisfy the *Roberts* test." If Koppelman's diagnosis of the Scouts is correct, then expressive association challenges to antidiscrimination law would likely generate a peculiar feedback loop in which any litigant serious enough to file suit could on that basis alone generate enough public attention to qualify as an expressive association. But if that were true—and if Koppelman is serious about granting those groups constitutional protections—then the judicial inquiry would morph from resolving a "case or controversy" to a kind of administrative advisory opinion. Viewed less charitably, it would amount to little more than a financially cumbersome "registration requirement" that required discriminatory groups to litigate their status as discriminatory expressive associations to receive constitutional protections. If Koppelman's ultimate objective is to create a financial disincentive of this kind, he would be better off arguing for either a direct tax or a loss of tax-exempt status for discriminatory groups, both of which would be more efficient alternatives to litigation (although whether these alternatives would be constitutionally defensible is a separate matter).[35]

In my view, we are better off with a *contextual* analysis that allows courts to examine how power operates on the ground. This approach would ask courts to evaluate challenges to the exercise of the right of assembly in the specific contexts in which those assemblies exist. Sometimes, but rarely, the power exerted by peaceable, noncommercial assemblies will overreach to such an extent that the right would give way to the interests of the state. In the first chapter of this book, I offered two examples of when this rare occurrence might warrant an incursion into the right of assembly: (1) the historical example of the Jaybird Association in *Terry v. Adams*; and (2) the thought experiment of membership in a Christian student group providing exclusive access to elite legal jobs in *Christian Legal Society v. Martinez*. When courts are unable to offer a convincing account of this overreaching of private power—supported with factual rigor rather than aspirational values—they should defer to the values of assembly that I have advocated throughout the book.

Koppelman at times gestures toward the kind of contextual analysis that I commend. He highlights the importance of resolving empirical questions in a given case and concludes his book with the warning that "efforts to produce more general rules produce astounding pathologies." In fact, when Koppelman shifts from defending the message-based approach to describing the quasi-public and quasi-monopolistic nature of the Boy Scouts, he raises precisely the kinds of questions that I believe ought to be addressed in challenges to the boundaries of the right of assembly.[36]

The importance of the fact-specific contextual analysis that I am advocating is illustrated by Amy Gutmann's attempt to limit the implications of *Roberts*. Gutmann suggests that a "small exclusive country club, whose activities consist of golf, tennis, swimming, and socializing, is private in a way that the Jaycees is not." But that argument depends on the location of the club and the supply and demand for the goods it offers. In some small towns, the country club may be the social hub in which networking occurs, deals are brokered, and careers are made or broken. Or the club may offer a good not elsewhere available—for example, if it were the only or perhaps simply the "best" option for golf in the area. In these circumstances, the club may be far more "public" than the St. Paul and Minneapolis Jaycees. Its exercise of private power may well cause it to lose the protections of assembly, but that conclusion requires assessing the underlying facts and circumstances.[37]

Some will no doubt disagree with my normative argument for assembly if it sacrifices antidiscrimination objectives in the ways that I have suggested. The challenge to those who reject the vision set forth in this book is for them to articulate an alternative that captures both normative aspirations and jurisprudential integrity. The current framework of intimate and expressive association does neither. It has failed us badly. On the issue of gay rights so divisive in our culture today, it leads to decisions like *Boy Scouts of America v. Dale* and *Christian Legal Society v. Martinez* that avoid the hard question at the root of the controversies that underlie them—whether we are willing to permit difference at the cost of equality. The neolibertarian and message-based proposals fare no better.

The Missing *Roberts* Dissent

Having sketched a political and constitutional theory of assembly, I conclude this chapter with an illustration of how we might apply it: a hypothetical dissent in *Roberts* premised on the right of assembly. Importantly, this thought experiment is written in a particular genre. It is not intended as a summary of the arguments of this book or a balanced consideration of the issues inherent in questions of group autonomy. As with many judicial dissents, it is provocative and argumentative in its attempts to weave together different modalities of constitutional interpretation. Because it responds to Justice Brennan's majority opinion and Justice O'Connor's concurrence, it is in some ways situated by those texts. And yet it is also a creative work, an attempt to envision a different constitutional outcome and, indeed, a different constitutional vision.

I have anachronistically attributed the *Roberts* dissent to Justice Rutledge, who wrote the majority opinion in *Thomas v. Collins*. That opinion, discussed in Chapter 2, marks the high point of the Court's recognition of the right of assembly. As Aviam Soifer has suggested,

Rutledge's "dynamic, relational language" emphasized that the right of assembly was "broad enough to include private as well as public gatherings, economic as well as political subjects, and passionate opinions as well as factual statements." Soifer argues that the principles articulated in *Thomas* "starkly contrast with the instrumental focus of more recent freedom of association decisions," a contrast evident in the dissent premised on the right of assembly that follows.[38]

SUPREME COURT OF THE UNITED STATES

No. 83–724

ROBERTS, ACTING COMMISSIONER,
MINNESTOTA DEPARTMENT OF HUMAN RIGHTS
ET AL. v. UNITED STATES JAYCEES

ON WRIT OF CERTIORARI TO THE UNITED STATES
COURT OF APPEALS FOR THE EIGHTH CIRCUIT

[July 3, 1984]

JUSTICE RUTLEDGE, dissenting.

The women's soccer team at the University of North Carolina has won the past three national championships, a dominance reminiscent of the UCLA men's basketball team a decade ago and unmatched anywhere else in amateur athletics today. Since 1950, the LPGA has hosted a women's professional golf tour and now includes nationally televised tournaments and millions of dollars in annual prize money. Music has thrived (or perhaps suffered, depending on one's perspective) with all-male groups like the Beatles and the Righteous Brothers, and all-female groups like the Pointer Sisters and the Bangles. All-black choirs perform gospel music, and the Mormon Tabernacle Choir consists of, well, Mormons. The Talmudical Institute of Upstate New York, the Holy Trinity Orthodox Seminary (Russian Orthodox), and Morehouse College admit only men to their programs; Barnard College,

Bryn Mawr College, and Wellesley College admit only women. During the women's movement in the early twentieth century, women organized around women-only banner meetings, balls, swimming races, potato sack races, baby shows, meals, pageants, and teatimes. Gay bars and gay political associations have flourished by limiting their membership to homosexuals. Sometimes discrimination is a good thing.

Of course, discrimination also has its costs. Those excluded—the Salt Lake atheist with perfect pitch, the male golfer with limited swing velocity but machinelike precision— are denied opportunities, privileges, and relationships they might otherwise have had. They may be harmed economically, socially, and psychologically. When groups exclude on the basis of characteristics like race, gender, or sexual orientation, the psychological harm of exclusion may also extend well beyond those who have actually sought acceptance to others who share their characteristics. For all of these reasons, there is much to be said for an antidiscrimination norm and the value of equality that underlies it. But our constitutionalism also recognizes values other than equality, including a meaningful pluralism that permits diverse groups to flourish within our polity. That liberty finds refuge in the freedom of assembly.

Respondent United States Jaycees is a nonprofit group that desires to exclude women from its membership. However much I may disagree with the Jaycees's principles and practices, they fall within the boundaries of peaceable assembly, *see* U.S. Const., Amend. I. The majority's decision to resolve this case under a different standard fails to account for the role of assembly in our constitutional framework and jeopardizes the tradition of dissent and free expression long recognized in this country.

I.

The right of peaceable assembly guards "not solely religious or political" causes but also "secular causes," great and small.

Thomas v. Collins. Although its "most pristine and classic form" may manifest in a physical gathering such as a protest or strike, *Edwards v. South Carolina,* our decisions have never limited assembly to protests and demonstrations. To the contrary, we have expressly relied on the right of assembly to invalidate convictions for participating in meetings (*De Jonge v. Oregon*), organizing local chapters of a national group (*Herndon v. Lowry*), and speaking publicly without a proper license (*Thomas v. Collins*). We noted in *NAACP v. Alabama* that our decision in *American Communications Association v. Douds* referred to "the varied forms of governmental action which might interfere with freedom of assembly" and concluded that "compelled disclosure of membership in an organization engaged in advocacy of particular beliefs is of the same order."

As Justice Douglas once observed:

> Joining a lawful organization, like attending a church, is an asso-
> ciational activity that comes within the purview of the First
> Amendment, which provides in relevant part: "Congress shall
> make no law . . . abridging the freedom of speech, or of the
> press; or the right of the people, peaceably to assemble, and to
> petition the government for a redress of grievances." "Peaceably
> to assemble" as used in the First Amendment necessarily
> involves a coming together, whether regularly or spasmodically.

Gibson v. Florida Legislative Investigation Committee (Douglas, J., concurring).

The right of assembly "cannot be denied without violating those fundamental principles of liberty and justice which lie at the base of all civil and political institutions." *De Jonge v. Oregon.* Indeed, as we announced in *West Virginia v. Barnette:*

> The very purpose of a Bill of Rights was to withdraw certain
> subjects from the vicissitudes of political controversy, to place
> them beyond the reach of majorities and officials and to estab-
> lish them as legal principles to be applied by the courts. One's
> right to life, liberty, and property, to free speech, a free press,

freedom of worship and assembly, and other fundamental rights may not be submitted to vote; they depend on the outcome of no elections.

See also Bates v. City of Little Rock ("Like freedom of speech and a free press, the right of peaceable assembly was considered by the Framers of our Constitution to lie at the foundation of a government based upon the consent of an informed citizenry—a government dedicated to the establishment of justice and the preservation of liberty."). In Justice Brandeis's well-known words:

> Those who won our independence . . . believed that freedom to think as you will and to speak as you think are means indispensable to the discovery and spread of political truth; that without free speech and assembly discussion would be futile; that with them, discussion affords ordinarily adequate protection against the dissemination of noxious doctrine; that the greatest menace to freedom is an inert people; that public discussion is a political duty; and that this should be a fundamental principle of the American government.

Whitney v. California (Brandeis, J., concurring). Only "the gravest abuses, endangering paramount interests, give occasion for permissible limitation." *Thomas v. Collins.*

II.

The majority fails to recognize the importance of protecting even those dissenting practices out of step with mainstream values. As we noted in *Gilmore v. Montgomery*, "the freedom to associate applies to the beliefs we share, and to those we consider reprehensible" and "tends to produce the diversity of opinion that oils the machinery of democratic government and insures peaceful, orderly change." In that same decision, we quoted approvingly Justice Douglas's assertion that "the associational rights which our system honors permit all white, all black, all brown, and all yellow clubs to be formed. They also permit all Catholic, all Jewish, or all agnostic clubs to be established. Government may not tell a man or woman who his or her associates must be. The individual can be as selective as he desires." *Gilmore v. Montgomery* (quoting *Moose Lodge No. 107 v. Irvis* (Douglas, J., dissenting)).

Our nation has long protected dissenting groups with the right of assembly. These groups often expressed views antithetical and even threatening to those who held political power. They included the Democratic-Republican Societies of the late eighteenth century, suffragists and abolitionists of the antebellum era, and groups advocating on behalf of labor, women, and racial minorities in the twentieth century. We have not always been so vigilant in our protection of civil liberties, and our fear-driven denials of the right of assembly mark some of the low points of our constitutional history. *See, e.g., Dennis v. United States* (upholding convictions of leaders of the Communist Party for their organizing and advocacy).

Notwithstanding our notable failures in cases like *Dennis*, we have usually sought to extend the right of assembly to favored and disfavored groups alike. Over the past few decades, we have carved out an important limitation on the protections of assembly in cases involving discrimination on the basis of race. Most of these cases involved places of public accommodation as that term is defined in the Civil Rights Act of 1964. *See, e.g., Heart of Atlanta Motel v. United States* (motel), *Katzenbach v. McClung* (restaurant), *Daniel v. Paul* (amusement park). We have never endorsed the legal fiction advanced by the Minnesota Supreme Court that a private *group* like the Jaycees is a *place* of public accommodation.

In a separate line of cases arising out of the civil rights era, we construed a Reconstruction era statute, the Civil Rights Act of 1866, to bar racial discrimination in the sale or lease of private property. In *Jones v. Alfred H. Mayer*, we reasoned that the 1866 Act reached these private transactions because "the exclusion of Negroes from white communities" reflected "the badges and incidents of slavery." We extended the reach of *Jones* to membership in a community park and playground in *Sullivan v. Little Hunting Park* and a private swimming pool in *Tillman v. Wheaton-Haven Recreation Association*. *Jones, Sullivan,* and *Tillman* all involved sales or leases related to real property covered under the Fair Housing Act of 1968. Justice Harlan dissented in *Sullivan* because he thought that relying on the Civil Rights Act of 1866 rather than a straightforward application of the Fair Housing Act required a "vague and open-ended" construction that risked "grave constitutional issues should [the former] be extended too far into some types of private discrimination." Today's decision confirms the wisdom of his warning.

The majority cites *Tillman, Sullivan,* and *Daniel* to support its contention that "the local chapters of the Jaycees are large and basically unselective groups." Ante, 630. The constitutional infirmity of the groups in these cases wasn't that they employed a single membership criterion. It was that the criterion was: (1) race; (2) used by whites to exclude blacks; (3) in membership groups closely tied to housing (in *Tillman* and *Sullivan*) or created as an obvious sham (in *Daniel*); and (4) in the midst of the Civil Rights Era. The constitutional rationale underlying these cases wasn't that unselective groups lacked an intimacy worthy of constitutional protection but that: (1) their lack of selectivity factored against qualifying them under the public club exception to the public accommodations laws of the Civil Rights Act of 1964; and (2) "the exclusion of Negroes from white communities" reflected "the badges and incidents of slavery." The majority makes no attempt to explain how these rationales justify denying constitutional protections to the Jaycees.

The majority also cites our decision in *Runyon v. McCrary,* which construed another provision of the Civil Rights Act of 1866 to bar racial discrimination by "private, commercially operated, nonsectarian schools." Justice Stewart's opinion in *Runyon* quoted with approval the Fourth Circuit's conclusion that "'there is no showing that discontinuance of [the] discriminatory admission practices would inhibit in any way the teaching in these schools of any ideas or dogma.'" That claim is unpersuasive. Equally implausible is the majority's suggestion that "the Jaycees has failed to demonstrate that the Act imposes any serious burdens on the male members' freedom of expressive association." Ante, 626. Ten years ago, the First Circuit made a more commonsense observation about the message conveyed by a group's very existence in upholding the associational rights of a gay student group: "beyond the specific communications at [its] events is the basic 'message' [Gay Students Organization] seeks to convey—that homosexuals exist, that they feel repressed by existing laws and attitudes, that they wish to emerge from their isolation, and that public understanding of their attitudes and problems is desirable for society." *Gay Students Organization of the University of New Hampshire v. Bonner* (1st Cir. 1974).

III.

The majority's category of "intimate association" builds upon a decontextualized understanding of privacy that artificially elevates certain groups to a special protected status. Its implicit distinction between intimate and nonintimate associations is unconvincing: all of the values, benefits, and attributes that the majority assigns to intimate associations are equally applicable to many if not most nonintimate associations. In my view, we should avoid creating a distinction of such constitutional significance where one is unwarranted.

The regrettable consequence of creating an unnecessary right of intimate association is that it jettisons those groups that fail to meet its arbitrary contours to a lower level of constitutional protection. In the majority's words, "the nature and degree of constitutional protection afforded freedom of association may vary depending on the extent to which [intimate or expressive association] is at stake in a given case." Ante, 618. Indeed, the majority's restriction of intimate associations to those "distinguished by such attributes as relative smallness, a high degree of selectivity in decisions to begin and maintain the affiliation, and seclusion from others in critical aspects of the relationship," ante, 620, would exclude most if not all of the groups that the right of assembly has protected throughout our nation's history.

IV.

The majority's category of "expressive association" improperly construes the Jaycees as a means of expression and ignores that both its membership and its acts of gathering are forms of expression. Justice O'Connor's concurrence makes a similar error in dismissing the expressive aspects of the Jaycees.

We noted in *NAACP v. Alabama* that the "close nexus between the freedoms of speech and assembly" demonstrates that "effective advocacy of both public and private points of view, particularly controversial ones, is undeniably enhanced by group association." The very existence of the Jaycees is a form of expression, and the forced inclusion of unwanted members unquestionably alters the content of that expression. As we stated in *Griswold v. Connecticut*, the related right of association "includes the right to express one's attitudes or philosophies by membership in a group or by affiliation with it or by other lawful means." As Justice Douglas once noted, "joining is a method of expression." *Lathrop v. Donahue* (Douglas, J., dissenting).

We observed in *Thomas v. Collins:*

> If the exercise of the rights of free speech and free assembly cannot be made a crime, we do not think this can be accomplished by the device of requiring previous registration as a condition for exercising them and making such a condition the foundation for restraining in advance their exercise and for imposing a penalty for violating such a restraining order. So long as no more is involved than exercise of the rights of free speech and free assembly, it is immune to such a restriction.

The reasoning expressed in *Thomas* is similar to our prior restraint doctrine for free speech. We recognize in that area of the law that preventing a message altogether by restraining a speaker is as anathema to free speech as punishing the message after the fact—it may send a "chilling effect" that discourages the speaker from even attempting to convey a message. The same is true with actions taken to constrain an assembly before its expression is manifest.

Justice O'Connor's concurrence today rightly notes that "protection of the association's right to define its membership derives from the recognition that the formation of an expressive association is the creation of a voice, and the selection of members is the definition of that voice." Ante, 633. And despite its disregard for the consequences to the Jaycees, the majority also recognizes the voice-altering nature of its decision:

> There can be no clearer example of an intrusion into the internal structure or affairs of an association than a regulation that forces the group to accept members it does not desire. Such a regulation may impair the ability of the original members to express only those views that brought them together. Freedom of association therefore plainly presupposes a freedom not to associate.

Ante, 623. In a critical comment reflecting the significance of what is at stake today, the majority acknowledges that: "according protection to collective effort on behalf of shared goals is especially important in preserving political and cultural diversity and in shielding dissident expression from suppression by the majority." Ante, 622.

Justice O'Connor's concurrence proposes an alternative assessment based on the commercial nature of a group. She concludes that the Jaycees is "first and foremost, an organization that, at both the national and local levels, promotes and practices the art of solicitation and management" and that "Minnesota's attempt to regulate the membership of the Jaycees chapters operating in that State presents a relatively easy case for application of the expressive-commercial dichotomy." Ante, 639.

I disagree with my colleague's conclusion on the record before us. As Judge Arnold wrote in the opinion below:

The Jaycees does not simply sell seats in some kind of personal-development classroom. Personal and business development, if they come, come not as products bought by members, but as by-products of activities in which members engage after they join the organization. These activities are variously social, civic, and ideological.

United States Jaycees v. McClure (8th Cir. 1983).

Justice O'Connor's classification of the Jaycees is illustrative of the dangers that arise when a court imposes its own interpretation of the meaning and purposes of a group or its practices. The record establishes that the Jaycees, like many similarly situated groups, has many purposes and activities. Each of its members will embrace certain values and activities more than others, and to some the Jaycees may well be first and foremost a commercial organization. But we cannot state with any certainty that the overall purposes, values, and activities of the Jaycees are primarily commercial in nature. The Jaycees is not a for-profit business incorporated for the purposes of generating revenue. It is a private group.

V.

In my view, the proper standard for determining the limits of group autonomy is through the right of assembly. We observed in *Thomas v. Collins* that because of the "preferred place given in our scheme to the great, the indispensable democratic freedoms secured by the First Amendment," only "the gravest abuses, endangering paramount interests, give occasion for permissible limitation." As we set forth in that opinion:

Where the line shall be placed in a particular application rests, not on such generalities, but on the concrete clash of particular interests and the community's relative evaluation both of them and of how the one will be affected by the specific restriction, the other by its absence. That judgment in the first instance is for the legislative body. But in our system where the line can constitutionally be placed presents a question this Court cannot escape answering independently, whatever the legislative judgment, in the light of our constitutional tradition. And the answer, under that tradition, can be affirmative, to support an intrusion upon this domain, only if grave and impending public danger requires this.

Id. at 531–32.

The Jaycees is a peaceable, noncommercial assembly that presents no "grave and impending public danger." Nor is this a case where the record evidences any compelling abuse of private power. The Jaycees is not the Jaybird Association. *See Terry v. Adams.*

VI.

This case involves the clash of two fundamental values: equality and autonomy. On the one hand, the Jaycees's membership requirements are inherently discriminatory and inconsistent with liberal ideals of equality. On the other hand, the group depends upon this discrimination for its very existence. We are left with a choice between two constitutional visions: a radical sameness that destroys dissenting traditions or the destabilizing difference of a meaningful pluralism. Honoring one ideal sacrifices the other.

The minimal constraints of peaceable assembly leave us with racists, bigots, and ideologues. They also leave us with difference. Peaceable assembly forces us to confront more honestly questions of what it means to live among dissenting, political, and expressive groups.

Because the Jaycees is a peaceable noncommercial assembly and is otherwise entitled under our precedent to protect its autonomy and message in the ways it deems desirable, I respectfully dissent.

CONCLUSION

This book has traced the history of the constitutional protections accorded to groups, beginning with the freedom of assembly in the Bill of Rights and culminating with what I have characterized as a weak right of association that emerged in the middle of the twentieth century and was refashioned a generation later. I have argued that American constitutionalism—as embodied by the people of this country even if not always in the opinions of the Supreme Court—has always recognized the importance of the dissenting, political, and expressive group. The modern right of association, in contrast, has lost sight of these attributes by drawing upon shifting justifications during its development over the past fifty years: first a pluralism that emphasized consensus and stability, then the penumbras of the First Amendment that linked association to privacy, and, most recently, a tenuous hierarchy of intimate and expressive association. This highly malleable doctrine arbitrarily extends constitutional protections to some groups and denies them to others, thus weakening group autonomy—and threatening liberty.[1]

The right of assembly protects the members of a group based not upon their principles or politics but by virtue of their coming together in a way of life. The kinds of unpopular, renegade, and even dangerous gatherings that have sought refuge in that right remind us of the importance of resisting all but the rarest of encroachments upon an assembled people. This caution is obscured in the shifting theoretical and jurisprudential justifications of association, which have too easily permitted incursions into group autonomy.

One eminently practical way to challenge the weakened right of association is to raise the freedom of assembly as an independent constitutional claim in First Amendment litigation. Although it is possible that courts would conclude that assembly is an antiquated precursor to the right of association, it would be odd for a judicially constructed right completely to subsume a right enumerated in the text of the Constitution. Moreover, the Court's previous decisions maintain an ambiguous link between assembly and association that falls short of equating the two concepts. On the other hand, if courts were to reaffirm the continued importance of the freedom of assembly, then they would need to explain its doctrinal framework and outline the relationship of assembly to other First Amendment freedoms.

The normative claims asserted in this book are not without consequences. They reintroduce a weighing of constitutional values that some would prefer remain suppressed. They strengthen protections for groups that you and I don't like. But they also strengthen protections for groups that we care about, against a state-enforced majoritarianism whose threat we might not recognize. As Justice Black once wrote: "I do not believe that it can be too often repeated that the freedoms of speech, press, petition and assembly guaranteed by the First Amendment must be accorded to the ideas we hate, or sooner or later they will be denied to the ideas we cherish."[2]

We ought to remember that "challenges to existing values and decisions to embody and express dissident values are precisely the choices and activities that cannot be properly evaluated by summations of existing preferences" and that "the constitutional right of assembly ought to protect activities that are *unreasonable* from the perspective of the existing order."[3] By losing touch with our past recognition of the freedom of assembly and the groups that have embodied it, we risk embracing too easily an attenuated right of association that cedes to the state the authority over what kinds of groups are acceptable in the democratic experiment. Democracy and stability may be easier in the short term, but in forgetting the freedom of assembly, we forget the kind of politics that has brought us this far.

NOTES

Acknowledgments

1. At the risk of enduring some (perhaps warranted) scoffing for including a footnote in my acknowledgments, my reference to the "poles of abuse" contrasts an increasingly liberalized freedom of assembly under the Weimar Republic that may have in some ways facilitated the Nazi Party's rise to power with the constraints on assembly and other civil liberties placed upon Japanese Americans in the United States during the Second World War.

Chapter 1. Overview of the Argument

1. Abraham Lincoln, *Uncollected Letters of Abraham Lincoln,* ed. Gilbert A. Tracy (New York: Houghton Mifflin, 1917), 127. John Rawls, *A Theory of Justice* (Cambridge, Mass.: Belknap Press of Harvard University Press, 1971), 53. Rawls usually refers to association rather than assembly in his later work. See, e.g., John Rawls, *Political Liberalism* (New York: Columbia University Press, 1993), 221 n.8, 291, 338, 418. But see ibid., 335 (mentioning assembly). Franklin Roosevelt's well-known four freedoms were preceded by a different "four freedoms" (speech, press, religion, and assembly) that captured the popular press, headlined the 1939 New York World's Fair, and formed the core of nationwide celebrations of the sesquicentennial anniversary of the Bill of Rights.

2. *Roberts v. United States Jaycees,* 468 U.S. 609, 618 (1984).

3. Andrew Koppelman with Tobias Barrington Wolff, *A Right to Discriminate? How the Case of* Boy Scouts of America v. James Dale *Warped the Law of Free Association* (New Haven: Yale University Press, 2009), xi ("Before *Dale*, there was a well-settled law of freedom of association. *Dale* has disrupted that law, capriciously and destructively. This book is a plea for the restoration of the *ancien regime*."). I take Koppelman's claim to be that *Boy Scouts of America v. Dale*, 530 U.S. 640 (2000), disrupted the framework first set in place sixteen years earlier in *Roberts v. United States Jaycees*, 468 U.S. 609 (1984). Koppelman acknowledges the "germinal case" of the right of association in *NAACP v. Alabama*, 357 U.S. 449 (1958), see Koppelman, *A Right to Discriminate?* 18–22, but it is clear that *Roberts* rather than *NAACP v. Alabama* does most of the work that he wants to embrace as the "well-settled law of freedom of association." Although *A Right to Discriminate?* lists its authors as "Andrew Koppelman with Tobias Barrington Wolff," I will refer only to Koppelman for ease of reference and because most of the arguments with which I engage flow out of earlier publications that Koppelman wrote exclusively. For examples of political theorists who implicitly or explicitly endorse the idea of expressive association, see Stephen Macedo, *Liberal Virtues: Citizenship, Virtue, and Community in Liberal Constitutionalism* (Oxford: Oxford University Press, 1990); Amy Gutmann, ed., *Freedom of Association* (Princeton: Princeton University Press, 1998); Rawls, *Political Liberalism*. For examples of constitutional arguments that rely upon the concept, see Brief for Petitioner at 2, *Christian Legal Society v. Martinez*, No. 08–1371 (Jan. 2010) (arguing that the Christian Legal Society is an expressive association); Brief for Petitioner at 32, *Boy Scouts of America v. Dale*, No. 99–699 (Feb. 28, 2000) (arguing that the Boy Scouts is an expressive association).

4. The claim about intelligibility is not meant to be universal. Some gatherings may present a relatively coherent message absent any shared practices or history. A group of strangers that meets in front of a prison to protest an execution is one example.

5. The example of the gay social club is taken from Brief of Gays and Lesbians for Individual Liberty as Amicus Curiae in Support of Petitioner at 11 *Christian Legal Society v. Martinez*, No. 08–1371 (Feb. 4, 2010) (noting that gay organizations "have relied on exclusively gay environments in which to feel safe, to build relationships, and to develop political strategy," including "many exclusively gay social and activity clubs, retreats, vacations, and professional organizations"). The prayer or meditation group is likely "nonexpressive" under the Court's doctrine of expressive association if its only verbal and symbolic expression is among its members and to its deity. To the extent that prayer qualifies as the free exercise of religion, it is unlikely to find constitutional protection in the rational basis scrutiny afforded general laws of neutral applicability under the test announced in *Employment Division v. Smith*, 494 U.S. 872 (1990). The example of the college fraternity comes from *Chi Iota Colony of Alpha Epsilon Pi Fraternity v. City University of New York*, 443 F.Supp. 2d 374, 376 (2006) (concluding that Chi Iota had not shown a clear or substantial likelihood of success on its expressive association claim), rev'd on other grounds by *Chi Iota Colony of Alpha Epsilon Pi Fraternity v. City University of New York*, 502 F.3d 136 (2007). Each of these groups is presumably a nonexpressive, nonintimate association.

6. *Truth v. Kent Sch. Dist.*, 542 F.3d 634 (9th Cir. 2008). See also *Roberts v. United States Jaycees*, 468 U.S. 609, 618 (1984) (all-male expressive association denied constitutional protections), *Board of Directors of Rotary International v. Rotary Club of Duarte*, 481 U.S. 537 (1987) (same); *Christian Legal Society v. Kane*, No. C04–04484, May 19, 2006, at *20 (relying on *Kent* to deny expressive association claim of religious student group), *affirmed on other grounds by Christian Legal Society v. Martinez*, 130 S. Ct. 2971 (2010).

7. *NAACP v. Alabama ex rel. Patterson*, 357 U.S. 449, 462 (1958). I have located at least twenty-five federal district and appellate court opinions referring to a "freedom of association" clause in the United States Constitution. See, e.g., *Swanson v. City of Bruce*, 105 Fed. Appx. 540, 542 (5th Cir. 2004) (unpublished opinion) (referring to "the freedom of association clause"); *Boyle v. County of Allegheny*, 139 F.3d 386, 394 (3d Cir. 1998) (asserting that the plurality opinion in *Elrod v. Burns*, 427 U.S. 247 (1976) "held that the discharge of a government employee because of his political affiliation violates the freedom of association clause of the First Amendment"); *Darnell v. Campbell County Fiscal Court*, 924 F.2d 1057 (6th Cir. 1991) (unpublished opinion) (discussing the requirements for a prima facie case under "the freedom of association clause of the first amendment"); *Grace United Methodist Church v. City of Cheyenne*, 427 F.Supp. 2d 1186, 1203 (D. Wyo. 2006) ("The First Amendment's Free Speech Clause and Freedom of Association Clauses apply to the states through the Fourteenth Amendment."); *Hyman v. City of Louisville*, 132 F.Supp. 2d 528, 543 (W.D. Ky. 2001) ("The Supreme Court has interpreted the First Amendment to provide little protection under the Freedom of Association Clause to commercial enterprises.").

8. I originally described the inherently political nature of assembly as "public." See John D. Inazu, "The Forgotten Freedom of Assembly," 84 *Tulane Law Review* 565, 570 (2010) (describing "the dissenting assembly, the public assembly, and the expressive assembly"). My initial use of "public" rather than "political" was an effort to avoid confusion over conventional understandings of "political" confined to the state's governance and attempts to influence it through groups like parties and lobbying organizations. I have since realized that the interminable debates over the boundaries of "public" and "private" make "public" in this context even more ambiguous than "political." Accordingly, I refer to the latter in this book. The underlying claim remains the same: "claims of assembly have been public claims that advocate for a visible political space distinguishable from government." Ibid.

9. C. Edwin Baker, *Human Liberty and Freedom of Speech* (New York: Oxford University Press, 1989), 134.

10. Robert Putnam's seminal work captures much of the texture of assembly that I am suggesting. See Robert D. Putnam, *Bowling Alone: The Collapse and Revival of American Community* (New York: Simon and Schuster, 2000). For related arguments, see generally, Alasdair C. MacIntyre, *After Virtue: A Study in Moral Theory* (Notre Dame: University of Notre Dame Press, 1981); Charles Taylor, *Sources of the Self: The Making of the Modern Identity* (Cambridge, Mass.: Harvard University Press, 1989); Michael J. Sandel, *Liberalism and the Limits of Justice* (New York: Cambridge University Press, 1998). See also Richard W.

Garnett, "The Story of Henry Adams's Soul: Education and the Expression of Associations," 85 *Minnesota Law Review* 1841, 1846 (2001) (describing "the indivisible process of acquiring beliefs, premises, and dispositions that are our windows on the world, that mediate and filter our experience of it, and that govern our evaluation and judgment of it"); Robert K. Vischer, *Conscience and the Common Good: Reclaiming the Space between Person and State* (New York: Cambridge University Press, 2010), 3 (describing "the relational dimension of conscience"). My arguments also share some affinities with Ethan Leib's work on friendship. See Ethan J. Leib, "Friendship and the Law," 54 *UCLA Law Review* 631–708 (2007). Among other salient observations, Leib highlights the importance of friendship to "keeping the private sphere private" and as a means of resistance to and "freedom from" the state. Ibid., 663–67, 674–80. It is possible that the Court's category of "intimate association" is meant to further similar aims. But as I explain in Chapter 4, the problem with intimate association is its artificial drawing of lines between "intimate" and "nonintimate" groups, both of which can embody the social vision that I ascribe to assembly.

11. Cf. *Christian Legal Society v. Walker*, 453 F.3d 853, 863 (7th Cir. 2006) ("Forcing [the Christian Legal Society] to accept as members those who engage in or approve of homosexual conduct would cause the group as it currently identifies itself to cease to exist."); Richard John Neuhaus, *The Naked Public Square: Religion and Democracy in America* (Grand Rapids: Eerdmans, 1984), 142 ("When an institution that is voluntary in membership cannot define the conditions of belonging, that institution in fact ceases to exist."). In *Christian Legal Society v. Martinez*, 130 S. Ct. 2971 (2010), the Court upheld Hastings College of the Law's refusal to recognize a student chapter of the Christian Legal Society because that group refused to allow non-Christians and those who affirmed homosexual conduct to become group members and leaders. In *Holder v. Humanitarian Law Project*, 130 S. Ct. 2705 (2010), the Court addressed a federal statute that prohibited "knowingly provid[ing] a foreign terrorist organization" with "material support or resources." 18 U.S.C. § 2339A(b)(1). The statute defined "material support or resources" to include, among other things, "training," "expert advice or assistance," "personnel," and "service." Ibid., §§ 2339B(a)(1), g(4). A group of United States citizens and associations challenged the application of the statute to their support of two groups, the Kurdistan Workers' Party (also known as the Partiya Karkeran Kurdistan, or PKK), which sought to establish an independent Kurdish state in southeastern Turkey, and the Liberation Tigers of Tamil Eelam (LTTE), which sought to create an independent Tamil state in Sri Lanka. *Holder*, 561 U.S. at *3. Specifically, they desired to "'(1) train members of the PKK on how to use humanitarian and international law to peacefully resolve disputes; (2) engage in political advocacy on behalf of Kurds who live in Turkey; (3) teach PKK members how to petition various representative bodies such as the United Nations for relief; and (4) engage in political advocacy on behalf of Tamils who live in Sri Lanka." Ibid., *2 (Breyer, J., dissenting) (internal quotation marks omitted). The government suggested that the statute "prohibits a lawyer hired by a designated group from filing on behalf of that group an *amicus* brief

before the United Nations or even before [the United States Supreme Court]." Ibid., *11 (citing Tr. of Oral Arg. 47–49, 53).

12. Stephen L. Carter, "Liberal Hegemony and Religious Resistance: An Essay on Legal Theory," in *Christian Perspectives on Legal Thought*, ed. Michael W. McConnell, Robert F. Cochran Jr., and Angela C. Carmella (New Haven: Yale University Press, 2001), 33. See also Michael W. McConnell, "The New Establishmentarianism," 75 *Chicago-Kent Law Review* 453, 466 (2000) ("Genuine pluralism requires group difference, and maintenance of group difference requires that groups have the freedom to exclude, as well as the freedom to dissent. Freedom of association is an essential structural principle in a liberal society.").

13. William N. Eskridge Jr., "A Jurisprudence of 'Coming Out': Religion, Homosexuality, and Collisions of Liberty and Equality in American Public Law," 106 *Yale Law Journal* 2411, 2415 (1997). See also David A. J. Richards, *Fundamentalism in American Religion and Law: Obama's Challenge to Patriarchy's Threat to Democracy* (New York: Cambridge University Press, 2010), 13 ("The best of American constitutional law rests, I have come to believe, on the role it accords resisting voice, and the worst on the repression of such voice."); Kenneth L. Karst, "The Freedom of Intimate Association," 89 *Yale Law Journal* 629, 688 (1980) ("One of the points of any freedom of association must be to let people make their own definitions of community."); *Roberts v. United States Jaycees*, 468 U.S. 609, 633 (1984) (O'Connor, J., concurring) ("Protection of the association's right to define its membership derives from the recognition that the formation of an expressive association is the creation of a voice, and the selection of members is the definition of that voice.").

14. Akhil R. Amar, *The Bill of Rights: Creation and Reconstruction* (New Haven: Yale University Press, 1998), 246.

15. The Court incorporated the assembly clause in *De Jonge v. Oregon*, 299 U.S. 353 (1937). Subsequent cases arising shortly after *De Jonge* included *Herndon v. Lowry*, 301 U.S. 242 (1937), *Hague v. Committee for Industrial Organization*, 307 U.S. 496 (1939), and *Thomas v. Collins*, 323 U.S. 516 (1945). The last time the Court applied the constitutional right of assembly appears to have been in *NAACP v. Claiborne Hardware Co.*, 458 U.S. 88 (1982)— thirty years ago. A majority opinion of the Supreme Court has only *mentioned* the right of assembly six times in the past twenty years. The language of assembly appears in the Religious Land Use and Institutionalized Persons Act of 2000 (RLUIPA), 42 U.S.C. §§ 2000cc, et seq. (limiting government restrictions on "the religious exercise of a person, including a religious assembly or institution").

16. *NAACP v. Alabama ex rel. Patterson*, 357 U.S. 449 (1958); *Roberts v. United States Jaycees*, 468 U.S. 609 (1984).

17. Mark DeWolfe Howe, "The Supreme Court, 1952 Term—Foreword: Political Theory and the Nature of Liberty," 67 *Harvard Law Review* 91–92 (1953) (describing "the heart of the pluralistic thesis" advanced by Gierke, Maitland, Figgis, and Laski); Arthur Bentley, *The Process of Government* (Chicago: University of Chicago Press, 1908); Louis Hartz, *The Liberal Tradition in America: An Interpretation of American Political Thought Since the Revolution* (New York: Harcourt, 1955).

18. *Griswold v. Connecticut*, 381 U.S. 479 (1965).

19. See Ronald Dworkin, *Freedom's Law* (New York: Oxford University Press, 1996) (rights as trumps); John Rawls, "The Idea of Public Reason Revisited," 64 *Chicago Law Review* 765 (1997) (public reason); Ronald Dworkin, *Law's Empire* (Cambridge, Mass.: Belknap Press of Harvard University Press, 1986) (law as integrity). I recognize that I am making a critical and perhaps controversial interpretation of Dworkin. For examples of others seeing similarities between the constraining effects of Rawls's public reason and Dworkin's law as integrity, see Paul F. Campos, "Secular Fundamentalism," 94 *Columbia Law Review* 1826–27 (1994) ("Law as integrity parallels the idea of public reason legitimating the exercise of coercive state power 'in accordance with a constitution the essentials of which all citizens may reasonably be expected to endorse in the light of principles and ideals acceptable to them as reasonable and rational.'"); Edward J. McCaffery, "Ronald Dworkin, Inside-Out," 85 *California Law Review* 1057 (1997) ("Dworkin's method can be understood as a form of public reason in the law."); George Rutherglen, "Private Law and Public Reason," 92 *Virginia Law Review* 1511 (2006) ("Dworkin would not have to modify much of his legal or political theory to limit the range of political discourse to what Rawls recognizes as reasonable."); Martin Shapiro, "Fathers and Sons: The Court, the Commentators, and the Search for Values," in *The Burger Court: The Counter-Revolution That Wasn't*, ed. Vincent Blasi (New Haven: Yale University Press, 1983), 224 (noting that "Rawls has given us a revived social contract theory that manages to render equality rather than freedom the central operating tenet of the contract" and "Dworkin is in the process of attempting to demonstrate that equality ought to be the central principle from which constitutional and other legal rules are to be deduced."). Dworkin himself has resisted comparisons between law as integrity and Rawlsian public reason, arguing recently that he has "great difficulties" with Rawls's distinction "between political values on the one hand and comprehensive moral convictions on the other." Ronald Dworkin, *Justice in Robes* (Cambridge, Mass.: Belknap Press of Harvard University Press, 2006), 253.

20. *Roberts v. United States Jaycees*, 468 U.S., 609, 618 (1984); *Boy Scouts of America v. Dale*, 530 U.S. 640 (2000).

21. Martha Minow, "Introduction," in *Narrative, Violence, and the Law: The Essays of Robert Cover*, ed. Martha Minow, Michael Ryan, and Austin Sarat (Ann Arbor: University of Michigan Press, 1992), 8 (describing the views of Robert Cover).

22. Nancy L. Rosenblum, *Membership and Morals: The Personal Uses of Pluralism in America* (Princeton: Princeton University Press, 1998), 37.

23. William A. Galston, *Liberal Pluralism: The Implications of Value Pluralism for Political Theory and Practice* (New York: Cambridge University Press, 2002), 3. Isaiah Berlin, *Four Essays on Liberty* (New York: Oxford University Press, 1969).

24. Cf. Alasdair C. MacIntyre, *Whose Justice? Which Rationality?* (Notre Dame: University of Notre Dame Press, 1988). See also MacIntyre, *After Virtue*; Taylor, *Sources of the Self*; Sandel, *Liberalism and the Limits of Justice*.

25. For examples from classical liberalism, see John Locke, *A Letter Concerning Toleration* (1689); John Stuart Mill, *On Liberty* (1859) (insisting upon "freedom to unite, for any purpose not involving harm to others."). The best-known libertarian account is Robert Nozick, *Anarchy, State, and Utopia* (New York: Basic Books, 1974). See also Chandran Kukathas, *The Liberal Archipelago* (New York: Oxford University Press, 2003), 133. Kukathas doesn't rely on Nozick but instead constructs a kind of "group libertarianism."

26. Koppelman, *A Right to Discriminate?* xii. See, e.g., Richard A. Epstein, "Should Antidiscrimination Laws Limit Freedom of Association? The Dangerous Allure of Human Rights Legislation," 25 *Social Philosophy and Policy* 123 (2008).

27. Koppelman, *A Right to Discriminate?* 5, 6.

28. Richard Hofstadter, *The Idea of a Party System: The Rise of Legitimate Opposition in the United States, 1780–1840* (Berkeley: University of California Press, 1969), 55, quoted in Steven G. Calabresi, "Political Parties as Mediating Institutions," 61 *University of Chicago Law Review* 1489 (1994). See also John Howard Yoder, "Response of an Amateur History and a Religious Citizen," 7 *Journal of Law and Religion* 417 (1989) ("The very term 'Bill of Rights' was borrowed from British history. No one in the colonies in the 1770s thought that the new thing they were doing was independent of the changes which had begun in Great Britain since the early 1600s. There was a long British Puritan history, from the age of Milton to the 1689 Bill of Rights, in the course of which the civil freedoms of speech, press, and assembly arose out of religious agitation, not the other way around."); Michael W. McConnell, "The Problem of Singling out Religion," 50 *DePaul Law Review* 16 (2000) ("The struggle for the freedom to publish religious tracts was a precursor to the struggle for the freedom of the press more generally, as the freedom to gather together for purposes of religious worship was for the freedom of assembly."). For more on the contemporary relevance of Williams and Penn, see John D. Inazu, "Between Liberalism and Theocracy," 33 *Campbell Law Review* 591 (2011).

29. See especially, Sheldon Wolin, *Politics and Vision: Continuity and Innovation in Western Political Thought* (Princeton: Princeton University Press, 2004).

30. *Jones v. Alfred H. Mayer Co.*, 392 U.S. 409 (1968).

31. See, e.g., *Grutter v. Bollinger*, 539 U.S. 306, 343 (2003) ("We expect that 25 years from now, the use of racial preferences will no longer be necessary to further the interest approved today."); *Green v. County School Board*, 391 U.S. 430, 435–38 (1968) (holding that a school district may be declared unitary and lacking racial discrimination based on satisfactory performance in five areas of a school district's operations); *Northwest Austin Municipal Util. Dist. No. One v. Holder* 129 S. Ct. 2504 (2009) ("More than 40 years ago, this Court concluded that 'exceptional conditions' prevailing in certain parts of the country justified extraordinary legislation otherwise unfamiliar to our federal system. In part due to the success of that legislation, we are now a very different Nation. Whether conditions continue to justify such legislation is a difficult constitutional question we do not answer today."); *Wygant v. Jackson Bd. of Educ.*, 476 U.S. 267, 276 (1986) (plurality opinion) ("In the absence of particularized findings, a court could uphold remedies that are ageless in their

reach into the past, and timeless in their ability to affect the future"); *Freeman v. Pitts,* 503 U.S. 467, 491–92 (1992) ("With the passage of time, the degree to which racial imbalances continue to represent vestiges of a constitutional violation may diminish").

32. The limitations inherent in the right of assembly are similar to those found in the free exercise of religion. A religious group that used its freedom to establish a theocracy would undermine the principles of the free exercise of religion (quite apart from establishment clause concerns). The relationship between the right of assembly and the religion clauses of the First Amendment is a yet unexplored dimension of constitutional law that might shed some light on the troubled jurisprudence surrounding "church-state" issues. For some very tentative thoughts along these lines, see Inazu, "Between Liberalism and Theocracy."

33. Koppelman, *A Right to Discriminate?* xiii.

34. See *Terry v. Adams,* 345 U.S. 461.

35. Steven G. Calabresi, "Political Parties as Mediating Institutions," 61 *University of Chicago Law Review* 1490 (1994). Howard Dickman suggests that the Wagner Act "created a hybrid social organization, private in origin but exercising public power over individual rights; the majority union became something akin to a private government, a legally created 'state within the state.'" Howard Dickman, *Industrial Democracy in America: Ideological Origins of National Labor Relations Policy* (La Salle: Open Court, 1987), 283, quoted in Paul Moreno, "Organized Labor and American Law: From Freedom of Association to Compulsory Unionism," 25 *Social Philosophy and Policy* 49 (2008). On the right of "political association," see *Tashjian v. Republican Party of Conn.,* 479 U.S. 208, 217 (1986); *Clingman v. Beaver,* 544 U.S. 581 (2005). On labor unions and the right of association, see, e.g., Sheldon Leader, *Freedom of Association: A Study in Labor Law and Political Theory* (New Haven: Yale University Press, 1992); Reuel E. Schiller, "From Group Rights to Individual Liberties: Post-War Labor Law, Liberalism, and the Waning of Union Strength," 20 *Berkeley Journal of Employment and Labor Law* 1 (1999). Schiller contends that mid-twentieth-century liberalism buttressed union rights at the expense of individual liberties but that "as the theory of interest-group pluralism declined in the early 1960s, labor law changed, reflecting that decline." Ibid., 4–5. Moreno writes that "American law has never denied organized labor's freedom of association." Moreno, "Organized Labor," 24. On the complicated relationship between the right of association and political parties, see, e.g., *California Democratic Party v. Jones,* 530 U.S. 567 (2000). For a general critique of the application of expressive association to political parties, see Samuel Issacharoff, "Private Parties with Public Purposes: Political Parties, Associational Freedoms, and Partisan Competition," 101 *Columbia Law Review* 274 (2001).

36. James Boyle, *Shamans, Software, and Spleens: Law and the Construction of the Information Society* (Cambridge, Mass.: Harvard University Press, 1996), 27. See also Gregory P. Magarian, "The First Amendment, the Public-Private Distinction, and Nongovernmental Suppression of Wartime Political Debate" 73 *George Washington Law Review* 101 (2004).

37. Robert Cover, "Nomos and Narrative," 97 *Harvard Law Review* 1, 10 (1983).

38. Philip Bobbitt, *Constitutional Fate: Theory of the Constitution* (New York: Oxford University Press, 1984) (discussing six "modalities" of constitutional argument: textual, structural, prudential, historical, precedential, and ethical); MacIntyre, *After Virtue;* MacIntyre, *Whose Justice? Which Rationality?* For an example of the kind of interpretive approach to which I am sympathetic, see H. Jefferson Powell, *The Moral Tradition of American Constitutionalism* (Durham: Duke University Press, 1993).

39. Cover, "Nomos and Narrative," 53.

Chapter 2. The Right Peaceably to Assemble

1. In highlighting the characteristic of dissent, I do not mean to suggest that all assemblies are dissenting. But as a constitutional matter, the assemblies whose boundaries and existence are most vulnerable to challenge are precisely those that dissent from consensus norms. Assemblies that do not annoy or offend those in power usually have little to fear from the state.

2. Caleb Nelson cautions against placing too much reliance on punctuation in the Constitution because at the time of the founding "punctuation marks [were] thought to lack the legal status of words." Caleb Nelson, "Preemption," 86 *Virginia Law Review* 225, 258 (2000). He notes that "[t]he ratification of the Constitution by the states reflects this relatively casual attitude toward punctuation" because many states that incorporated a copy of the Constitution in the official form of ratification varied its punctuation." Ibid., 259, n.102. Nelson cites as an example the copy of the Constitution in the Pennsylvania form of ratification, which used "different punctuation marks than the Constitution engrossed at the Federal Convention" in roughly thirty-five places. Ibid. My approach to the text, debates, and context of the assembly clause of the First Amendment has benefited from Michael Curtis's observations about history and method. See Michael Kent Curtis, *No State Shall Abridge: The Fourteenth Amendment and the Bill of Rights* (Durham: Duke University Press, 1986), 9 ("We may seek from history more than history can provide. The fact that the likely intent of the framers of a constitutional provision (narrowly read) may provide one form of legitimacy does not mean that it provides the only form. Still, appeal to historically existing common values is one characteristic of a community. Where valid, the appeal should not be discarded simply because the method may not answer all possible questions correctly from the critic's point of view.").

3. Neil H. Cogan, *The Complete Bill of Rights: The Drafts, Debates, Sources, and Origins* (New York: Oxford University Press, 1997), 129, 140. Willi Paul Adams has argued that the bills of rights and constitutions that arose from the states "did not reach a definition of the common good that resolved the ambiguities inherent in the concept as it was developed in the decade prior to 1776. The common good and the sum of private interests were seen as synonymous, and the possibility of conflict between them was belittled." Willi Paul Adams, *The First American Constitutions: Republican Ideology and the Making of State Constitutions in the Revolutionary Era* (New York: Rowan and Littlefield, 2001), 221.

4. Congressional Register, August 15, 1789, vol. 2, quoted in Cogan, *Complete Bill of Rights,* 145. Cf. Melvin Rishe, "Freedom of Assembly," 15 *DePaul Law Review* 317, 337 (1965) ("Were the courts truly bound to delve into whether or not an assembly served the common good, it is likely that many assemblies that have been held to be protected by the constitution would lose this protection.").

5. Congressional Register, August 15, 1789, vol. 2, quoted in Cogan, *Complete Bill of Rights,* 143. This version also changed the semicolon after "common good" to a comma. The motion to strike is reported in *Senate Journal (1st Congress)* (September 3, 1789), 70. The following day the Senate adopted similar language: "That Congress shall make no law abridging the freedom of speech, or of the press, or the [r]ight of the people peaceably to assemble and consult for their common good, and to petition the government for a redress of grievances." Ibid., September 4, 1789, 71. The merged text read: "Congress shall make no law establishing articles of faith or a mode of worship, or prohibiting the free exercise of religion, or abridging the freedom of speech, or the press, or the right of the people peaceably to assemble, and petition to the government for the redress of grievances." Ibid., September 9, 1789, 77. The amendment took its final form on September 24, 1789: "Congress shall make no law respecting an establishment of religion, or prohibiting the free exercise thereof; or abridging the freedom of speech, or of the press; or the right of the people peaceably to assemble, and to petition the government for a redress of grievances." Cogan, *Complete Bill of Rights,* 136. A number of state constitutional provisions retained references to the common good. See George P. Smith, "The Development of the Right of Assembly: A Current Socio-Legal Investigation," 9 *William and Mary Law Review* 359 (1967) (cataloging state constitution assembly clauses).

6. Jason Mazzone, "Freedom's Associations," 77 *Washington Law Review* 639, 712–13 (2002). But see Akhil R. Amar, *The Bill of Rights: Creation and Reconstruction* (New Haven: Yale University Press, 1998), 26 (referring to assembly and petition as separate clauses); William W. Van Alstyne, *First Amendment: Cases and Materials* (Westbury: Foundation Press, 1995), 32 (referring to a distinct "'peaceably to assemble' clause"); James E. Leahy, *The First Amendment: 1791–1991: Two Hundred Years of Freedom* (Jefferson: McFarland, 1991), 202 ("The final wording of the First Amendment indicates that the first Congress intended to protect the right of the people to assemble for whatever purposes and at the same time to be assured of a separate right to petition the government if they chose to do so."). The only other recent article to address the history of the right of assembly is Tabatha Abu El-Haj, "The Neglected Right of Assembly," 56 *UCLA Law Review* 543 (2009).

7. Cogan, *Complete Bill of Rights,* 143. The earlier version derived in turn from Madison's draft. Ibid., 129. Mazzone recognizes that "in Madison's draft, assembly is separated from petitioning by a semi-colon, perhaps indicating that while the right of assembly is related to the right of petition, assembly is not necessarily limited to formulating petitions." Mazzone, "Freedom's Associations," 715 n.409. Mazzone addresses the comma in a footnote and argues that because it "mirrors the comma" preceding the

words "or prohibit the free exercise thereof" in the first half of the First Amendment, "it does not therefore signal a right of petition separate from the right of assembly." Ibid., 713 n.392. The argument for textual parallelism doesn't hold because the free exercise clause explicitly refers back to "religion" (before the comma) with the word "thereof." A closer parallel—which illustrates the problem with Mazzone's interpretation—is the suggestion that the comma separating speech and press connotes that they embody only a singular freedom. My quibbles with Mazzone do not diminish my appreciation for his work. He is one of the few scholars in recent years to notice the relationship between assembly and association, and his thoughtful article posits a number of ideas with which I am highly sympathetic. See, e.g., ibid., 646 (arguing that assembly and petition provide "a much firmer constitutional basis for protecting the rights of citizens to come together in collective activities" than "expressive association").

8. Cogan, *Complete Bill of Rights,* 144 (quoting Congressional Register, August 15, 1789, vol. 2); Irving Brant, *The Bill of Rights: Its Origin and Meaning* (Indianapolis: Bobbs-Merrill, 1965).

9. The Conventicle Act is *16 Charles II c. 4* (1664). The act was renewed in 1667 and again in 1670. William Dixon, *William Penn: An Historical Biography* (Philadelphia: Blanchard and Lea, 1851), 75, 76. In 1715, an "Act for preventing Tumults and riotous Assemblies" made it a felony if twelve or more people unlawfully assembled failed to disperse within an hour after authorities read a proclamation. Smith, "The Development of the Right of Assembly," 363 n.22. On Penn's trial, see Brant, *Bill of Rights,* 56, 57, 61. Penn and Mead were fined for contempt of court for wearing their hats after being ordered by an officer of the court to put them on. In addition to its pronouncement on the right of assembly, the case became an important precedent for the independence of juries. Following their verdict of acquittal, the trial judge had imprisoned the jurors, who were later vindicated in habeas corpus proceedings. Ibid.

10. Cogan, *Complete Bill of Rights,* 145 (quoting Congressional Register, August 15, 1789, vol. 2). The final text read: "Congress shall make no law respecting an establishment of religion, or prohibiting the free exercise thereof; or abridging the freedom of speech, or of the press; or the right of the people peaceably to assemble, and to petition the government for a redress of grievances." Ibid., 136.

11. Robert M. Chesney, "Democratic-Republican Societies, Subversion, and the Limits of Legitimate Political Dissent in the Early Republic," 82 *University of North Carolina Law Review,* 1525, 1536 n.46 (2004). Mazzone also highlights the importance of the Democratic-Republican Societies to early interpretations of assembly and association. Mazzone, "Freedom's Associations," 734–42.

12. Philip S. Foner, *The Democratic-Republican Societies, 1790–1800 (A Documentary Sourcebook)* (Westport, Conn.: Greenwood Press, 1976), 6, 7. Foner, *Democratic-Republican Societies,* 7; Chesney, "Democratic-Republican Societies," 1538 n.54; Eugene Link, *Democratic-Republican Societies, 1790–1800* (Morningside Heights, N.Y.: Columbia University Press, 1942), 71–74. The term "Democratic-Republican Societies" comes from historians.

Chesney, "Democratic-Republican Societies," 1527 n.5. Although the exact number is disputed, there were probably around forty societies. Ibid., 1537 n.52.

13. Foner, *Democratic-Republican Societies,* 11; ibid. (quoting *North-Carolina Gazette* (New Bern), April 19, 1974); ibid., 25 (quoting *Independent Chronicle* (Boston), January 16, 1794) (original emphasis); ibid., 393 (quoting "Resolution Adopted Upholding the Cause of France," *South Carolina State Gazette* (April 29, 1794)).

14. Foner, *Democratic-Republican Societies,* 10; Chesney, "Democratic-Republican Societies," 1539; Simon P. Newman, *Parades and the Politics of the Street: Festive Culture in the Early American Republic* (Philadephia: University of Pennsylvania Press, 1997), 2, 3. These rituals were "vital elements of political life" practiced by ordinary Americans in the early Republic. Ibid., 5. While Newman cautions that some participants may have been interested only in "the festive aspects of public occasions and holidays," he writes that it was "all but impossible for these people, whatever their original motives for taking part, to avoid making public political statements by and through their participation: both their presence and their participation involve some degree of politicization and an expression of political identity and power in a public setting." Ibid., 8–9. El-Haj notes "the centrality of large gatherings of people in public places as part of the election festivities—to eat, drink, and parade and by implication to affirm their role as participants in the new nation." El Haj, "The Neglected Right of Assembly," 555.

15. Newman, *Parades and the Politics of the Street,* 3, 120, 122, 128–29. It is important not to overstate these societies' egalitarianism: their officers were "virtually without exception men of considerable substance." Eric McKitrick and Stanley Elkins, *The Age of Federalism* (New York: Oxford University Press, 1993), 458.

16. Chesney, "Democratic-Republican Societies," 1546, 1557; ibid., 1526 (quoting Letter from President George Washington to Burges Ball (September 25, 1794)); ibid., 1559 (quoting Letter from President George Washington to Governor Henry Lee (August 26, 1794)); *Annals of Congress,* vol. 4 (1794), 788 (Statement of President George Washington); Chesney, "Democratic-Republican Societies," 1558 (not ordinary political criticism); Irving Brant, *James Madison: Father of the Constitution, 1787–1800* (Indianapolis: Bobbs-Merrill, 1950), 417.

17. Chesney, "Democratic-Republican Societies," 1563; *Annals of Congress,* vol. 4 (1794), 934 (Statement of Representative Madison).

18. Foner, *Democratic-Republican Societies,* 33; ibid., 34 (quoting *New York Journal,* January 17, 1795); ibid., 327 (quoting James McCullough, "The Patriotic Society of New-Castle county, in the State of Delaware, To the Patriotic Societies throughout the United States" (undated)). See also James McCullough, "The Address of the Patriotic Society of the County of Newcastle, State of Delaware: To the People of the United States of America" (January 8, 1795), in Foner, *Democratic-Republican Societies,* 333 ("All we mean is simply to assert, that any individual citizen (and of consequence a society which is a collection of individuals) can never be blamed for a constitutional resistance to a law, which he believes from the bottom of his heart to be a bad one; and that if in consequence of his constitutional resistance, any unfortunate event should follow, the [burden] of the blame should

lay upon the shoulders of that legislature who passed it, rather than on him, if it must rest upon either.").

19. Foner, *Democratic-Republican Societies*, 40. See also Chesney, "Democratic-Republican Societies," 1526.

20. Benjamin L. Oliver, *The Rights of an American Citizen* (1832), 187 (emphasis omitted). Oliver limited his conception of assembly to discussions of "public measures." Ibid., 95. His lukewarm description warned that assemblies "called on the most unexceptionable business," and serve "chiefly as occasions for haranguing the people, and exciting their passions by loud and florid declamation, delivered with the regulated and precise gesture of the academy, and with all the generous and glowing ardor of holiday patriotism" but are nevertheless "a great improvement on the affrays, tumults, riots and public disturbances, which in many countries invariably attend numerous and irregular assemblies of the people." Ibid.

21. Francis Lieber, *Manual of Political Ethics: Designed Chiefly for the Use of Colleges and Students of Law* (2d ed. 1881), vol. 2, 295; ibid., 468–69. Lieber refers to "public meetings" at 471.

22. *Leavitt v. Truair*, 13 Pick. 111, 113, 30 Mass. 111, 113 (Mass. 1832) (emphasis added). At the time, Massachusetts required state support for sectarian religion. See, e.g., *Oakes v. Hill*, 10 Pick. 333, 351, 27 Mass. 333, 351 (Mass. 1830) ("A religious establishment and public worship ought to be maintained by legal coercion" and "the religion thus to be established and supported ought to be not only Christianity, but the *Protestant* Christian religion."). As of the Statute of 1823, the state exempted from taxation and membership anyone who could "[show] himself to be a member of some other religious society." Ibid., 351.

23. *First Parish in Sudbury v. Stearns*, 21 Pick. 148, 153, 38 Mass. 148, 153 (Mass. 1838). The opinion stressed that the society at issue was a poll parish rather than a territorial parish, which was "all voluntary and optional." Ibid. Unlike a territorial parish that drew its membership from within territorial limits, a poll parish "only incorporates as members those particular individuals who may voluntarily unite with the society." *Taylor v. Edson*, 58 Mass. 522, 527 (Mass. 1849).

24. Petition to the General Assembly of the State of North Carolina (November 24, 1818), microformed on *Race, Slavery, and Free Blacks: Petitions to Southern Legislatures, 1777–1867*, PAR 11281803 (University Publications of America, 1998); Petition to the General Assembly of the State of North Carolina (December 3, 1858), microformed on *Race, Slavery, and Free Blacks*, PAR 11285802; Petition to South Carolina General Assembly (circa 1820), microformed on *Race, Slavery, and Free Blacks*, PAR 11382008; Petition to the Senate and House of Representatives of the State of Mississippi (circa 1852), microformed on *Race, Slavery, and Free Blacks*, PAR 11085201. For examples from Virginia and Delaware, see, e.g., Petition to the General Assembly of Virginia (December 21, 1859), microformed on *Race, Slavery, and Free Blacks*, PAR 11685902 (asserting "two existing & wide-spread evils" in relationships with slaves and free negroes); Petition to the Senate and House of Representatives of the State of Delaware in General Assembly (January 26, 1847),

microformed on *Race, Slavery, and Free Blacks*, PAR 10384703 (white citizens are "greatly annoyed by the assemblages of Negroes and others in the streets of said town of Milford after night and on Sabbath days using all manner of profane language yelling and bawling, boxing, wrestling & fighting.").

25. William Goodell, *The American Slave Code* (New York: Negro Universities Press, 1968 (1853)), 329; June Purcell Guild, *Black Laws of Virginia: A Summary of the Legislative Acts of Virginia Concerning Negroes from Earliest Times to the Present* (Richmond: Whittet and Shepperson, 1936), 175–76.

26. John W. Cromwell, "The Aftermath of Nat Turner's Insurrection," 5 *Journal of Negro History* 208, 218, 223, 230 (1920); ibid., 219 (quoting *The Journal of the House of Delegates* (1831), 9, 10). On the additional restrictions, see Guild, *Black Laws of Virginia*, 106–7 ("no slave, free Negro or mulatto shall preach, or hold any meeting for religious purposes either day or night."). In 1848, Chapter 120 of the Criminal Code decreed: "It is an unlawful assembly of slaves, free Negroes or mulattoes for the purpose of religious worship when such worship is conducted by a slave, free Negro, or mulatto, and every such assembly for the purpose of instruction in reading and writing, by whomsoever conducted, and every such assembly in the night time, under whatsoever pretext." Ibid., 178–79. The law also stated that "any white person assembling with slaves or free Negroes for purpose of instructing them to read or write, or associating with them in any unlawful assembly, shall be confined in jail not exceeding six months and fined not exceeding $100.00." Ibid., 179.

27. Cromwell, "The Aftermath of Nat Turner's Insurrection," 231–33. For example, Tennessee's 1831 act restricted "all assemblages of slaves in unusual numbers, or at suspicious times and places, not expressly authorized by the owners." *Leetch v. State*, 2 Head 140 (Tenn. 1858). In upholding a fine against a slave owner for violating the provisions of the act, the Supreme Court of Tennessee opined: "The argument is unsound, that to constitute the offence the slaves, when assembled, must do some other unlawful act. That is not made an element by the Legislature, and we are not authorized to add it. It is a police regulation, founded on sound policy." Ibid. See also *State v. Brown*, 27 Tenn. 89 (Tenn. 1847) (similar construction of 1831 act in appeal by grocerykeeper); C. Peter Ripley, *The Black Abolitionist Papers* (Chapel Hill: University of North Carolina Press, 1985), 443 n.9 ("most southern states"); Theodore Dwight Weld, "The Power of Congress over Slavery in the District of Columbia," reprinted in Jacobus tenBroek, *Equal under Law* (New York: Collier Books, 1965), 271. Jacobus tenBroek describes Weld's tract as "a restatement and synthesis of abolitionist constitutional theory as of that time." tenBroek, *Equal under Law*, 243. See also Harry Kalven, *The Negro and the First Amendment* (Columbus: Ohio State University Press, 1965). Akhil Amar writes that the right of assembly for religious worship was "a core right that southern states had violated." Amar, *Bill of Rights*, 245.

28. *African Methodist Episcopal Church v. City of New Orleans*, 15 La. Ann. 441 (La. 1860).

29. Eric Foner, ed., *Nat Turner* (Englewood Cliffs, N.J.: Prentice-Hall, 1971), 74 (quoting James L. Smith, *Autobiography of James L. Smith* (Norwich, Conn., 1881), 26–30); William

Goodell's 1853 book *The American Slave Code* observed that "religious liberty is the precursor of civil and political liberty and enfranchisement." Goodell, *The American Slave Code*, 328.

30. Linda Lumsden, *Rampant Women: Suffragists and the Right of Assembly* (Knoxville: University of Tennessee Press, 1997), xxiii. Lumsden has suggested that "virtually the entire suffrage story can be told through the prism of the right of assembly." Ibid., 144; Nancy Isenberg, *Sex and Citizenship in Antebellum America* (Chapel Hill: University of North Carolina Press, 1998), 16 (quoting John Alexander Jameson, *A Treatise on the Principles of American Constitutional Law and Legislation: The Constitutional Convention* (Chicago: E. B. Meyers, 1869)).

31. Jean Fagan Yellin and John C. Van Horne, eds., *The Abolitionist Sisterhood: Women's Political Culture in Antebellum America* (Ithaca: Cornell University Press, 1994), ix (New York and Philadelphia conventions); Isenberg, *Sex and Citizenship in Antebellum America*, 15 (quoting "To the Women of Ohio," *Anti-Slavery Bugle*, March 30, 1850) (Salem convention); ibid. (describing Salem forum).

32. Isenberg, *Sex and Citizenship in Antebellum America*, 46.

33. Isenberg, *Sex and Citizenship in Antebellum America*, 46; Lumsden, *Rampant Women*, xxvi, xxvii.

34. *Annual Report of the Boston Female Anti-Slavery Society* (1836), 27–28 (quoting *Boston Commercial Gazette*). Antiabolitionists reviled Thompson, calling him an "artful, cowardly fellow" who "always throws himself under the protection of the female portion of his audience when in danger." Ibid., 12. On Garrison's escape, see John L. Thomas, *The Liberator: William Lloyd Garrison* (Boston: Little, Brown, 1963). For Garrison's response, see William Lloyd Garrison, *Selections from the Writings and Speeches of William Lloyd Garrison* (Boston: R. F. Wallcut, 1852), 377.

35. C. Peter Ripley, ed., *The Black Abolitionist Papers* (Chapel Hill: University of North Carolina Press, 1991), vol. 3, 166 n.17 ("cause célèbre"); John W. Blassingame, John R. McKivigan, and Peter P. Hinks, eds., *The Frederick Douglass Papers* (New Haven: Yale University Press, 1982), series 1, vol. 2, 207–8, 268 n.14 (on Douglass's visit).

36. Michael Kent Curtis, *Free Speech, "The People's Darling Privilege": Struggles for Freedom of Expression in American History* (Durham: Duke University Press, 2000), 362, 363; Curtis, *No State Shall Abridge*, 135 ("statute books groaned").

37. Curtis, *No State Shall Abridge*, 137 (quoting *Washington* (D.C.) *Evening Chron.*, Sept. 9, 1866, at 1, col. 5) ("if these persons assemble"); ibid., 136 (quoting Michael Les Benedict, *A Compromise of Principle: Congressional Republicans and Reconstruction, 1863–1869* (New York: Norton, 1974), 205–6) (describing Louisiana massacre).

38. Charles Lane, *The Day Freedom Died: The Colfax Massacre, the Supreme Court, and the Betrayal of Reconstruction* (New York: Henry Holt, 2008), 3–4. See also David M. Chalmers, *Hooded Americanism: The History of the Ku Klux Klan* (Durham: Duke University Press, 1987), 8–21 (describing growth and violence of the Klan from 1865 to 1871).

39. 16o Stat 141 (1870); *United States v. Cruikshank*, 92 U.S. 542, 548 (1875)); Lane, *The Day Freedom Died*, 114.

40. *United States v. Hall,* 26 F. Cas. 79, 81 (C.C.S.D. Ala. 1871); Lane, *The Day Freedom Died,* 115.

41. Lane, *The Day Freedom Died,* 58, 62, 68. See also Aviam Soifer, *Law and the Company We Keep* (Cambridge, Mass.: Harvard University Press, 1995), 120–21.

42. *United States v. Cruikshank,* 551, 552. Cf. Lane, *The Day Freedom Died,* 246. After decades of relative obscurity, *Cruikshank* has recently garnered renewed attention for its discussion of the Second Amendment. See *District of Columbia v. Heller,* 554 U.S. 570 (2008); *McDonald v. Chicago,* 130 S. Ct. 3020 (2010).

43. *Cruikshank,* 542, 552. Although unremarkable as a legal proposition today, *Cruikshank's* holding had severe implications for the protection of African Americans in southern jurisdictions where the rule of law was in peril. It is possible to read the text of the opinion so that the additional clause modifies "petitioning" rather than "assemble," as if Waite were referring to "the right of the people peaceably to assemble for the purpose of petitioning Congress for any thing else connected with the powers or the duties of the national government" rather than "the right of the people peaceably to assemble for any thing else connected with the powers or the duties of the national government." Either way, the sentence cannot be read as limiting assembly to petitioning Congress for a redress of grievances.

44. *Presser v. Illinois,* 116 U.S. 252, 267 (1886). For later suggestions by the Court that assembly and petition are distinct rights, see *McDonald v. City of Chicago,* 130 S. Ct. 3020 (2010) ("In [*United States v. Cruikshank*], the Court held that the general "right of the people peaceably to assemble for lawful purposes," which is protected by the First Amendment, applied only against the Federal Government and not against the states. Nonetheless, more than sixty years later the Court held that the right of peaceful assembly was a "fundamental righ[t] . . . safeguarded by the due process clause of the Fourteenth Amendment."); *District of Columbia v. Heller,* 554 U.S. 570 (2008) ("State constitutions of the founding period routinely grouped multiple (related) guarantees under a singular 'right,' and the First Amendment protects the 'right [singular] of the people peaceably to assemble, and to petition the Government for a redress of grievances.'"); *Thomas v. Collins,* 323 U.S. 516, 530 (1945) (referring to "the *rights* of the people peaceably to assemble and to petition for redress of grievances" (emphasis added)). Cf. *Chisom v. Roemer,* 501 U.S. 380, 409 (1991) (Scalia, J., dissenting) (The First Amendment "has not generally been thought to protect the right peaceably to assemble only when the purpose of the assembly is to petition the Government for a redress of grievances."). The scholarship interpreting *Cruikshank* as narrowing the right of assembly is voluminous. In 1908, a commentator writing in *Bench and Bar* cited *Cruikshank* in support of his contention that "the right to assemble is merely incidental to the right to petition" and concluded that "the right to assemble except for the purpose of petitioning the government is not expressly guaranteed by . . . the Federal Constitution." "The Right of Assembly," 13 *Bench and Bar* 9 (1908). This incorrect reading of assembly has persisted in more recent scholarship. See Note, "Freedom of Association: Constitutional Right or Judicial Technique," 46 *Virginia Law*

Review 730, 736 (1960) ("The first case to construe this provision of the first amendment construed freedom of assembly to mean the right to assemble *in order to* petition the government."); Charles E. Rice, *Freedom of Association* (New York: New York University Press, 1962), 109 (citing *Cruikshank* for the view that the language in the First Amendment "constituted the right of petition as the primary right, and the right of assembly as the ancillary right, thereby guaranteeing a right to assemble in order to petition"); Glenn Abernathy, *The Right of Assembly and Association* (Columbia: University of South Carolina Press, 1961), 152 ("It is important to note that the Cruikshank dictum *narrowed* the federal right from that of 'the right to peaceably assemble and petition for redress of grievances' to 'the right of the people peaceably to assemble for the purpose of petitioning Congress for a redress of grievances, or for anything else connected with the powers or the duties of the National Government.'") (emphasis added); Edward S. Corwin, Harold W. Chase, and Craig R. Ducat, *Edwin S. Corwin's The Constitution and What It Means Today*, 14th ed. (Princeton: Princeton University Press, 1978), 332 (citing *Cruikshank* for the view that historically "the right of petition is the primary right, the right peaceably to assemble a subordinate and instrumental right, as if Amendment I read: 'the right of the people peaceably to assemble' *in order to* 'petition the government'"). *Presser* has also been cited as limiting assembly to the purpose of petition. See Frank Easterbrook, "Implicit and Explicit Rights of Association," 10 *Harvard Journal of Law and Public Policy* 97 (1987) (citing *Presser* for the view that the freedom of assembly is "the exercise by groups of the right to petition for redress of grievances").

45. *Richardson v. Union Congregational Society of Francestown*, 58 N.H. 187 (N.H. 1877).

46. *People ex rel. Rice v. Board of Trade of Chicago*, 80 Ill. 134, 135 (Ill. 1875). The court noted that the board of trade "is not maintained for the transaction of business or for pecuniary gain, but simply to promulgate and enforce amongst its members correct and high moral principles in the transaction of business. It is not engaged in business, but only prescribes rules for the transaction of business." Ibid., 136.

47. *State ex rel. Poulson v. Grand Lodge of Missouri I.O.O.F.*, 8 Mo. App. 148, *4 (Mo. App. 1879). See also *Josich v. Austrian Benevolent Soc. of San Jose*, 51 P. 18, 19 (Cal. 1897) (quoting part of this passage from *Poulson*).

48. Frederick H. Bacon, *A Treatise on the Law of Benefit Societies and Life Insurance: Voluntary Associations, Regular Life, Beneficiary and Accident Insurance*, 2d ed. (St. Louis, 1894), vol. 1, 99.

49. Jameson, *A Treatise on the Principles of American Constitutional Law and Legislation*, 4, 5, 104. Jameson also refers to "spontaneous conventions" and "spontaneous assemblages." Ibid., 4; Albert Orville Wright, *An Exposition of the Constitution of the United States*, 13th ed. (Madison, 1884), 21. Cf. Thomas McIntyre Cooley, *The General Principles of Constitutional Law in the United States of America* (Boston, 1880), 268 ("The right to assemble may be important for religious, social, industrial, or political purposes; but it was no doubt its political value that was in view in adopting the amendment.").

50. *Poyer v. Village of Des Plaines*, 18 Ill. App. 225, *3 (Ill. App. 1 Dist. 1885). The opinion left open the factual determination of whether the particular assembly in question had

qualified as a nuisance. Ibid., *5 ("Our conclusion is that so much of the ordinance as declares all public picnics and open air dances, regardless of their character, to be a nuisance, is invalid; and that the court erred in refusing to so instruct the jury. Whether the gathering on July 31st was of such a character as to bring it within the second clause of the ordinance which declares the use of the grounds for the assembling of disorderly persons, etc., to be a nuisance, was a question of fact for the jury, to be decided according to the evidence, under proper instructions by the court.").

51. *Anderson v. City of Wellington*, 40 Kan. 173, 19 P. 719, 721, 722 (Kan. 1888). The leading case appears to be *In re Frazee*, 63 Mich. 396, 30 N.W. 72, 75 (Mich. 1886) ("It has been customary, from time immemorial, in all free countries, and in most civilized countries, for people who are assembled for common purposes to parade together, by day or reasonable hours at night, with banners and other paraphernalia, and with music of various kinds. These processions for political, religious, and social demonstrations are resorted to for the express purpose of keeping unity of feeling and enthusiasm, and frequently to produce some effect on the public mind by the spectacle of union and numbers. They are a natural product and exponent of common aims, and valuable factors in furthering them. They are only found to any appreciable extent in places having collected inhabitants, for spectators are generally as important as members."). See also *Rich v. City of Naperville*, 42 Ill. App. 222, 223–24 (Ill. App. 1891) ("Ever since the landing of the Pilgrims from the Mayflower the right to assemble and worship according to the dictates of one's conscience, and the right to parade in a peaceable manner and for a lawful purpose, have been fostered and regarded as among the fundamental rights of a free people. The spirit of our free institutions allows great latitude in public parades and demonstrations, whether religious or political, and if they do not threaten the public peace, or substantially interfere with the rights of others, every measure repressing them, whether by legislative enactment, or municipal ordinance, is an encroachment upon fundamental and constitutional rights.").

52. *Von Rueden v. State*, 96 Wis. 671, 71 N.W. 1048, 1049 (Wis. 1897). The Court noted that antecedent versions of the statute had gradually expanded its coverage from "any assembly of people, met for the worship of God, within the place of meeting or out of it," to "when meeting or met together for the performance of any duties enjoined on or pertaining to them, as members of any religious society, or for the recitation or performance of, or instruction in vocal music," to "any wedding party, or other company or assembly of peaceable citizens" to "all lawful meetings of the people." Ibid., 1049. That same year, Judge Caldwell's dissent in *Hopkins v. Oxley Stave* included an extended discussion of William Penn's trial for freedom of assembly. *Hopkins v. Oxley Stave Co.*, 83 F. 912 (8th Cir. 1897) (Caldwell, J., dissenting). Aziz Rana, *The Two Faces of American Freedom* (Cambridge, Mass.: Harvard University Press, 2010), 206. Rana continues: "Instead of popular participation being consigned to the occasional vote, the centrality of party identification meant that public involvement through a vast array of campaign activities—'ratification meetings, pole-raisings, parades, marches, barbeques, rallies, and bonfires'—created a permanently engaged citizenry." Ibid., 207.

53. Lumsden, *Rampant Women*, 3, 186 n.8, 146.

54. Lumsden, *Rampant Women*, 3, 17–19; Jennifer L. Borda, "The Woman Suffrage Parades of 1910–1913: Possibilities and Limitations of an Early Feminist Rhetorical Strategy," 66 *Western Journal of Communication* 25 (2002) (quoting Blatch). On the relationship between grassroots movements and larger institutional structures, see generally, Theda Skocpol, *Diminished Democracy: From Membership to Management in American Civic Life* (Norman: University of Oklahoma Press, 2003).

55. James P. Roche, "Civil Liberty in the Age of Enterprise," 31 *University of Chicago Law Review* 119 (1963); Langston Hughes, *Fight for Freedom: The Story of the NAACP* (New York: Norton, 1962), 22 (quoting Oswald Garrison Villard's "Call for a Conference"); Adam Fairclough, *Better Day Coming: Blacks and Equality 1890–2000* (New York: Viking, 2001), 83. Fairclough credits Du Bois with "provid[ing] the intellectual force that transmuted the carping criticism of a few individuals into something much more powerful: an organized movement with a clear program and a coherent ideology." Ibid. On the rise in the NAACP's membership, see Gilbert Jonas, *Freedom's Sword: The NAACP and the Struggle against Racism in America, 1909–1969* (New York: Routledge, 2005), 13–15; Theodore Kornweibel Jr., *Seeing Red: Federal Campaigns against Black Militancy, 1919–1925* (Bloomington: Indiana University Press, 1998), 67.

56. Fairclough, *Better Day Coming*, 99, 111, 112, 129–31.

57. John Hope Franklin and Alfred A. Moss Jr., *From Slavery to Freedom: A History of African Americans* (New York: Alfred A. Knopf, 1994), 363, 376, 377.

58. Alexis J. Anderson, "The Formative Period of First Amendment Theory, 1870–1915," 24 *American Journal of Legal History* 58 (1980); Philip Foner, *The Great Labor Uprising of 1877* (New York: Monad Press, 1977), 8, 10, 27. Louis Adamic reported that by May of 1886, the Knights of Labor had surpassed one million members. Louis Adamic, *Dynamite: The Story of Class Violence in America* (New York: Viking Press, 1931), 86. Despite these numbers, the Knights of Labor were "anything but effectual" throughout their history. Ibid., 58–59, 87; Richard Schneirov, Shelton Stromquist, and Nick Salvatore, "Introduction," in *The Pullman Strike and the Crisis of the 1890s*, ed. Richard Schneirov, Shelton Stromquist, and Nick Salvatore (Urbana: University of Illinois Press, 1999), 4 ("decade of labor unrest").

59. *Fiske v. Kansas*, 274 U.S. 380, 383 (1927) (quoting Preamble); David M. Rabban, "The IWW Free Speech Fights and Popular Conceptions of Free Expression Before World War I," 80 *University of Virginia Law Review* 1076 n.114 (1994) (citing *Industrial Worker* (Seattle), "A Call to Action," February 26, 1910, 2); *New York Times*, "Paterson Checks Weavers' Strike," February 27, 1927; David M. Rabban, *Free Speech in Its Forgotten Years* (New York: Cambridge University Press, 1997), 85 (quoting *Solidarity*, " 'Heroic' Contrasts," July 26, 1913, 2).

60. Irwin M. Marcus, "The Johnstown Steel Strike of 1919: The Struggle for Unionism and Civil Liberties," 63 *Pennsylvania History* 100 (1996); John Heaton, *Cobb of "The World": A Leader in Liberalism* (New York: E. P. Dutton, 1924), 269–70. There has been some debate as to when or even whether the conversation between Wilson and Cobb occurred. See

Jerold S. Auerbach, "Woodrow Wilson's 'Prediction' to Frank Cobb: Words Historians Should Doubt Ever Got Spoken," 54 *Journal of American History* 608 (1967); Arthur S. Link, "That Cobb Interview," 72 *Journal of American History* 7 (1985). On the Palmer Raids, see Soifer, *Law and the Company We Keep,* 57.

61. Rabban, *Free Speech in Its Forgotten Years,* 7. Chafee's important works in this period are Zechariah Chafee Jr., "Freedom of Speech in War Time," 32 *Harvard Law Review* 932–73 (1919); Zechariah Chafee Jr., *Freedom of Speech* (New York: Harcourt, Brace, and Howe, 1920). For the importance of Chafee's work to Holmes and Brandeis, see Rabban, *Free Speech in Its Forgotten Years,* 5. See also John Wertheimer, "Freedom of Speech: Zechariah Chafee and Free-Speech History," 22 *Reviews in American History* 367, 374 (1994). On problems with Chafee's scholarship, see ibid., 374–75 (Chafee's "record as a scholar rightly gives us pause."). Wertheimer also notes that Chafee's advocacy was not without personal risk: "A group of conservative Harvard Law School alumni, with behind-the-scenes help from J. Edgar Hoover and the Justice Department, launched a campaign to have Chafee fired from Harvard on the grounds that his free-speech writings rendered him unfit to continue teaching there." Ibid., 368.

62. *Washington Post,* "Pertinent Points in Republican Acceptance Speech," July 23, 1920, 4; *New York Times,* "College Liberals Organize League," April 4, 1921; *New York Times,* "Gompers Fights Sedition Bill," January 19, 1920, 15 (Sterling-Graham sedition bill "can be used to kill free speech and free assembly"); ibid., "Labor Will Fight for Every Right, Gompers Asserts," June 13, 1922, 1 (arguing against the denial of "freedom of expression, freedom of press, and the freedom of assembly"); ibid., "Gompers Assails Harding on Unions," July 1, 1923, 3 (Daugherty injunction "sought to deny the constitutional rights of freedom of speech, freedom of assembly, and freedom of the press to railroad workers"). In 1951, President Truman, speaking at the dedication of a memorial to Gompers, said: "Above all, he fought the labor injunction because it was used to violate the constitutional rights to free speech and freedom of assembly." Harry S. Truman, *Address at the Dedication of a Square in Washington to the Memory of Samuel Gompers* (October 27, 1951), courtesy of John T. Woolley and Gerhard Peters, *The American Presidency Project* (online). Santa Barbara: University of California (host).

63. *Whitney v. California,* 274 U.S. 357 (1927) (Brandeis J., concurring). The decision was formally overruled in *Brandenburg v. Ohio,* 395 U.S. 444 (1969) (per curiam). Brandeis concurred rather than dissented in *Whitney* on procedural grounds, but his opinion strongly rebuked the majority's reasoning. See generally, Philippa Strum, *Louis D. Brandeis: Justice for the People* (Cambridge, Mass.: Harvard University Press, 1984), 306; Vincent Blasi, "The First Amendment and the Ideal of Civic Courage: The Brandeis Opinion in *Whitney v. California,*" 29 *William and Mary Law Review* 653 (1988).

64. *Whitney,* 375 (Brandeis, J. concurring). Judges and scholars have written volumes about these words and those that followed, but almost all of them focus on speech alone rather than speech and assembly. Justice Brennan, writing for the Court in the landmark case *New York Times v. Sullivan,* deemed Brandeis's Whitney concurrence the "classic

formulation" of the fundamental principle underlying free speech. *New York Times v. Sullivan*, 376 U.S. 254, 270 (1964). Cf. H. Jefferson Powell, *A Community Built on Words: The Constitution in History and Politics* (Chicago: University of Chicago Press, 2002), 194. See also Robert Cover, "The Left, the Right, and the First Amendment: 1918–1928," 40 *Maryland Law Review* 371 (1981) ("classic statement of free speech"). The only mention of "speech and assembly" prior to *Whitney* is *New York ex rel. Doyle v. Atwell*, 261 U.S. 590, 591 (1923) (noting that petitioners alleged a deprivation of the "rights of freedom of speech and assembly").

65. See, e.g., *Poulos v. New Hampshire*, 345 U.S. 395, 423 (1953) (Douglas, J., dissenting) ("There is no free speech in the sense of the Constitution when permission must be obtained from an official before a speech can be made. That is a previous restraint condemned by history and at war with the First Amendment."); *Kingsley International Pictures Corp. v. New York*, 360 U.S. 684, 697–98 (1959) (Douglas, J., dissenting) ("I can find in the First Amendment no room for any censor whether he is scanning an editorial, reading a news broadcast, editing a novel or a play, or previewing a movie."); *New York Times v. United States*, 403 U.S. 713, 720–25 (1971) (Douglas, J., concurring). As Ashutosh Bhagwat has noted, Brandeis believed that "the textual right of assembly protects membership in political organizations." Ashutosh Bhagwat, "Associational Speech," 120 *Yale Law Journal* 978 (2011). See also *American Communications Assn. v. Douds*, 339 U.S. 382, 402 (1950) ("the fact that no direct restraint or punishment is imposed upon speech or assembly does not determine the free speech question. Under some circumstances, indirect 'discouragements' undoubtedly have the same coercive effect upon the exercise of First Amendment rights as imprisonment, fines, injunctions or taxes."); *NAACP v. Alabama ex rel. Patterson*, 357 U.S. 449, 462 (1958) (noting that *Douds* referred to "the varied forms of governmental action which might interfere with freedom of assembly" and concluding that "compelled disclosure of membership in an organization engaged in advocacy of particular beliefs is of the same order"). The principle that assembly encompasses membership is also evidenced by the now discredited logic underlying a number of the communist cases decided prior to the Court's recognition of the right of association. See, e.g., *Joint Anti-Fascist Refugee Committee v. Clark*, 177 F.2d 79, 84 (D.C. Cir. 1949) ("Nothing in the Hatch Act or the loyalty program deprives the Committee or its members of any property rights. Freedom of speech and assembly is denied no one. Freedom of thought and belief is not impaired. Anyone is free to join the Committee and give it his support and encouragement. Everyone has a constitutional right to do these things, but no one has a constitutional right to be a government employee."); *Bailey v. Richardson*, 182 F.2d 46 (D.C. Cir. 1950) (Edgerton, J., dissenting) ("Guilt by association . . . denies both the freedom of assembly guaranteed by the First Amendment and the due process of law guaranteed by the Fifth.").

66. *New York ex rel. Bryant v. Zimmerman*, 278 U.S. 63, 66, 72 (1928). Justice McReynolds's lone dissent reflected his belief that the Court lacked jurisdiction in the case. Ibid., 77 (McReynolds, J., dissenting).

67. *NAACP v. Alabama*, 360 U.S. 240 (1959); Chalmers, *Hooded Americanism*, 2–5; *Brandenburg v. Ohio*, 395 U.S. 444 (1969). By the 1960s, Klan membership numbered no more than fifty thousand, "including the ladies' auxiliaries." Chalmers, *Hooded Americanism*, 387. No more than ten thousand of these were "hard core" members who "lived their lives completely in a Klan world." Ibid. George Bryant's trial and appeals had unfolded at the height of the Klan's reign—Bryant was arrested following a shooting in September 1924 that alerted Buffalo authorities to the possibility of a secret Klan organization in violation of the Walker Law. "To Bring Criminal Action Against Buffalo Klan Heads," *New York Times*, September 9, 1924, 1.

68. Cover, "The Left, the Right, and the First Amendment," 354.

69. Cover, "The Left, the Right, and the First Amendment," 442.

70. Jerold S. Auerbach, "The La Follette Committee: Labor and Civil Liberties in the New Deal," 51 *Journal of American History* 440, 440 n.30, 442, 442 n.32 (1964).

71. *New York Times*, "Hoover's Warning of the Perils to Liberty," September 18, 1935, 10; *New York Times*, "Long and Coughlin Classed by Ickes as 'Contemptible,'" April 23, 1935, 1.

72. *De Jonge v. Oregon*, 299 U.S. 353, 357, 358 (1937). De Jonge was sentenced to seven years' imprisonment. Ibid., 358. See also Leahy, *First Amendment*, 316.

73. *De Jonge*, 362, 364, 365. Brandeis had called the right of assembly fundamental in his *Whitney* concurrence ten years earlier. *Whitney v. California*, 373.

74. *Herndon v. Lowry*, 301 U.S. 242, 258 (1937); *Herndon v. State*, 178 Ga. 832, 174 S.E. 597, 599 (Ga. 1934); J. C. Chunn, "Herndon Awaits Fate: Judge Reverses Decision; Will Study the Facts," *Pittsburgh Courier*, November 16, 1935 ("Negro Republic"); *Herndon v. State*, 615; Charles H. Martin, *The Angelo Herndon Case and Southern Justice* (Baton Rouge: Louisiana State University Press, 1976), xii ("white liberals"); *Herndon v. Lowry*, 258.

75. John Dewey, "Creative Democracy: The Task Before Us," in *John Dewey: The Later Works, 1925–1953*, ed. Jo Ann Boydston (Carbondale: Southern Illinois University Press, 1976), vol. 14, 227, 228; *Hague v. Committee for Industrial Organization*, 101 F.2d 774 (3d Cir. 1939); The Committee on the Bill of Rights, "Brief of the Committee on the Bill of Rights of the American Bar Association" (hereinafter "Committee Brief") (February 27, 1939), 4, 7, 19.

76. "Association's Committee Intervenes to Defend Right of Public Assembly," 25 *American Bar Association Journal* 7 (1939); *New York Times*, "A Brief for Free Speech," December 23, 1938, 18. The *Times* later wrote that the brief "was received all over the country with approval as a lucid exposition and defense of the fundamental guarantee of American liberty. *New York Times*, "Bar and Civil Liberties," July 17, 1939, 10. Zechariah Chafee had a substantial role in drafting the brief. When he published *Free Speech in the United States* two years later, his thirty-page discussion of the freedom of assembly consisted almost entirely of verbatim sections of the brief. See Zechariah Chafee, *Free Speech in the United States* (Cambridge, Mass.: Harvard University Press, 1941), 409–38. The committee submitted a revised version of its amicus brief when the case reached the Supreme Court.

77. *New York Times*, "Mile-Long Mall Feature of Fair," December 12, 1937, 57.

78. *New York Times*, "Fair to Broadcast to World Today," January 1, 1939, 13. Thompson was at the time a news commentator for the *New York Herald Tribune*. She was considered by some to be "the most influential woman in the United States after Eleanor Roosevelt," and her syndicated column, "On the Record," reached an estimated eight to ten million readers three times a week. Susan Ware, *Letter to the World: Seven Women Who Shaped the American Century* (New York: Norton, 1998), 45. Thompson's portrait graced the cover of *Time* on June 13, 1939. Ibid., 47. Her speech pitted the free assembly of democracy against the abuses of fascism. Dorothy Thompson, "Democracy," Dorothy Thompson Papers, Series VII, Box 6 (Syracuse University Library) (January 1, 1939), 1.

79. Nicholas Murry Butler, "The Four Freedoms," *New York Times*, March 5, 1939, AS5 (pictures of Friedlander's statues accompanied Butler's editorial); Henry Steele Commager, "To Secure the Blessings of Liberty," *New York Times*, April 9, 1939, SM3.

80. *New York Times*, "Mayor Dedicates Plaza of Freedom," May 1, 1939, 4; *Hague v. Committee for Industrial Organization*, 307 U.S. 496 (1939). Roberts reached his assembly analysis through a somewhat contorted interpretation of the privileges and immunities clause. Justice Stone's concurrence pointed out that neither of the parties had raised this argument, and that *De Jonge's* analysis of the due process clause should have been controlling. Ibid., 518 (Stone, J., concurring); *New York Times*, "A Fundamental Liberty Upheld in Hague Case," June 11, 1939, E7; *Wall Street Journal*, "Public Mind in Good Health," January 7, 1941, 4.

81. Franklin Delano Roosevelt, Annual Message to Congress, The "Four Freedoms" Speech (January 6, 1941). See also The Franklin D. Roosevelt Four Freedoms Awards Home Page, http://www.fourfreedoms.nl (last visited April 2, 2011).

82. *Time*, "Of Thee They Sing," February 24, 1941; *Time*, "Freely Criticized Company," April 28, 1941.

83. Orson Welles, "His Honor, the Mayor," in *The Free Company Presents: A Collection of Plays about the Meaning of America* (New York: Dodd, Mead, 1941), 143; Charles Higham, *Orson Welles: The Rise and Fall of an American Genius* (New York: St. Martin's Press, 1985), 175; *Time*, "Freely Criticized Company"; Matthew F. McGuire, *Memorandum for the Assistant to the Attorney General* (April 24, 1941).

84. *Washington Post* (December 15, 1941); Henry Steele Commager, "Charter of Our Way of Life," *New York Times*, December 14, 1941, SM6; *New York Times*, "Day Will Honor Bill of Rights," November 29, 1941, 19.

85. Emily Roxworthy, *The Spectacle of Japanese American Trauma: Racial Performativity and World War II* (Honolulu: University of Hawaii Press, 2008), 70; Greg Robinson, *A Tragedy of Democracy: Japanese Confinement in North America* (New York: Columbia University Press, 2009), 131.

86. *Hirabayashi v. United States*, 320 U.S. 81 (1943); *Korematsu v. United States*, 323 U.S. 214 (1944); *West Virginia v. Barnette*, 319 U.S. 624, 638 (1943).

87. *Thomas v. Collins*, 323 U.S. 516 (1945); "Test for Texas Labor Law: Thomas of the Auto Union Will Argue His Case Before High State Court," *New York Times*, October 10,

1943. See also "Thomas Will Test Texas Labor Law," *Atlanta Constitution*, September 25, 1943 ("I came to Texas to test the constitutionality of the Manford act.").

88. *Thomas v. Collins*, 530–31 (emphasis added), 534. The "preferred place" language originated in Justice Douglas's opinion for the Court in *Murdock v. Pennsylvania*, 319 U.S. 105, 115 (1943) ("Freedom of press, freedom of speech, freedom of religion are in a preferred position.").

89. *To Secure These Rights: The Report of the President's Committee on Civil Rights* (New York: Simon and Schuster, 1947), 47, 48. President Truman established the committee with Executive Order 9808 (December 5, 1946).

90. Some of the last cases to address the right of assembly were *Edwards v. South Carolina*, 372 U.S. 229 (1963); *Cox v. Louisiana*, 379 U.S. 536 (1965); *Brown v. Louisiana*, 383 U.S. 131 (1966); *Shuttlesworth v. City of Birmingham*, 394 U.S. 147 (1969); and *Gregory v. City of Chicago*, 394 U.S. 111 (1969). Cf. *Coates v. City of Cincinnati*, 402 U.S. 611, 615 (1971) ("The First [Amendment does] not permit a State to make criminal the exercise of the right of assembly simply because its exercise may be 'annoying' to some people."). The right of petition suffered a similar fate. See Stephen H. Higginson, "A Short History of the Right to Petition Government for a Redress of Grievances," 96 *Yale Law Journal* 142, 142 (1986) ("the right of petition was collapsed into the right of free speech and expression"). See also David C. Frederick, "John Quincy Adams, Slavery, and the Disappearance of the Right of Petition," 9 *Law and History Review* 113, 141 (1991) (the Supreme Court "merged the right of petition with other first amendment rights in a doctrine that obscures both the original meaning and the form of the right"). The references from Dr. King are taken from Martin Luther King Jr., *Letter from a Birmingham Jail* (April 16, 1963) (asserting that the Birmingham ordinance denied "citizens the First Amendment privilege of peaceful assembly and protest"); Martin Luther King Jr., *I've Been to the Mountaintop* (April 3, 1968) ("But somewhere I read of the freedom of assembly").

91. *Perry Education Association v. Perry Local Educators' Association*, 460 U.S. 37, 45 (1983). Cf. C. Edwin Baker, *Human Liberty and Freedom of Speech* (New York: Oxford University Press, 1989), 316 n.18 ("An interesting, and perhaps ideologically telling, practice of the Supreme Court is its focus on 'speech' and expression in cases in which it has the option of using either a speech or an assembly analysis."); *Boos v. Barry*, 485 U.S. 312, 315 (1988); *Boos v. Barry*, Brief for Petitioner at *74, *64 (1987 U.S. S. Ct. Briefs LEXIS 417).

Chapter 3. The Emergence of Association in the National Security Era

1. Shortly after the September 11, 2001, terrorist attacks, concerns over additional acts of domestic terrorism prompted then deputy assistant attorney general John Yoo to advise the White House and Department of Defense that "First Amendment speech and press rights may also be subordinated to the overriding need to wage war successfully." See John Yoo, "Authority for Use of Military Force to Combat Terrorist Activities within the United States," October 23, 2001, 24.

2. Formed at the urging of Congressman Martin Dies of Texas, the investigative body was popularly known as the "Dies Committee" from 1938 to 1945. From 1945 to 1957, the House Committee on Un-American Activities (HUAC) conducted more than 230 public hearings and examined more than three thousand witnesses, 135 of whom were cited for contempt. See Carl Beck, *Contempt of Congress: A Study of the Prosecutions Initiated by the Committee on Un-American Activities, 1945–1957* (New Orleans: Hauser Press, 1959), 181. See generally Thomas Emerson and David Helfeld, "Loyalty among Government Employees," 58 *Yale Law Journal* 1, 8–19 (1948) (discussing the development of federal government's loyalty program); *To Secure These Rights: The Report of the President's Committee on Civil Rights* (New York: Simon and Schuster, 1947), 50.

3. Samuel Walker, *In Defense of American Liberties: A History of the ACLU* (New York: Oxford University Press, 1990), 176 (quoting Executive Order 9835, March 22, 1947). By 1951, the FBI had initiated fourteen thousand full-scale investigations of federal employees, which had led to more than two thousand resignations. Melvin Urofsky, *Felix Frankfurter: Judicial Restraint and Individual Liberties* (Boston: Twayne, 1991), 107. The loyalty determination standard is taken from Executive Order 9835, March 22, 1947. Clark's response is reported in Emerson and Helfeld, "Loyalty among Government Employees," 32. The story of the Attorney General's List of Subversive Organizations (AGLOSO) is chronicled in Robert Justin Goldstein, *American Blacklist: The Attorney General's List of Subversive Organizations* (Lawrence: University of Kansas Press, 2008), 64. By 1955, the list included almost three hundred organizations. Ibid., 62. The AGLOSO designation was "usually a kiss of death to an organization." Ibid. (quoting Ellen Schrecker, *The Age of McCarthyism* (Boston: Bedford, 2002), 47).

4. Emerson and Helfeld, "Loyalty among Government Employees," 70, 79, 81, 83. Emerson and Helfeld's article drew a fiery response from J. Edgar Hoover, whose comments were printed in the next issue of the journal.

5. Charles Wyzanski Jr., "The Open Window and the Open Door: An Inquiry into Freedom of Association," 35 *California Law Review* 336, 336–37, 338, 346 (1947). Roosevelt appointed Wyzanski to the federal bench in 1941. He served in that capacity for forty-five years, presided over the Harvard University Board of Overseers, and served as a trustee of the Ford Foundation. Eric Pace, "Charles E. Wyzanski, 80, is Dead," *New York Times*, September 5, 1986, A20. Frankfurter had mentored Wyzanski at Harvard and called him "one of the most brilliant students I ever had." Ibid.

6. Victor Navasky, *Naming Names* (New York: Viking Press, 1980), 80, 83. Hollywood executives issued the "Waldorf-Astoria Policy Statement," which announced that producers would "not knowingly employ a Communist." Harold Horowitz, "Loyalty Tests for Employment in the Motion Picture Industry," 6 *Stanford Law Review* 443 (1954). The *New York Times* called the statement "an action unprecedented in American industrial fields." Ibid.

7. Lucas A. Powe, *The Warren Court and American Politics* (Cambridge, Mass.: Belknap Press of Harvard University Press, 2002), 77–78.

8. Powe, *The Warren Court and American Politics,* 15. The McCarran Internal Security Act, 50 U.S.C. § 781, et seq. (1950), was also known as the Subversive Activities Control Act of 1950. Registered individuals were denied employment in government, defense, and labor unions. Powe, *The Warren Court and American Politics,* 77; Walker, *In Defense of American Liberties,* 198. Truman's veto is mentioned in Geoffrey R. Stone, *Perilous Times: Free Speech in Wartime* (New York: Norton, 2004), 313.

9. *American Communications Association v. Douds,* 339 U.S. 382, 388 (1950). The statutory language is found in 61 Stat. 136, 146, 29 U. S. C. (Supp. III) § 141, § 159 (h), amending National Labor Relations Act of 1935, 49 Stat. 449, 29 U. S. C. § 151 et seq. I rely on *Douds* advisedly, as the case involves a labor union in the context of a statutory regulatory scheme. In the context of this narrative, it is most helpful for its rhetorical use of assembly rather than as marking the outer boundaries of autonomy for labor unions. See, e.g., ibid., 399 (recognizing "the high place in which the right to speak, think, and assemble as you will was held by the Framers of the Bill of Rights and is held today by those who value liberty both as a means and an end").

10. *Dennis v. United States,* 341 U.S. 494 (1951); Walker, *In Defense of American Liberties,* 187 (quoting Baldwin); Martin H. Redish, *The Logic of Persecution: Free Expression and the McCarthy Era* (Stanford: Stanford University Press, 2005), 81–83, 87. Redish calls *Dennis* "one of the most troubling free speech decisions ever handed down by the United States Supreme Court." Ibid., 81.

11. *Dennis v. United States,* 507, 511; Milton R. Konvitz, *Fundamental Liberties of a Free People: Religion, Speech, Press, Assembly* (Ithaca: Cornell University Press, 1957), 307; *Dennis v. United States,* 581 (Black, J., dissenting); Allida M. Black, *Casting Her Own Shadow: Eleanor Roosevelt and the Shaping of Postwar Liberalism* (New York: Columbia University Press, 1996), 154, 155. Black reports that "the furor [Roosevelt's] stance generated cut into her lecture tour and deprived her of income she needed." Ibid.

12. Michal R. Belknap, *Cold War Political Justice: The Smith Act, the Communist Party, and American Civil Liberties* (Westport, Conn.: Greenwood Press, 1977), 156, 157; Fred Jerome, *The Einstein File: J. Edgar Hoover's Secret War against the World's Most Famous Scientist* (New York: St. Martin's Press, 2002), 238–39, 246, 247. McCarthy labeled Einstein "an enemy of America." Ibid., 240. Einstein also advised that educators refuse to answer questions about association based on First Amendment rights of "free speech and free association." *New York Times,* "Balky Teacher Cites Dr. Einstein's Advice," December 19, 1953. Einstein remained inflamed by the rampant McCarthyism. A few months before his death, he wrote: "If I were a young man again . . . I would not try to become a scientist or teacher, I would rather choose to be a plumber or a peddler, in the hope of finding that modest degree of independence still available under present circumstances." Jerome, *The Einstein File,* 355.

13. Belknap, *Cold War Political Justice,* 157–58 (Belknap writes that "juries ground out Smith Act convictions with monotonous regularity." Ibid., 157); *Adler v. Board of Education,* 342 U.S. 485, 489–90, 493 (1952). Black, Douglas, and Frankfurter filed separate dissents.

Black protested the Court's endorsement of a law "which effectively penalizes school teachers for their thoughts and their associates." Ibid., 497 (Black, J., dissenting). Douglas refused to accept "the recent doctrine that a citizen who enters the public service can be forced to sacrifice his civil rights." Ibid., 508 (Douglas, J., dissenting). Frankfurter's lengthy dissent rested largely on procedural grounds. Ibid., 497 (Frankfurter, J., dissenting).

14. *Wieman v. Updegraff,* 344 U.S. 183, 186, 191 (1952).

15. *Wieman v. Updegraff,* 195 (Frankfurter, J., concurring) (citation omitted). The Court had mentioned a "freedom of association" in *Douds.* See 339 U.S. at 409 ("the effect of [a] statute in proscribing beliefs—like its effect in restraining speech or freedom of association—must be carefully weighed by the courts in determining whether the balance struck by Congress comports with the dictates of the Constitution"). Its only mention of a right of association prior to *Douds* had been a passing reference to "the rights of free speech, assembly, and association" in *Whitney v. California,* 274 U.S. 357, 371 (1927); Thomas I. Emerson and David Haber, *Political and Civil Rights in the United States* (Buffalo: Dennis, 1952), 248. Emerson and Haber wrote: "It is generally accepted that the rights in the First Amendment to freedom of speech, press and assembly, and to petition the government for redress of grievances, taken in combination, establish a broader guarantee to the right of political association." Ibid.

16. Powe, *The Warren Court and American Politics,* 90 ("most important jurist"). At a 1972 memorial service for Harlan, Justice Stewart quipped: "I can assure you that a very interesting law review article could someday be written on 'The Liberal Opinions of Mr. Justice Harlan.'" Norman Dorsen, "John Marshall Harlan," in *The Warren Court: A Retrospective,* ed. Bernard Schwartz (New York: Oxford University Press, 1996), 241. The "McCarthyite garbage" reference comes from Tinsley E. Yarbrough, *John Marshall Harlan: Great Dissenter of the Warren Court* (New York: Oxford University Press, 1992), 338 (quoting Charles Fried). Frankfurter also "privately deplored the excesses of McCarthyism and the witch-hunts conducted in the name of national security," and "risked personal opprobrium in his defense of some of the accused." Melvin I. Urofsky, *Felix Frankfurter: Judicial Restraint and Individual Liberties* (New York: Twayne, 1991), 105.

17. *Poe v. Ullman,* 367 U.S. 497, 542–43 (1961) (Harlan, J., dissenting).

18. *Service v. Dulles,* 354 U.S. 363 (1957); *Watkins v. United States,* 354 U.S. 178 (1957); *Yates v. United States,* 354 U.S. 298, 318–20 (1957). On the effect of *Yates* on Smith Act prosecutions, see Walker, *In Defense of American Liberties,* 243 (*Yates* "halted further Smith Act prosecutions"); Yarbrough, *John Marshall Harlan,* 191 ("Following [*Yates*], Smith Act prosecutions were drastically curtailed, then abandoned entirely."). Following the decisions, outraged conservatives in the Senate led by William Jenner of Indiana introduced a "court-stripping" bill to deprive the Court of certain subject matter jurisdiction.

19. *Sweezy v. New Hampshire,* 354 U.S. 234 (1957) (plurality opinion); N.H. Rev. Stat. Ann.1955, c. 588, §§ 1–16 (New Hampshire Subversive Activities Act of 1951); *Wyman v. Sweezy,* 100 N. H. 103, 113 (N.H. 1956). *Sweezy v. New Hampshire,* 247. Warren paid particular attention to Sweezy's role as a university professor, noting that "scholarship cannot

flourish in an atmosphere of suspicion and distrust" and "teachers and students must always remain free to inquire, to study and to evaluate, to gain new maturity and understanding; otherwise our civilization will stagnate and die." Ibid., 250.

20. *Sweezy v. New Hampshire,* Jurisdictional Statement of Appellant, filed June 19, 1956 ("Jurisdictional Statement"), 27, 4, 19. These arguments weren't at issue in *Scales, Watkins,* and *Dulles,* all of which involved federal rather than state action.

21. See *Barron v. Mayor and City Council of City of Baltimore,* 32 U.S. 243 (1833); *United States Constitution,* Amendment XIV. This clause restricted state action that deprived "liberty" without due process, but it remained to be seen what exactly that encompassed. Soon after passage of the Fourteenth Amendment, the Court focused on a different provision of the Bill of Rights, the Privileges and Immunities Clause. In the *Slaughter-House Cases,* 16 Wall. (83 U.S.) 36 (1873), the Court intimated that the Bill of Rights might be applicable to the states through the Fourteenth Amendment as "privileges and immunities" of citizenship. This is the theory that Justice Roberts relied upon to hold the freedom of assembly applicable to Mayor Hague's actions in *Hague v. Committee for Industrial Organization,* 307 U.S. 496 (1939). But besides *Hague,* the Court has usually cited the Due Process Clause rather than the Privileges and Immunities Clause in applying the rights of the First Amendment to state action.

22. *Prudential Ins. Co. v. Cheek,* 259 U.S. 530, 543 (1922); *Gitlow v. New York,* 268 U.S. 652, 666 (1925); *De Jonge v. Oregon,* 299 U.S. 353 (1937).

23. *Palko v. Connecticut,* 302 U.S. 319, 324–26 (1937). Cardozo continued: "These, in their origin, were effective against the federal government alone. If the Fourteenth Amendment has absorbed them, the process of absorption has had its source in the belief that neither liberty nor Justice would exist if they were sacrificed." Ibid., 325 (citations omitted). Later that year, Chief Justice Hughes reached a similar conclusion about the right of assembly in *De Jonge v. Oregon:* "The First Amendment of the Federal Constitution expressly guarantees [the right of assembly] against abridgment by Congress. But explicit mention there does not argue exclusion elsewhere. For the right is one that cannot be denied without violating those fundamental principles of liberty and justice which lie at the base of all civil and political institutions—principles which the Fourteenth Amendment embodies in the general terms of its due process clause." *De Jonge v. Oregon,* 364.

24. *Murdock v. Pennsylvania,* 319 U. S. 105, 108 (1943); *Everson v. Board of Education,* 330 U.S. 1, 8 (1947); *Wolf v. Colorado,* 338 U.S. 25, 26 (1949). Black concurred and Douglas dissented, arguing that entirety of Fourth Amendment applied to the states.

25. *Murdock v. Pennsylvania,* 108 (Rutledge had used the same language with respect to the freedom of assembly in *Thomas v. Collins,* 530–31). Black and Douglas didn't share the exact same views about incorporation. Douglas joined Black's dissent in *Adamson v. California,* which argued that the Fourteenth Amendment had incorporated *all* of the civil liberties provisions of the Bill of Rights. *Adamson v. California,* 332 U. S. 46, 71–72 (1947) (Black, J., dissenting). But elsewhere Douglas backed away from Black's "total incorporation" theory; *Kovacs v. Cooper,* 336 U.S. 77, 90, 95–96 (1949) (Frankfurter, J., concurring);

West Virginia State Board of Education v. Barnette, 319 U.S. 624, 639 (1943). There were, of course, phrasings ambiguous enough to be consistent with both alternatives. See, e.g., *Staub v. City of Baxley*, 355 U.S. 313, 325 (1958) (the "fundamental right [of speech] is made free from congressional abridgment by the First Amendment and is protected by the Fourteenth from invasion by state action").

26. See *Griswold v. Connecticut*, 381 U.S. 479, 484 (1965).

27. *Sweezy v. New Hampshire*, 250; ibid., 255–56, 266–67 (Frankfurter, J., concurring). Justice Clark's dissent erroneously concluded that Frankfurter concurred "on the ground that Sweezy's rights under the First Amendment had been violated." Ibid., 268 (Clark, J., dissenting).

28. Powe, *The Warren Court and American Politics*, 35 (quoting *Brown v. Board of Education*, Amicus Brief of the United States of America); ibid. (quoting *New York Times*, May 18, 1954, 19); "Equal Education for All," *Washington Post*, May 19, 1954, 19. See generally, Mary L. Dudziak, "*Brown* as a Cold War Case," 91 *Journal of American History* 32 (2004).

29. Jeff Woods, *Black Struggle, Red Scare: Segregation and Anti-Communism in the South, 1948–1968* (Baton Rouge: Louisiana State University Press, 2004), 49 (citing Aldon D. Morris, *The Origins of the Civil Rights Movement: Black Communities Organizing for Change* (New York: Free Press, 1984), 26–33); Charles H. Martin, *The Angelo Herndon Case and Southern Justice* (Baton Rouge: Louisiana State University Press, 1976), xii; Woods, *Black Struggle, Red Scare*, 5, 53. Neil McMillen asserts that "the region had virtually no Communists." Neil R. McMillen, *The Citizens' Council: Organized Resistance to the Second Reconstruction, 1954–64* (Urbana: University of Illinois Press, 1971), 193. But see *Gibson v. Florida Legislative Investigation Committee*, 372 U.S. 539, 580 (1963) (Harlan, J., dissenting) ("it is not amiss to recall that government evidence in Smith Act prosecutions has shown that the sensitive area of race relations has long been a prime target of Communist efforts at infiltration"). In 1950, the NAACP adopted an "anti-communism" resolution that acknowledged that "certain branches of the National Association for the Advancement of Colored People are being rocked by internal conflicts between groups who follow the Communist line and those who do not, which threaten to destroy the confidence of the public in the Association and which will inevitably result in its eventual disruption" and "there is a well organized, nationwide conspiracy by Communists either to capture or split and wreck the NAACP." Ibid., 580, 581 (quoting Statement from Forty-First Convention of the National Association for the Advancement of Colored People).

30. Powe, *The Warren Court and American Politics*, 42 (Powe writes that the footnote "reduced both the legal and moral force" of the opinion. Ibid., 44); ibid., 39; McMillen, *The Citizens' Council*, 195 (Eastland followed this argument with a frontal assault in a publication called "Is the Supreme Court Pro-Communist?" Ibid., 195–96. Another segregationist, Medford Evans, wrote that "forced integration is communism in action." Ibid., 197); Woods, *Black Struggle, Red Scare*, 5; Powe, *The Warren Court and American Politics*, 68; McMillen, *The Citizens' Council*, 198. Brady told one council gathering that the NAACP "was a willing and ready tool in the hands of Communist front organizations." *NAACP v. Alabama*, Brief

Supporting Petition for Certiorari ("NAACP Cert Brief"), 21 n.20 (citing Brady comments made on June 22, 1955). He was careful to make a clear distinction between the councils and the "nefarious Ku Klux Klans." McMillen, *The Citizens' Council*, 18.

31. Powe, *The Warren Court and American Politics*, 68; NAACP Cert Brief at 20 (quoting *Southern School News*, vol. 1, no. 5: 2); Powe, *The Warren Court and American Politics*, 68, 165.

32. Powe, *The Warren Court and American Politics*, 165 (quoting Mark Tushnet, *Making Civil Rights Law: Thurgood Marshall and the Supreme Court, 1936–1961* (New York: Oxford University Press, 1994), 283).

33. *NAACP v. Alabama*, Petition for Certiorari, 17, 18; Petitioner's Brief, 21, 22, 24; Respondent's Brief, 2. Alabama insisted that the only harm articulated by the NAACP and its members was "the mere speculation of injury by private persons to its members." Ibid., 12. Citing *United States v. Cruikshank*, 92 U.S. 542 (1875), the state contended that "private action is not state action" and did not constitute a violation of constitutional rights. Ibid.

34. *NAACP v. Alabama*, Amicus Brief of American Jewish Congress et al. ("Pfeffer Amicus Brief"), October 3, 1957; *NAACP v. Alabama*, 355 U.S. 860 (1957) (denying motion for leave to file amicus brief); Leo Pfeffer, *The Liberties of an American: The Supreme Court Speaks* (Boston: Beacon Press, 1956), 111.

35. Pffefer Amicus Brief, 8, 10–11, 15.

36. *NAACP v. Alabama*, January 15, 1958 Oral Argument Tr. at 32:15; *NAACP v. Alabama*, January 16, 1958, Oral Argument Tr. at 51:30–1:01:20. Rinehart instead challenged the NAACP's attempt to assert the right as a corporation or on behalf of its members. He argued that *Watkins* and *Sweezy* had addressed assertions of individual rights, not the rights of a group. He intimated only once that the state could constrain an individual right of association, arguing unconvincingly that a member of the NAACP asked during a hearing to confirm his membership would be required to make such a disclosure. Ibid., 1:00:20–1:01:13. Rinehart also argued vehemently that the right of association wasn't implicated, because the case involved no state action: any adverse treatment following disclosure of membership in the NAACP would come from private persons or businesses, not the state. Ibid. For good measure, Rinehart implausibly contended that the possibility of these private actions was "pure speculation." Ibid., 55:00.

37. Yarbrough, *John Marshall Harlan*, 161 (quoting John M. Harlan, Memorandum for the Conference, April 22, 1958, Harlan Papers, Box 495).

38. *NAACP v. Alabama*, 461; *De Jonge v. Oregon*, 353; *Thomas v. Collins*, 516; *NAACP v. Alabama*, 460; *De Jonge v. Oregon*, 364 and *Thomas v. Collins*, 528 n.12; *NAACP v. Alabama*, 460 (citing *American Communications Association v. Douds*, 339 U.S. 382, 402 (1950)).

39. *NAACP v. Alabama*, 460, 462, 463, 466; Thomas I. Emerson, "Freedom of Association and Freedom of Expression," 74 *Yale Law Journal* 2 (1964); George P. Smith, "The Development of the Right of Assembly: A Current Socio-Legal Investigation," 9 *William and Mary Law Review* 366 (1967). See also David Fellman, *The Constitutional Right of Association* (Chicago: University of Chicago Press, 1963), 3 ("The broader rights of association have developed, in part, out of the right of assembly, and in part out of broader due

process concepts."); Melvin Rishe, "Freedom of Assembly," 15 *DePaul Law Review* 317 (1965) ("To refer to [association] as a new freedom would be amiss for it is only a further development of the freedom of assembly so plainly stated in the first amendment."). But see Andrew Koppelman with Tobias Barrington Wolff, *A Right to Discriminate? How the Case of* Boy Scouts of America v. James Dale *Warped the Law of Free Association* (New Haven: Yale University Press, 2009), 17, 18 (asserting that "*NAACP v. Alabama* made clear that freedom of association was firmly rooted in the First Amendment" and describing the right of association as a "speech-based right").

40. Yarbrough, *John Marshall Harlan*, 125 (quoting *NAACP v. Alabama*, Harlan opinion draft, Harlan Papers, Box 533); ibid. (quoting Felix Frankfurter to John M. Harlan, April 23, 1958, Harlan Papers, Box 46). The justices realized that "unanimity was considered crucial in racial cases." Ibid., 162. Yarbrough cites letters from Erwin Griswold and Edward Corwin congratulating Harlan on the opinion. Ibid., 165 n.35 (citing Erwin Griswold to John M. Harlan, July 8, 1958, Harlan Papers, Box 538; Edward S. Corwin to John M. Harlan, July 7, 1958, Harlan Papers, Box 511).

41. William O. Douglas, *The Douglas Letters: Selections from the Private Papers of Justice William O. Douglas,* ed. Melvin I. Urofsky (Bethesda: Adler and Adler, 1987), 198 (quoting William O. Douglas to John Marshall Harlan, April 22, 1958). Dissenting from an opinion handed down the same day as *NAACP v. Alabama,* Douglas wrote that the liberties contained in the First Amendment include "the right to believe what one chooses, the right to differ from his neighbor, the right to pick and choose the political philosophy that he likes best, the right to associate with whomever he chooses, the right to join the groups he prefers, the privilege of selecting his own path to salvation." *Beilan v. Board of Public Education,* 357 U.S. 399, 412–13 (1958) (Douglas, J., dissenting).

42. Yarbrough, *John Marshall Harlan*, 126–27; 126 (quoting Hugo L. Black to John M. Harlan, May 2, 1958, Harlan Papers, Box 46); 162. Clark threatened to dissent on procedural grounds, but Frankfurter persuaded him to join the majority on the merits. Ibid., 162, 163.

43. *Bryant v. Zimmerman,* 278 U.S. 63, 72 (1928); *NAACP v. Alabama,* 465–66. Harlan also attempted a less plausible distinction, noting that "the situation before us is significantly different from that in *Bryant,* because the organization there had made no effort to comply with any of the requirements of New York's statute but rather had refused to furnish the State with any information as to its local activities." Ibid., 465–66.

44. "Freedom of Association," *Washington Post,* July 3, 1958, A12 (emphasis added); "Freedom to Associate," *New York Times,* July 2, 1958, 28. The *Ohio State Law Journal* tied the new freedom of association to the freedom of assembly and suggested that the decision reinforced that "first amendment rights occupy a high position in the hierarchy of constitutional freedoms and may be limited only when the state has a compelling interest." Frank M. Hays, "State May Not Compel Association to Disclose Names of Members," 20 *Ohio State Law Journal* 123, 124–25, 124 n.8 (1959). Cf. ibid., 126 (the Court followed "quite closely its previous holdings in the area of free speech and assembly").

The *Brooklyn Law Review* concluded that the freedom of association, although not mentioned in the First Amendment, was "included therein." "Freedom of Association—Right to Privacy," 25 *Brooklyn Law Review* 123 (1985). The *George Washington Law Review* suggested that "the new freedom of association is a cognate of . . . first amendment freedoms and enjoys coordinately their preferred status." Myron Solter, "Freedom of Association—A New and Fundamental Civil Right," 27 *George Washington Law Review* 653, 672 (1959). The *Harvard Law Review*'s summary of *Alabama* noted that the holding rested on "freedom of association" but did not elaborate on the nature or source of that freedom. "Disclosure of Membership Lists," 72 *Harvard Law Review* 193, 194 (1958).

45. *Uphaus v. Wyman,* 360 U.S. 72 (1959); *Barenblatt v. United States,* 360 U.S. 109 (1959); Anthony Lewis, "High Court Term a Significant One," *New York Times,* July 6, 1958, 29. It is important to keep in mind that the Supreme Court's application of the new right of association in communist cases came after the height of McCarthyism. See generally, Goldstein, *American Blacklist,* 205 (noting the Senate's censure of McCarthy in late 1954 and emphasizing that by 1955, the government's loyalty program had come "under increasingly withering and sustained attack from broad sectors of American society.").

46. *Uphaus v. Wyman,* 77, 81; ibid., 82, 103 (Brennan, J., dissenting). Brennan wrote: "The Court describes the inquiry we must make in this matter as a balancing of interests. I think I have indicated that there has been no valid legislative interest of the State actually defined and shown in the investigation as it operated, so that there is really nothing against which the appellant's rights of association and expression can be balanced." Ibid., 106. Brennan's dissent conflated speech, expression, assembly, association, and privacy, referring at times to the "rights of association and expression," ibid., 106, and "the interest in privacy as it relates to freedom of speech and assembly." Ibid., 107–8. But he made his most frequent appeals to the constitutional rights of "speech and assembly." Ibid., 82, 83, 97, 105, 106, 107–8. Black, Douglas, and Warren joined Brennan's dissent.

47. Compare United States Constitution, Amendment I ("Congress shall make no law . . .") with Amendment V (forbidding the deprivation of "liberty . . . without due process of law" by the federal government). The right of association couldn't be applied to the federal government through the Due Process Clause of the Fourteenth Amendment because that provision applied only to "States"; *Barenblatt,* 126. See also ibid. ("Undeniably, the First Amendment in some circumstances protects an individual from being compelled to disclose his associational relationships."). Harlan's conclusion that the right of association limiting the federal government was found in the First Amendment is not inconsistent with his view that the right of association limiting state action was in the Fourteenth Amendment. That was, in essence, how he viewed rights specifically enumerated in the First Amendment.

48. *Barenblatt,* 113–14; Yarbrough, *John Marshall Harlan,* 201 (quoting Frankfurter); *Barenblatt,* 125.

49. Yarbrough, *John Marshall Harlan,* 202 (quoting Felix Frankfurter to John M. Harlan, June 3, 1959); *Barenblatt,* 120.

50. Powe, *The Warren Court and American Politics*, 144; *Barenblatt*, 134; ibid., 143 (Black, J., dissenting) (Douglas and Warren joined Black's dissent, and Brennan dissented separately); ibid., 150–51. Black rested his dissent on the First Amendment rights of speech and association.

51. *Barenblatt*, 127; *Uphaus*, 78, 77.

52. *Bates v. Little Rock*, 361 U.S. 516, 522–23 (1960); ibid., 527–28 (Black and Douglas, JJ., concurring) (emphasis added). On the intent of the ordinances, see Joseph B. Robison, "Protection of Associations from Compulsory Disclosure of Membership," 58 *Columbia Law Review* 614 (1958). Similar statutory efforts unfolded in Virginia, Texas, and Tennessee. Ibid., 616. Louisiana attacked the NAACP through an existing state law that had originally been drafted against the Ku Klux Klan. A note in the *Virginia Law Review* published after *Bates* suggested that "the concept of 'freedom of association' illustrates the development of a judicial technique" for dealing with the particular kind of situation at issue in *NAACP v. Alabama* and *Bates* rather than "an enunciation of an independent constitutional right." Peter R. Fisher, "Freedom of Association: Constitutional Right or Judicial Technique?" 46 *Virginia Law Review* 730 (1960).

53. *Shelton v. Tucker*, 364 U.S. 479, 486 (1960); ibid., 496 (Harlan, J., dissenting) (citations omitted). B. T. Shelton had refused to file the affidavit due to his membership in the NAACP. Ibid., 483. He had originally challenged both the affidavit requirement and a separate Arkansas statue making it unlawful for any member of the NAACP to be employed by the state of Arkansas. Ibid., 484 n.2.

54. *Louisiana ex rel. Gremillion v. NAACP*, 366 U.S. 293, 294, 296, 297 (1961).

55. Walker, *In Defense of American Liberties*, 241. Membership in the NAACP in the South had fallen from 128,000 in 1955 to 80,000 in 1957, and almost 250 branches had closed. Michael J. Klarman, *From Jim Crow to Civil Rights: The Supreme Court and the Struggle for Racial Equality* (New York: Oxford University Press, 2004), 383. In Louisiana, membership plummeted from 13,000 to 1,700, and in South Carolina it fell from 8,200 to 2,000. Ibid. The litigation that led to *NAACP v. Alabama* effectively shut down the NAACP in that state from the time of the 1956 injunction until the case was finally resolved in 1964 (following additional litigation after the Supreme Court's decision). Ibid. On the demise of the communist party, see generally Robert Justin Goldstein, *Political Repression in Modern America: From 1870 to the Present* (Cambridge, Mass.: Schenkman, 1978), 369 ("The most dramatic and easily documentable effect of the Truman-McCarthy period was the virtual annihilation of the Communist Party.").

56. *Communist Party v. Subversive Activities Control Board*, 367 U.S. 1, 93 (1961) ("*SACB*"); Harry Kalven Jr., *A Worthy Tradition: Freedom of Speech in America* (New York: Harper and Row, 1988), 264. Kalven contends that the 212 pages of opinions by the justices and the belief that the case involved legislation limited in scope to the Communist Party has led the decision to be "treated as outside the mainstream of First Amendment precedent." Ibid. He argues that despite its verbosity, *SACB* "is quite possibly the precedent which carries the greatest threat to political freedoms in the future" and deserves a "central

place" in First Amendment case law. Ibid. Frankfurter entitled a section of his opinion "The Freedoms of Expression and Association Protected by the First Amendment." *SACB*, 88. He asserted that "the power of Congress to regulate Communist organizations [subject to foreign control] is extensive," but that power was "limited by the First Amendment." Ibid., 95, 96. Frankfurter concluded that the act's registration provisions were "not repugnant to the First Amendment," and that certain accounting provisions did not violate "First Amendment rights." Ibid., 103. Douglas's dissent noted that "[f]reedom of association is included in the bundle of First Amendment rights[.]" Ibid., 171 (Douglas, J., dissenting) (citing *NAACP v. Alabama*, 460). Brennan's partial dissent referred to "the rights of freedom of advocacy and association guaranteed by the First Amendment." Ibid., 191 (Brennan, J., dissenting in part). Warren joined Brennan's partial dissent. Black's dissent never explicitly referenced a "First Amendment right of association," but his opinion made clear that he accepted the First Amendment argument. See, e.g., ibid., 148 (Black, J., dissenting) ("The freedom to advocate ideas about public matters through associations of the nature of political parties and societies was contemplated and protected by the First Amendment."). Although *SACB* suggested that all nine justices accepted that the right of association applied against the federal government came from the First Amendment, the source of the right of association constraining state action remained unclear.

57. *Scales v. United States*, 367 U.S. 203 (1961). The Court also issued its opinion in *Noto v. United States*, 367 U.S. 290 (1961), which unanimously reversed a conviction under the Smith Act's membership clause. But *Noto* relied exclusively on a sufficiency of the evidence analysis. Ibid., 291 ("The only one of petitioner's points we need consider is his attack on the sufficiency of the evidence, since his statutory and constitutional challenges to the conviction are disposed of by our opinion in *Scales*, and consideration of his other contentions is rendered unnecessary by the view we take of his evidentiary challenge.").

58. Walker, *In Defense of American Liberties*, 240; Kalven, *A Worthy Tradition*, 259. Cf. Walker, *In Defense of American Liberties*, 240 (referring to "a double standard for political groups").

59. See Yarbrough, *John Marshall Harlan*, 339 (noting Harlan's "reluctance as a Justice to second-guess the judgments of government officials regarding national security matters"); ibid., 212; ibid. (quoting Brennan Papers, Box 407).

60. Powe, *The Warren Court and American Politics*, 155.

61. Yarbrough, *John Marshall Harlan*, 210; Powe, *The Warren Court and American Politics*, 155; Yarbrough, *John Marshall Harlan*, 210.

62. Powe, *The Warren Court and American Politics*, 156; *Gibson v. Florida Legislative Investigation Committee*, 372 U.S. 539 (1963); Walker, *In Defense of American Liberties*, 241. Powe writes that Goldberg was "looking for a way to protect the NAACP without having to overrule all the legislative-investigation cases." Powe, *The Warren Court and American Politics*, 221. Harlan's dissent argued that the Court's decision forced the legislative committee "to prove in advance the very things it is trying to find out." *Gibson*, 576 (Harlan, J., dissenting). Cf. Milton R.

Konvitz, *Expanding Liberties: The Emergence of New Civil Liberties and Civil Rights in Postwar America* (New York: Viking Press, 1967), 109 ("if Alabama or Arkansas or Florida or Louisiana had won in the Court, a way would have opened for the South to paralyze the N.A.A.C.P. and any other civil rights or civil liberties organization; and since the Bill of Rights is not self-executing, but is dependent upon vindication through litigation, the struggle for freedom and equality would have been effectively arrested."). The Court acknowledged its attenuated application of the right of association in communist cases in *Keyishian v. Board of Regents*, 385 U.S. 589 (1967). Justice Clark's dissent, joined by Harlan, Stewart, and White, lamented that "the majority has, by its broadside, swept away one of our most precious rights, namely, the right of self-preservation." Ibid., 620 (Clark, J., dissenting).

63. *Gibson*, 559 (Black, J., concurring); ibid., 560 n.2, 562–63, 569–570 (Douglas, J., concurring). Douglas reiterated his arguments for association (some of which were taken verbatim from his *Gibson* concurrence) in a lecture that he delivered at Brown University and subsequently published in the *Columbia Law Review*. See William O. Douglas, "The Right of Association," 63 *Columbia Law Review* 1361 (1963). Harlan's dissent in *Gibson* (joined by Clark, Stewart, and White) ignored Douglas's attacks on the liberty argument for association.

64. Glenn Abernathy, *The Right of Assembly and Association* (Columbia: University of South Carolina Press, 1961); Charles E. Rice, *Freedom of Association* (New York: New York University Press, 1962); David Fellman, *The Constitutional Right of Association* (Chicago: University of Chicago Press, 1963); Rice, *Freedom of Association*, xvii–xviii; Carl Beck, *Contempt of Congress: A Study of the Prosecutions Initiated by the Committee on Un-American Activities, 1945–1957* (New Orleans: Hauser Press, 1959), viii.

65. Glenn Abernathy, "The Right of Association," 6 *South Carolina Law Quarterly* 32, 33–34, 72, 75–77 (1953).

66. Abernathy, *The Right of Assembly and Association*, 240.

67. Abernathy, *The Right of Assembly and Association*, 4, 173, 236–37 (emphasis added), 237. The right of assembly, of course, requires judgment by limiting its protections to groups that don't pose a threat of imminent harm to the state. That judgment is a subjective political one made by the state. But the right of association also includes this political judgment *and* other subjective assessments like the one that Abernathy identified.

68. Emerson, "Freedom of Association and Freedom of Expression," 2, 3.

69. On my reading, postwar pluralists like Dahl and Truman exhibit both the balance and the consensus assumptions, but these are sometimes split between "interest group pluralists" and "consensus thinkers," respectively. See, e.g., Morton J. Horwitz, *The Transformation of American Law, 1870–1960: The Crisis of Legal Orthodoxy* (New York: Oxford University Press, 1992), 251. Horwitz acknowledges that "in some formulations, in fact, both consensus and equilibrium theories might converge, as the interest group pluralists conceded that what underlay the substantive conflict over ends was a more fundamental agreement about process." Ibid. See also ibid., 257 (describing the "close relationship

between interest group pluralist theories of politics modeled on equilibrium theories in economics and consensus theories that sought to find fundamental agreement over ends and values").

70. Alexis de Tocqueville, *Democracy in America,* trans. Henry Reeve (New York: D. Appleton, 1899); James Madison, "*Federalist* No. 10," in *The Federalist,* ed. Benjamin F. Wright (New York: Barnes and Noble, 2004).

71. John Gunnell, "The Genealogy of American Pluralism: From Madison to Behavioralism," 3 *International Political Science Review* 254, 256 (1996). For a more detailed account of Lieber's role, see John Gunnell, *Descent of Political Theory* (Chicago: University of Chicago Press, 1993), 24–32. Gunnell writes that Lieber's *Manual of Political Ethics* sought "to distinguish the state from the family, the church, and other social entities and to establish the primacy of the state." Ibid., 28. By the 1880s, the theory of the state was "a distinct and influential paradigm" in American political thought. Ibid., 36. The primacy of the state in classical liberalism is evident in Hobbes's *Leviathan* but also in Locke's more familiar liberal thought. Even when Locke discusses a freedom of religious association in his *Letter Concerning Toleration,* he makes clear that when minority practices collide with majority will, the latter prevails. See John Locke, *A Letter Concerning Toleration* (Indianapolis: Hackett, 1983 (1689)), 49 ("No opinions contrary to human Society, or to those moral Rules which are necessary to the preservation of Civil Society, are to be tolerated by the Magistrate.").

72. Arthur Bentley, *The Process of Government* (Chicago: University of Chicago Press, 1908), xxxiv, 258–59 (original emphasis), 208–9. Bentley doesn't develop the concept of "balance" to the degree of later pluralists. He describes law as "the pressures being assumed to have worked themselves through to a conclusion or balance" but notes that "the pressures never do as a matter of fact work themselves through to a final balance, and law, stated as a completed balance, is therefore highly abstract." Ibid., 272. On the demise of German idealism, see Gunnell, *The Genealogy of American Pluralism,* 254.

73. Earl Latham, "The Group Basis of Politics: Notes for a Theory," 46 *American Political Science Review* 379 (1952) (describing Laski's views); Herbert H. Deane, *The Political Ideas of Harold J. Laski* (New York: Columbia University Press, 1955), 13; Harold Laski, *Authority in the Modern State* (New Haven: Yale University Press, 1919), 65, 75–81, 384–85; Gunnell, "The Genealogy of American Pluralism," 257. Laski drew from other British pluralists, including John Figgis, Frederic Maitland, and G. D. H. Cole. Deane, *The Political Ideas of Harold J. Laski,* 17, 26–27. A separate prong of Laski's attack against the state challenged legal positivists like Bentham and Austin who maintained that the state was sovereign and that law itself was nothing more than the command of the sovereign. Ibid., 14–15. Deane writes that Laski's distrust of consolidated political power led him to desire "to see power split up, divided, set against itself, and thrown widespread among men by various devices of decentralization." Ibid., 17. Cf. Grant McConnell, *Private Power and American Democracy* (New York: Knopf, 1966), 119 ("the private association . . . has been linked with the values of decentralization and federalism. It has also been pictured as the source of stability in politics and held up as the medium of the public interest.").

74. Gunnell, "The Genealogy of American Pluralism," 260; Gunnell, *Descent of Political Theory*, 204; Gunnell, "The Genealogy of American Pluralism," 259; John Kenneth Galbraith, *American Capitalism: The Concept of Countervailing Power* (Boston: Houghton Mifflin, 1952); David Riesman, *The Lonely Crowd: A Study of the Changing American Character* (New Haven: Yale University Press, 1950), 246–51; Godfrey Hodgson, *America in Our Time* (Garden City: Doubleday, 1976), 12, quoted in Stephen M. Feldman, *American Legal Thought from Premodernism to Postmodernism: An Intellectual Voyage* (New York: Oxford University Press 2000), 119. Other important works building on Laski's pluralist concepts included *A History of Political Theories: Recent Times*, ed. Charles Meriam and Henry Elmer Barnes (New York: Macmillan, 1924), and Pendleton Herring, *Group Representation before Congress* (Baltimore: Johns Hopkins Press, 1929). Laski himself drifted away from pluralism in favor of socialism. Deane writes that by the early 1930s, Laski found "the essence of the state to be its power to enforce its norms upon all who live within its boundaries and its supremacy over all other forms of social grouping." Deane, *The Political Ideas of Harold J. Laski*, 84.

75. David Bicknell Truman, *The Governmental Process: Political Interests and Public Opinion* (New York: A. Knopf, 1951), 502, 503, 506, 514.

76. Gunnell, *Descent of Political Theory*, 221 (quoting Dahl); ibid., 265. Morton Horowitz calls Dahl's *Preface to Democratic Theory* "perhaps the most influential book of democratic theory during the post-war period." Horwitz, *The Transformation of American Law*, 256. Richard Merelman suggests that Dahl's 1956 *A Preface to Democratic Theory* and his 1970 *After the Revolution?* bookend the era of postwar pluralist dominance. Richard Merelman, *Pluralism at Yale: The Culture of Political Science in America* (Madison: University of Wisconsin Press, 2003), 17. Merelman observes that the claims that Dahl considers as "settled" in the former are "up for grabs" in the latter. Ibid., 18. On Dahl's indebtedness to Laski, see Avigail Eisenberg, *Reconstructing Political Pluralism* (Albany: State University of New York Press, 1995), 96; Robert Dahl, *Democracy, Liberty, and Equality* (New York: Oxford University Press, 1986), 281–82 n.11.

77. Robert Dahl, *Democracy in the United States: Promise and Performance* (Chicago: Rand McNally, 1972), 35; C. Wright Mills, *The Power Elite* (Oxford: Oxford University Press, 1956); Robert Dahl, *A Preface to Democratic Theory* (Chicago: University of Chicago Press, 1956), 133; Eisenberg, *Reconstructing Political Pluralism*, 141; Dahl, *A Preface to Democratic Theory*, 151. Eisenberg suggests that stability became the motivation behind Dahl's research program: "Pluralist politics did not interest Dahl because it provided the highest ideals of democracy. Rather, pluralism was prized because it stabilizes what might otherwise be an unstable and conflict-ridden environment." Eisenberg, *Reconstructing Political Pluralism*, 158.

78. Robert Dahl, *Pluralist Democracy in the United States: Conflict and Dissent* (Chicago: Rand McNally, 1967), 24; Dahl, *Democracy in the United States*, 41–42; Robert Dahl, *Modern Political Analysis* (Englewood Cliffs, N.J.: Prentice-Hall, 1963), 73.

79. Gunnell, *Descent of Political Theory*, 263. Cf. ibid., 106 (the controversy about "state and pluralism" was "in the end, one about the identity of political theory and political science"). These trends in some ways continue today, with graduate work in political science increasingly focused on mastering statistical techniques and formal modeling. Cf.

Powe, *The Warren Court and American Politics*, xii ("There was a time when political scientists had as much interest in the Court as did academic lawyers and when the major journals of political science regularly published articles in this genre. . . . Today a nonquantitative article on the Supreme Court and politics in a political science journal would stick out like an article on physics in a law journal."). See also Sheldon S. Wolin, "Political Theory as a Vocation," 63 *American Political Science Review* 1063 (1969) ("Like all technique-oriented activity, the behavioral movement presupposes that the fundamental purposes and arrangements served by its techniques have been settled and that, accordingly, it reinforces, tacitly or explicitly, those purposes and arrangements and operates according to a notion of alternatives tightly restricted by these same purposes and arrangements.").

80. Alan Brinkley, *The End of Reform: New Deal Liberalism in Recession and War* (New York: Knopf, 1995), 226, 271.

81. Bentley, *The Process of Government*, 372; Myron Hale, "The Cosmology of Arthur F. Bentley," in *The Bias of Pluralism*, ed. William Connolly (New York: Atherton Press, 1971), 45.

82. John Dewey, *Freedom and Culture* (New York: G. P. Putnam, 1939), 134, 175; Daniel Boorstin, *The Genius of American Politics* (Chicago: University of Chicago Press, 1953) (Boorstin claimed that "we all actually have a common belief, have glossed over sectarian differences in religion and produced a kind of generalized, non-denominational faith" and "this kind of faith, taken together with the lack of distinctions in our political philosophy, has tended to break down the boundaries between religious and political thought." Ibid., 162); Louis Hartz, *The Liberal Tradition in America: An Interpretation of American Political Thought Since the Revolution* (New York: Harcourt, 1955), 11 (Hartz's book began with an epigraph from *Democracy in America* and praised Tocqueville for "a series of deep insights into the American liberal community." Ibid., i, 31); Laura Kalman, *The Strange Career of Legal Liberalism* (New Haven: Yale University Press, 1996), 23 (Charles Beard's famous study is *An Economic Interpretation of the Constitution of the United States* (New York: Macmillan, 1913)); Daniel Bell, *The End of Ideology: On the Exhaustion of Political Ideas in the Fifties* (Glencoe, Ill.: Free Press, 1960) (Bell argued that the changing face of the American labor movement no longer evoked calls to Marxism or other ideologies. Ibid.).

83. Truman, *The Governmental Process*, 506, 507, 512–15, and 515 n.15. Potential groups didn't require a physical association because "[i]f the claims implied by the interests of these potential groups are quickly and adequately represented, interaction among those people who share the underlying interests or attitudes is unnecessary." Ibid., 506. The rules of the game were "dominant with sufficient frequency in the behavior of enough important segments of the society" that "both the activity and the methods of organized interest groups are kept within broad limits." Ibid., 515.

84. Truman, *The Governmental Process*, 520, 521, 523.

85. Truman, *The Governmental Process*, 513; Latham, "The Group Basis of Politics," 384. The state "establishes the norms of permissible behavior in group relations, and it enforces these norms." Ibid, 383. For Latham, this normative role of the state ultimately traced to its laws, which required "popular consent and understanding" to be effective.

Ibid., 389. With respect to "the abolition of groups," consider Robert Goldstein's observation that actual or proposed inclusion on the Attorney General's List of Subversive Organizations likely triggered the dissolution of groups that included the Abraham Lincoln School of Chicago, American Poles for Peace, the American Committee for Yugoslav Relief, the Benjamin Davis Freedom Committee, the China Welfare Appeal, the Committee for the Negro in the Arts, Everybody's Committee to End War, the Maritime Committee to Defend Al Lannon, and the National Association of Mexican Americans. Goldstein, *American Blacklist*, 67.

86. Dahl, *A Preface to Democratic Theory*, 132–33. Behavioralism convinced Dahl and other pluralists that their functionalist account of democracy honored the fact-value distinction exalted by positivist thought.

87. Robert Dahl, *Who Governs? Democracy and Power in an American City* (New Haven: Yale University Press, 1961), 316, 317; Dahl, *Democracy in the United States*, 52, 50; Dahl, *A Preface to Democratic Theory*, 150.

88. Madison, "Federalist No. 10." Cf. Bernard Brown, "Tocqueville and Publius," in *Reconsidering Tocqueville's Democracy in America*, ed. Abraham Eisenstadt (New Brunswick: Rutgers University Press, 1988), 48 (Madison "postulates a critical difference between faction (even when it is embodied by a majority) on the one hand and justice or the public good on the other. Throughout *The Federalist* the warning is sounding that the immediate interests of individuals as well as of majorities may not further the long-term good of the collectivity.").

89. Truman, *The Governmental Process*, 6; Theodore Lowi, *The End of Liberalism: The Second Republic of the United States* (New York: Norton, 1979), 55. Cf. ibid., 36 (in contemporary pluralism, "groups became virtuous; they must be accommodated, not regulated"). See also Paul F. Bourke, "The Pluralist Reading of James Madison's Tenth Federalist," 9 *Perspectives in American History* 272 (1975) ("Madison's discussion of faction and interest establishes the close fit of modern pluralist theory and the wider American political culture.").

90. Dahl, *A Preface to Democratic Theory*, 15, 26, 29, 18, 22.

91. Lance Banning, *The Sacred Fire of Liberty: James Madison and the Founding of the Federal Republic* (Ithaca: Cornell University Press, 1995), 205; Ralph Ketcham, *James Madison*, 2d ed. (Charlottesville: University of Virginia Press, 1990), ix. Cf. Brown, "Tocqueville and Publius," 45–46 (suggesting that Dahl reads *The Federalist* to reflect "the ideology of a wealthy and advantaged elite"); Lowi, *The End of Liberalism*, 55.

92. Sheldon Wolin, *Tocqueville between Two Worlds: The Making of a Political and Theoretical Life* (Princeton: Princeton University Press, 2001), 240; Tocqueville, *Democracy in America*, 203–4. Tocqueville had carefully studied both *The Federalist* and Story's *Commentaries on the Constitution*, the latter of which reproduced *Federalist* No. 10 in its entirety. Brown, "Tocqueville and Publius," 43–45. Early in Book I of *Democracy in America*, Tocqueville wrote in a footnote that he would "often have occasion to quote *The Federalist* in this work." Tocqueville, *Democracy in America*, 134 n.8. He opined that "*The Federalist* is a fine book which, although it particularly concerns America, should be familiar to statesmen of all countries." Ibid. See also Brown, "Tocqueville and Publius," 53, 54 (Tocqueville

thought that "men of virtue would filter the raw passions and demands of the people," and "thus would egoistic individualism (Madison's factionalism) be transcended and an era of enlightened self-interest (Madison's public good) ushered in."); George Kateb, "Some Remarks on Tocqueville's View of Voluntary Associations," in *Nomos XI: Voluntary Associations*, ed. J. Roland Pennock and John W. Chapman (New York: Atherton Press, 1969), 142 ("The Madisonian vision of democratic politics as the struggle of potentially transgressive factions is absent from Tocqueville's account.").

93. Dahl, *Democracy in the United States*, 87 (Dahl notes that African Americans were an exception here but maintains that there was otherwise immense equality among the "free white population." Ibid.); Dahl, *Who Governs?* 312, 318, 2, 3. Dahl criticized Tocqueville's argument "that the stability of the American democratic system depends . . . on an almost universal belief in the basic rules of the democratic game." Ibid., 312. But while Dahl highlighted disagreement over "specific applications" of democratic principles to "crucial cases," he maintained a basic agreement with those principles.

94. Rogers M. Smith, *Civic Ideals: Conflicting Visions of Citizenship in U.S. History* (New Haven: Yale University Press, 1997), 17; McConnell, *Private Power and American Democracy*, 349. Cf. ibid., 358 ("Federalism and interest group 'pluralism' with which it is associated today are instruments of conservatism and particularism. The ideology of 'grass roots democracy' and the gradual growth of power in small units by the institutional processes of accommodation have probably betrayed us into yielding too much of the republic's essential values of liberty and equality.").

95. Rogers M. Smith, *Liberalism and American Constitutional Law* (Cambridge, Mass.: Harvard University Press, 1985), 14. Cf. Mark E. Warren, *Democracy and Association* (Princeton: Princeton University Press, 2001) ("because [Tocqueville's] bipolar state-civil society model fails to conceive economic and social power effects, it produces a limited conception of what counts as 'political.' ").

96. An important exception to the separation of public and private that I am describing was the role of state-sponsored churches in some areas of the country.

97. Tocqueville, *Democracy in America*, vol. 1, 290. For example, the nation that Tocqueville observed in 1830 had fewer than twelve thousand federal employees (almost nine thousand of whom worked for the Post Office) out of a population of more than thirteen million. Dahl, *Pluralist Democracy in the United States*, 60–61. As Mark Warren has written, "Tocqueville linked capacities for mediation and representation to civic habits developed within the associational fabric of civil society, which he in turn related to a strong meaning of democracy located in associational capacities for collective action." Warren, *Democracy and Association*, 30.

98. Morton J. Horwitz, "The History of the Public/Private Distinction," 130 *University of Pennsylvania Law Review* 1424, 1426, 1428 (1981); Kalman, *The Strange Career of Legal Liberalism*, 17; Lowi, *The End of Liberalism*, 42, 43. Cf. Theodore Lowi, "The Public Philosophy: Interest-Group Liberalism," 61 *American Political Science Review* 6 (1967) ("Once the principle of positive government in a growing and indeterminable political sphere was established, criteria arising out of the very issue of *whether* such a principle should be

established became extinguished. They were extinguished by the total victory of one side of the old dialogue over the other."). As Morton Horwitz suggests, it was "the emergence of the market as a central legitimating institution" that "brought the public/private distinction into the core of legal discourse during the nineteenth century." Horwitz, "The History of the Public/Private Distinction," 1424. Horwitz elaborates that "one of the central goals of nineteenth century legal thought was to create a clear separation between constitutional, criminal, and regulatory law—public law—and the law of private transactions—torts, contracts, property, and commercial law." Ibid.

99. Henry Kariel, *The Decline of American Pluralism* (Stanford: Stanford University Press, 1961), 1, 10; Sheldon Wolin, *Politics and Vision: Continuity and Innovation in Western Political Thought* (Princeton: Princeton University Press, 2004), 374; Kariel, *The Decline of American Pluralism*, 2; John Dewey, *The Public and Its Problems* (New York: Henry Holt, 1927), 126, 137.

100. McConnell, *Private Power and American Democracy*, 362, 146, 341–42. Cf. ibid., 362 (The government can be neither arbiter nor mediator when "the distinction between public and private is lost."). For example, the 1933 National Industrial Recovery Act and the 1935 Wagner Act bestowed upon labor unions "a substantial measure of public power." Ibid., 146. Professional and trade associations had been "given the power to nominate personnel, virtually as a form of representation, to official licensing boards" and "on occasion, to policy-making boards." Ibid., 147. And "private" associations like the American Farm Bureau Federation and the Chamber of Commerce of the United States had "direct government encouragement in their formation." Ibid.

101. McConnell, *Private Power and American Democracy*, 123, 124.

102. Michael Paul Rogin, *The Intellectuals and McCarthy: The Radical Specter* (Cambridge, Mass.: MIT Press, 1967), 10, 271, 16; Lowi, *The End of Liberalism*, 38, 55; William Connolly, "The Challenge to Pluralist Theory," in *The Bias of Pluralism*, ed. William Connolly (New York: Atherton Press, 1971), 5. Connolly suggests that Madison and Tocqueville provided the "intellectual springboards" for many pluralist thinkers. Ibid., 4. Lowi explained that interest group liberalism "is liberalism because it is optimistic about government, expects to use government in a positive and expansive role, is motivated by the highest sentiments, and possesses a strong faith that what is good for government is good for the society. It is interest-group liberalism because it sees as both necessary and good a policy agenda that is accessible to all organized interests and makes no independent judgment of their claims. It is interest-group liberalism because it defines the public interest as a result of the amalgamation of various claims." Lowi, *The End of Liberalism*, 51.

103. See generally, Wolin, *Politics and Vision*, 315–92, 557–606.

104. Madison, "Federalist No. 10." Tocqueville, *Democracy in America*, 305, 305–6, 303; Wolin, *Tocqueville between Two Worlds*, 250–51. Wolin believes that Tocqueville "concluded that in America there were insufficient legal safeguards against the tyranny of the majority." Wolin, *Tocqueville between Two Worlds*, 250.

105. Ronald Kahn, *The Supreme Court and Constitutional Theory, 1953–1993* (Lawrence: Kansas University Press, 1994), 89; Stephen M. Feldman, "From Modernism to

Postmodernism in American Legal Thought: The Significance of the Warren Court," in *The Warren Court: A Retrospective*, ed. Bernard Schwartz (New York: Oxford University Press, 1996), 335; Kalman, *The Strange Career of Legal Liberalism*, 26; Richard A. Posner, "The Decline of Law as an Autonomous Discipline: 1962–1987," 100 *Harvard Law Review* 761, 765 (1987). Cf. ibid. ("At least in the academy, the radical right had been discredited first by its isolationism and then by its racism, and the radical left had been squashed by the Cold War. Secular, humanistic, patriotic, and centrist, the American intellectual scene in the late 1950s and early 1960s was remarkably free from ideological strife."). Feldman elsewhere elaborates that "these 'legal process' professors shared easily in the idea of a social consensus party because of a lack of diversity among themselves" and "during the 1940s and 1950s, the overwhelming majority were white males." Stephen M. Feldman, *American Legal Thought from Premodernism to Postmodernism*, 119.

106. Arthur J. Goldberg, "New Frontiers for Lawyers and the Law," American Law Institute (May 19, 1961), in *The Defenses of Freedom: The Public Papers of Arthur J. Goldberg*, ed. Daniel Patrick Moynihan (New York: Harper and Row, 1964), 145; Charles Nesson, "The Harlan-Frankfurter Connection: An Aspect of Justice Harlan's Judicial Education," 36 *New York Law School Law Review* 179 (1991); Joseph P. Lash, *From the Diaries of Felix Frankfurter* (New York: Norton, 1975); *AFL v. American Sash & Door Co.*, 335 U.S. 538, 546 (1949) (Frankfurter, J., concurring) (in the quote that Frankfurter cited, Laski had warned of the dangers of "personify[ing] the idea" of an association). Harold J. Laski, "Morris Cohen's Approach to Legal Philosophy," 15 *University of Chicago Law Review* 575, 581 (1948); John M. Harlan, "Thoughts at a Dedication: Keeping the Judicial Function in Balance," 49 *American Bar Association Journal* 944 (1963); William J. Brennan Jr., "Some Aspects of Federalism," 39 *New York University Law Review* 945–961, 945, 960 (1964). Frankfurter's view was consistent with his more general deference to an interest in national unity. See, e.g., *Minersville Sch. Dist. v. Gobitis*, 310 U.S. 586, 600 (1940) (defending "the educational process for inculcating those almost unconscious feelings which bind men together in a comprehending loyalty, whatever may be their lesser differences and difficulties."). The Court overruled *Gobitis* three years later in *West Virginia State Bd. of Educ. v. Barnette*, 319 U.S. 624 (1943). Jeffrey Hockett suggests that "Frankfurter's understanding of the political process anticipated the tenets of pluralist political thought." Jeffrey D. Hockett, "Justices Frankfurter and Black: Social Theory and Constitutional Interpretation," 107 *Political Science Quarterly* 487 n.36 (1992). Brennan's later thinking evinced greater skepticism about the national unity toward which he gestured in his 1964 address. See, e.g., *FCC v. Pacifica Foundation*, 438 U.S. 726, 777 (1978) (Brennan, J., dissenting) ("The Court's decision may be seen for what, in the broader perspective, it really is: another of the dominant culture's inevitable efforts to force those groups who do not share its mores to conform to its way of thinking, acting, and speaking."). Ronald Kahn has argued that the Warren Court "rejected the apologetic pluralism of its age, as represented in the scholarship of Robert Dahl and David Truman, and placed into its jurisprudence a critical pluralist interpretation of politics, as later represented in the scholarship of Grant McConnell and Theodore

Lowi." Kahn, *The Supreme Court and Constitutional Theory*, 251. That conclusion may be reflected in some dimensions of the Warren Court's jurisprudence, but it is not borne out in the way that the justices shaped the right of association.

Chapter 4. The Transformation of Association in the Equality Era

1. Herbert Wechsler, "Toward Neutral Principles of Constitutional Law," 73 *Harvard Law Review* 34 (1959) (Wechsler argued that "the question posed by state-enforced segregation [was] not one of discrimination at all" but represented "the denial by the state of the freedom to associate."); *Brown v. Board of Education*, 347 U.S. 483 (1954); Andrew Koppelman, *Antidiscrimination Law and Social Equality* (New Haven: Yale University Press, 1996), 179 ("Wechsler's objection to *Brown* is silly with respect to public schools").

2. Gerald Rosenberg, *The Hollow Hope: Can Courts Bring About Social Change?* (Chicago: University of Chicago Press, 1993), 65, 97. For examples of integration in public places, see, e.g., *Brown v. Board of Education; Boynton v. Virginia*, 364 U.S. 454 (1960) (interstate transportation); *Turner v. Memphis*, 369 U.S. 350 (1962) (airports); *Johnson v. Virginia* 373 U.S. 61 (1963) (per curiam) (courtrooms); *Brown v. Louisiana*, 383 U.S. 131 (1966) (libraries); *Watson v. Memphis*, 373 U.S. 526 (1963); *Muir v. Louisville Park Theatrical Assn.*, 347 U.S. 971 (1954); *Holmes v. City of Atlanta*, 350 U.S. 879 (1955); *New Orleans City Park Improvement Assn. v. Detiege*, 358 U. S. 54 (1958); *Burton v. Wilmington Parking Authority*, 365 U.S. 715 (1961) (private restaurant owner who refused service based on customer's race violated Fourteenth Amendment because restaurant was located in a building leased from a state entity).

3. Pub. L. 88–352, 78 Stat. 241 (July 2, 1964); 42 U.S.C. §§ 2000a(b) and (e); *Bell v. Maryland*, 378 U.S. 226, 314 (1964) (Goldberg, J., concurring); *Daniel v. Paul*, 395 U.S. 298, 301–2 (1969) (rejecting an amusement park's contention that it was a private club exempt from the act because it charged patrons a twenty-five-cent "membership" fee and distributed "membership" cards). *Bell* addressed the trespass convictions of African Americans who had participated in a sit-in at a Baltimore restaurant in light of city and state public accommodations laws enacted after their convictions. The Court issued its decision ten days prior to the enactment of the Civil Rights Act of 1964 and remanded the case to the Maryland Court of Appeals. Ibid., 239. Justice Goldberg, joined by Justice Douglas and Chief Justice Warren, argued that the Fourteenth Amendment "resolves this apparent conflict of liberties in favor of the Negro's right to equal public accommodations." Ibid., 314 (Goldberg, J., concurring). Some of the constitutional momentum against discrimination in places of public accommodation preceded the act. See, e.g., *Marsh v. Alabama*, 326 U.S. 501, 506 (1946) ("Ownership does not always mean absolute dominion. The more an owner, for his advantage, opens up his property for use by the public in general, the more do his rights become circumscribed by the statutory and constitutional rights of those who use it."). For a more comprehensive history, see Joseph William Singer, "No Right to Exclude: Public Accommodations and Private Property," 90 *Northwestern University Law Review* 1283 (1996).

4. *Jones v. Alfred H. Mayer*, 392 U.S. 409, 444, 441, 442 (1968); *Sullivan v. Little Hunting Park*, 396 U.S. 229 (1969); *Tillman v. Wheaton-Haven Recreation Assn.*, 410 U.S. 431 (1973); 42

U.S.C. §§ 3601–3631; *Sullivan v. Little Hunting Park*, 241, 248 (Harlan, J., dissenting). In *Sullivan*, the Court characterized Little Hunting Park's exclusion of African Americans as "a device functionally comparable to a racially restrictive covenant." 396 U.S. at 236. In *Tillman*, a unanimous Court concluded that "the structure and practices of Wheaton-Haven . . . are indistinguishable from those of Little Haven Park." 410 U.S. at 438.

5. *Runyon v. McCrary*, 427 U.S. 160 (1976); *Norwood v. Harrison*, 413 U.S. 455, 463 (1973). For cases enjoining state tuition grants, see, e.g., *Brown v. South Carolina Board of Education*, 296 F.Supp. 199 (D.C.S.C. 1968), aff'd per curiam, 393 U.S. 222 (1968); *Poindexter v. Louisiana Financial Assistance Comm'n*, 275 F.Supp. 833 (E.D. La. 1967), aff'd per curiam, 389 U.S. 571 (1968).

6. *Norwood v. Harrison*, 470 (Burger was referring to Section 2 of the Thirteenth Amendment and also noted that "Congress has made such discrimination unlawful in other significant contexts"), 463, 469.

7. *Gilmore v. City of Montgomery*, 417 U.S. 556, 572, 573, 574, 575 (1974). The decision came after repeated instances of Montgomery's blatant disregard of mandates to integrate its public facilities. Ibid., 575.

8. *Runyon v. McCrary*, 427 U.S. 160, 168, 173, 176 (1976); *Norwood v. Harrison*, 455, 469–70 (emphasis added); *Runyon v. McCrary*, 176. See George Rutherglen, "Civil Rights in Private Schools: The Surprising Story of *Runyon v. McCrary*," in *Civil Rights Stories*, ed. Myriam E. Gilles and Risa Lauren Goluboff (New York: Foundation Press, 2008), 111 (*Runyon* "subordinated private choice to civil rights policy and extended federal law beyond the limitations of the state action doctrine").

9. John Hope Franklin, "The Civil Rights Act of 1866 Revisited," 41 *Hastings Law Journal* 1135, 1138 (1990). See Rutherglen, "Civil Rights in Private Schools," 111. Ibid., 122 (noting that in *Patterson v. McLean Credit Union*, 491, U.S. 164, 171–75 (1989), the Court asked for briefing on whether *Runyon* should be overruled but decided against overruling it and that *Patterson* was superseded by the Civil Rights Act of 1991, "which amended section 1981 to make clear that it covered all aspects of contractual relations and applied to all contracts").

10. *Runyon v. McCrary*, 427 U.S. at 176 (quoting *McCrary v. Runyon*, 515 F.2d 1082, 1087 (4th Cir. 1975)). See Andrew Koppelman with Tobias Barrington Wolff, *A Right to Discriminate? How the Case of* Boy Scouts of America v. James Dale *Warped the Law of Free Association* (New Haven: Yale University Press, 2009), 19 ("If the schools are integrated, it is hard to imagine that this will not have some effect on the ideas taught."); William Buss, "Discrimination by Private Clubs," 67 *Washington University Law Quarterly* 815, 831 (1989) ("The assertion that forcing a school to admit black children will 'in no way' inhibit the school's intended message that racial integration is bad proves too much to swallow. Just as government-mandated school segregation conveys a powerful message that black people are unworthy to associate with whites, state-mandated integration conveys a powerful message that blacks and whites are human beings with equal worth and dignity. That message must blunt any merely verbal message, taught in the school, that

segregation is a good thing."). Some scholars have nevertheless left Stewart's reasoning here unchallenged, arguing instead that the defendants in *Runyon* never contended that they should be protected as "expressive associations" (notwithstanding the fact that the Court had yet to recognize such a category). See, e.g., David E. Bernstein "The Right of Expressive Association and Private Universities' Racial Preferences and Speech Codes," 9 *William and Mary Bill of Rights Journal* 619, 626–27 (2001) ("A close reading of *Runyon* and the briefs filed in it reveal that *Runyon* was not an "expressive association" case. The defendants in *Runyon* made what amounts to a short, throw-away argument that their right to 'freedom of association,' floating somewhere in the penumbral ether of the Constitution, was violated by compelled integration. However, the defendants did not make an expressive association claim grounded in the First Amendment. They did not argue in their briefs that the school's ability to promote segregation would be compromised, nor did they provide evidence at trial on that issue.").

11. Stewart soon reiterated this distinction between act and message in cases beyond the civil rights context. Writing for the majority in *Abood v. Detroit Board of Education*, a 1977 case involving an "agency shop" arrangement for state government employees, he described "the freedom of an individual to associate *for the purpose of advancing beliefs and ideas.*" *Abood v. Detroit Board of Education*, 431 U.S. 209, 233 (1977) (emphasis added). And four years later, writing for the Court in *Democratic Party of the United States v. Wisconsin*, a case involving political parties, Stewart referred to the "freedom to gather in association *for the purpose of advancing shared beliefs.*" *Democratic Party of the United States v. Wisconsin*, 450 U.S. 107, 121 (1981) (emphasis added). That same year, Burger echoed Stewart's view in *Citizens Against Rent Control v. Berkeley*. *Citizens Against Rent Control v. Berkeley*, 454 U.S. 290 (1981). Although acknowledging that "the practice of persons sharing common views banding together *to achieve a common end* is deeply embedded in the American political process," Burger asserted that the real value of association was "that by collective effort individuals can *make their views known*, when, individually, their voices would be faint or lost." Ibid., 294 (emphasis added). Three years later, Brennan adopted Stewart's distinction between belief and practice and rendered association wholly instrumental to other First Amendment freedoms. *Roberts v. United States Jaycees*, 468 U.S. 609, 618 (1984).

12. See *Sweezy v. New Hampshire*, 354 U.S. 234, 266–67 (1957) (Frankfurter, J., concurring), and *Gibson v. Florida Legislative Investigation Committee*, 372 U.S. 539, 560 (1963) (Douglas, J., concurring); *NAACP v. Alabama*, 462 (Harlan continued: "Inviolability of privacy in group association may in many circumstances be indispensable to preservation of freedom of association, particularly where a group espouses dissident beliefs."); *Griswold v. Connecticut*, 381 U.S. 479 (1965).

13. Louis Brandeis and Sam Warren, "The Right to Privacy," 4 *Harvard Law Review* 193, 195 (1890); *NAACP v. Alabama ex rel. Patterson*, 357 U.S. 449, 462 (1958).

14. Bernard Schwartz, *The Unpublished Opinions of the Warren Court* (New York: Oxford University Press, 1985), 237, 235. Douglas's only mention of privacy in the draft came in the concluding paragraph, where he linked privacy to association, as he had done in his

Gibson concurrence: "The prospects of police with warrants searching the sacred precincts of marital bedrooms for telltale signs of the use of contraceptives is repulsive to the idea of privacy and association that make up a goodly part of the penumbra of the Constitution and Bill of Rights." Ibid., 236 (quoting Douglas's draft opinion). Schwartz writes that Douglas's sole mention of privacy in the last sentence of his draft "is scarcely enough to make it the foundation for any constitutional right of privacy, particularly for the broadside right established by the final Griswold opinion." Ibid., 230.

15. Schwartz, *The Unpublished Opinions of the Warren Court*, 237; *Griswold v. Connecticut*, 484. Brennan argued that Douglas's expanded view of association would extend First Amendment protection to the Communist Party. Schwartz, *The Unpublished Opinions of the Warren Court*, 237–38.

16. *Griswold v. Connecticut*, 483; *Zemel v. Rusk*, 381 U.S. 1, 24 (1965) (Douglas, J., dissenting) (quoting the papal encyclical *Pacem in Terris*); *Griswold v. Connecticut*, 483.

17. *Thomas v. Collins*, 323 U.S. 516, 540 (1945); *Communist Party of the United States v. Subversive Activities Control Board*, 367 U.S. 1, 170 (1961) (Douglas, J., dissenting). See *Poulos v. New Hampshire*, 345 U.S. 395, 423 (1953) (Douglas, J., dissenting) ("There is no free speech in the sense of the Constitution when permission must be obtained from an official before a speech can be made. That is a previous restraint condemned by history and at war with the First Amendment."); *Kingsley International Pictures Corp. v. New York*, 360 U.S. 684, 697–98 (1959) (Douglas, J., dissenting) ("I can find in the First Amendment no room for any censor whether he is scanning an editorial, reading a news broadcast, editing a novel or a play, or previewing a movie."); *New York Times v. United States*, 403 U.S. 713, 720–25 (1971) (Douglas, J., concurring).

18. *Griswold v. Connecticut*, 483; *Lathrop v. Donohue*, 367 U.S. 820, 882 (1961) (Douglas, J., dissenting).

19. *Griswold v. Connecticut*, 499, 500 (Harlan, J., concurring); ibid., 509 (Black, J., dissenting).

20. *Eisenstadt v. Baird*, 405 U.S. 438 (1972); *Griswold v. Connecticut*, 486; Brandeis and Warren, "The Right to Privacy," 215; *Eisenstadt v. Baird*, 453; H. Jefferson Powell, *The Moral Tradition of American Constitutionalism* (Durham: Duke University Press, 1993), 176, 177. Powell writes that *Eisenstadt* "clearly marked the reemergence of substantive due process as a mode of constitutional argument that the Court considered legitimate." Ibid., 176.

21. John Rawls, *A Theory of Justice*, rev. ed. (Cambridge, Mass.: Belknap Press of Harvard University Press, 1999 (1971)); John Gunnell, "The Real Revolution in Political Science," 37 *PS: Political Science* 49 (2004). Gunnell's important insight has gone largely unexamined within political theory. Rawls has inspired an enormous secondary literature, and it is not my intention here to summarize the many applications and critiques of his theory of justice. Rather, I am only interested in covering the background necessary to interrogate his views about the freedom of association. Because Rawls's work developed throughout the equality era, and because more refined articulations appear in his later writings, I draw upon some of these later sources and assume that they are in continuity with his original theory unless otherwise indicated.

22. John Rawls, *Political Liberalism* (New York: Columbia University Press, 1995), xvii and 148 (sectarian religious violence), 35 ("well-ordered society"); Rawls, *A Theory of Justice*, 232 ("Archimedean point"); Rawls, *Political Liberalism*, 135 ("incommensurable doctrines"), 148 (modus vivendi), 36 ("overlapping consensus"); Rawls, *A Theory of Justice*, 6, 79, 386. Rawls's premise about sectarian religious violence has not gone unchallenged. See, e.g., William T. Cavanaugh, *The Myth of Religious Violence: Secular Ideology and the Roots of Modern Conflict* (New York: Oxford University Press, 2009) (challenging conventional and historical understandings of "religion" and "secular").

23. Rawls, *Theory of Justice*, 457, 458, 462, 186. Rawls omits the freedom of association from his list of these liberties in *A Theory of Justice* but includes it in *Political Liberalism*. Compare Rawls, *A Theory of Justice*, 53 (listing "freedom of speech and assembly" but not association) with Rawls, *Political Liberalism*, 291, 335. Kevin Kordana and David Tabachnick have suggested that "the Rawlsian texts appear not to be consistent with regard to the status of the right to freedom of association" and "[t]he status of a right to freedom of association" among the basic liberties is "neither obvious nor uncontroversial." Kevin A. Kordana and David Blankfein Tabachnick, "The Rawlsian View of Private Ordering," 25 *Social Philosophy and Policy* 288, 290 (2008). I am not convinced by this interpretation; Rawls certainly seems to describe something akin to freedom of association in his account of the basic liberties in *A Theory of Justice* even if he does not name it as such. See Rawls, *A Theory of Justice*, 195–96 ("There are firm constitutional protections for certain liberties, particularly freedom of speech and assembly, and liberty to form political associations. The principle of loyal opposition is recognized, the clash of political beliefs, and of the interests and attitudes that are likely to influence them, are accepted as a normal condition of human life. . . . Without the conception of loyal opposition, and an attachment to constitutional rules which express and protect it, the politics of democracy cannot be properly conducted or long endure."); cf. John Rawls, "Constitutional Liberty and the Concept of Justice," in *John Rawls: Collected Papers*, ed. Samuel Freeman (Cambridge, Mass.: Harvard University Press, 1999), 94 (writing in 1962 that "although tolerant sects have a right not to tolerate an intolerant sect when they sincerely and with reason believe that their own security and that of the institution of liberty is in danger, they have this right only in this case"). And as early as 1975, Rawls noted that a well-ordered society "ensures an equal liberty and freedom of association." John Rawls, "Fairness to Goodness," in *John Rawls: Collected Papers*, ed. Samuel Freeman (Cambridge, Mass.: Harvard University Press, 1999), 275. But this quibble is tangential to my consideration of Rawls's understanding of association because Kordana and Tabachnick agree that at least some component of the right of association is included among the basic liberties. Kordana and Tabachnick, "The Rawlsian View of Private Ordering," 290 (freedom of association is a "complex right").

24. Rawls, *Theory of Justice*, 140 (to this end, Rawls advocated that a "political conception" of justice could be attained "without reference" to comprehensive doctrines. Ibid., 12. For Rawls, comprehensive doctrines "belong to what we may call the 'background

culture' of civil society," which "is the culture of the social, not of the political." Ibid., 14. Rawls's distinction between the "social" and the "political" is particularly troubling, as if "the culture of daily life, of its many associations," could exist in a social realm uninhibited by the legal framework established by the political. Ibid.); John Rawls, "The Idea of Public Reason Revisited," 64 *Chicago Law Review* 765 (1997); ibid., 776 (emphasis added). This "proviso" echoes his view in *Political Liberalism* that citizens can invoke comprehensive doctrines "provided they do this in ways that strengthen the idea of public reason itself." Rawls, *Political Liberalism*, 247.

25. Frank Michelman, "Foreword: On Protecting the Poor through the Fourteenth Amendment," 83 *Harvard Law Review* 7 (1969) (Laura Kalman writes that by 1973, Michelman was less enamored of Rawlsian solutions. Laura Kalman, *The Strange Career of Legal Liberalism* (New Haven: Yale University Press, 1996), 67); Kenneth Karst, "Foreword: Equal Citizenship under the Fourteenth Amendment," 91 *Harvard Law Review* 4 (1977); Kalman, *The Strange Career of Legal Liberalism*, 67.

26. Ronald Dworkin, *Freedom's Law* (New York: Oxford University Press, 1996), 17, 25; Alexander M. Bickel, *The Least Dangerous Branch: The Supreme Court at the Bar of Politics* (Indianapolis: Bobbs-Merrill, 1962) (discussing the "counter-majoritarian difficulty"). For purposes of this argument, I am assuming that liberal rights (including the right to group autonomy) are *individual* rights. An individual's right to group autonomy is violated if the state imposes unwanted membership requirements upon that person's group. It may be that some of these arguments can be reached by considering assembly as a "group right." See, e.g., Frederick Mark Gedicks, "The Recurring Paradox of Groups in the Liberal State," 2010 *Utah Law Review* 47 (2010).

27. *Roberts v. United States Jaycees*, 614; *United States Jaycees v. McClure*, 709 F.2d 1560, 1563 (8th Cir. 1983); Minn. Stat. § 363.03(3) (1982). An important fact sometimes lost in the retelling of *Roberts* is that the litigation reflected an internal debate among the Jaycees— the national organization had sued the local Minnesota chapters. At stake were two competing visions of the future of the organization. It is plausible—perhaps even likely— that the vision favoring the full inclusion of women would have won out absent interference by the courts. In fact, as Judge Arnold pointed out in the lower court opinion, the question about whether to admit women had "been vigorously debated within the organization," and while the national organization had defeated a resolution favoring the admission of women on three occasions prior to the *Roberts* litigation, each time a larger minority had voted in favor of the resolution. *United States Jaycees v. McClure*, 1561.

28. *Roberts v. United States Jaycees*, 617, 618, 622. Burger and Blackmun recused themselves from the case: Burger had been chapter president of the St. Paul Jaycees, and Blackmun had been a former member of the Minneapolis Jaycees.

29. *Roberts v. United States Jaycees*, 618.

30. *Roberts v. United States Jaycees*, 618, 623, 622.

31. *Roberts v. United States Jaycees*, 623, 626, 627. I am not suggesting that the limitations imposed on associate individual members are insignificant. But the pertinent legal inquiry is

whether prohibiting these limitations furthers the compelling interest in eradicating gender discrimination, and it is difficult to see how it does given the opportunities available to women as associate individual members. The right to vote in a Jaycees referendum is not the same as the right to vote in a governmental election. At the very least, the Court failed to show how its remedy of forced inclusion furthered the compelling interest that it identified.

32. *Roberts v. United States Jaycees,* 631, 633 (O'Connor, J., concurring). For favorable interpretations of O'Connor's concurrence, see, e.g., Seana Valentine Shiffrin, "What Is Really Wrong with Compelled Association?" 99 *Northwestern University Law Review* 876 (2005) ("Justice O'Connor's concurrence in Jaycees was largely correct."); Douglas O. Linder, "Freedom of Association after *Roberts v. United States Jaycees,*" 82 *Michigan Law Review* 1896 (1984) ("On balance, the O'Connor approach seems to enjoy several distinct advantages over the majority approach."); Eugene Volokh, "Freedom of Speech in Cyberspace from the Listener's Perspective: Private Speech Restrictions, Libel, State Action, Harassment, and Sex," 1996 *University of Chicago Legal Forum* 395 (1996).

33. *Roberts v. United States Jaycees,* 639, 640, 638, 636 (O'Connor, J., concurring).

34. As Larry Alexander notes, "Laws regulating membership in *any* organization—including commercial ones—will affect the content of that organization's expression." Larry Alexander, "What Is Freedom of Association and What Is Its Denial?" 25 *Social Philosophy and Policy* 7 (2008). One of the clearest illustrations of the consequences of the condition that an association be "predominantly engaged" in protected expression is the effect of charitable solicitation regulation on small or unpopular charities. See, e.g., *Riley v. National Federation of the Blind of North Carolina,* 487 U.S. 781, 799 (1988). See also John D. Inazu, "Making Sense of *Schaumburg:* Seeking Coherence in First Amendment Charitable Solicitation Law," 92 *Marquette Law Review* 551 (2009).

35. On the elevation of intimate over expressive association, see Aviam Soifer, *Law and the Company We Keep* (Cambridge, Mass.: Harvard University Press, 1995), 41 (contending that Brennan regarded expressive association "as instrumental and therefore subject to greater government intrusion"); George Kateb, "The Value of Association," in *Freedom of Association,* ed. Amy Gutmann (Princeton: Princeton University Press, 1998), 46 ("Running through Brennan's opinion is the assumption that all nonintimate relationships are simply inferior to intimate ones."); Koppelman, *A Right to Discriminate?* x (Under *Roberts,* "intimate associations of small groups of people had a stronger right [than expressive associations], to refuse association with anyone for any reason."); David E. Bernstein, "Expressive Association after *Dale,*" 21 *Social Philosophy and Policy* 202 (2004) ("The Court's apparent disdain for expressive association claims had a marked effect on lower courts."). For examples of the lack of protections for nonexpressive groups, see, e.g., *City of Dallas v. Stanglin,* 490 U.S. 19, 24 (1989) (applying rational basis scrutiny to city ordinance governing activity that "qualifies neither as a form of 'intimate association' nor as a form of 'expressive association' as those terms were described in *Roberts*"); *Swank v. Smart,* 898 F.2d 1247, 1251–52 (7th Cir. 1990) (First Amendment doesn't protect nonintimate nonexpressive associations); *Conti v. City of Fremont,* 919 F.2d 1385, 1388 (9th Cir. 1990) ("an activity receives no

special first amendment protection if it qualifies neither as a form of 'intimate association' nor as a form of 'expressive association,' as those terms were described in *Roberts*.").

36. Kenneth L. Karst, "The Freedom of Intimate Association," 89 *Yale Law Journal* 629 (1980). The one distinction that may have been plausible when Karst wrote in 1980 is no longer true today. Karst claimed that intimate association "implies an expectation of access of one person to another particular person's physical presence, some opportunity for face-to-face encounter." Ibid., 630. While physical presence may have been a distinguishing characteristic of intimate associations thirty years ago, that is no longer true today. Many people now bridge physical separation and connect in emotionally rich ways with friends and family through online social networking sites, blogs, and video conferencing. Others project their identities or create new ones through virtual representations ranging from simple text (like an online profile) to avatars. Some of these online relationships foster deep feelings of intimacy and connectedness. See, e.g., Howard Rheingold, *The Virtual Community: Homesteading on the Electronic Frontier*, rev. ed. (Cambridge, Mass.: MIT Press, 2000); Jerry Kang, "Cyber-Race," 113 *Harvard Law Review* 1130, 1171–72 (2000) (noting that in online forums, "pregnant women share experiences; the elderly console each other after losing love ones, patients fighting cancer provide information and support; disabled children find friends who do not judge them immediately on their disability; users share stories about drug addiction; and gays and lesbians on the brink of coming out give each other emotional shelter.").

37. Karst, "The Freedom of Intimate Association," 629, 629 n.26, 632, 634–35, 688.

38. Karst, "The Freedom of Intimate Association," 633. Cf. ibid., 688–89 ("any constitutional protection of enduring sexual relationships can be effective only if it is extended to the choice to engage in casual ones.").

39. Karst, "The Freedom of Intimate Association," 636, 637, 654, 658.

40. *Lawrence v. Texas*, 539 U.S. 558 (2003); *Bowers v. Hardwick*, 478 U.S. 186 (1986); ibid., 214 (Stevens, J., dissenting); ibid., 199 (Blackmun, J., dissenting); *Lawrence v. Texas*, 578 ("Justice Stevens' analysis, in our view, should have been controlling in *Bowers* and should control here."). Karst saw freedom of intimate association on "the cutting edge" of "the current revival of substantive due process." Karst, "The Freedom of Intimate Association," 665. In contrast, he believed that "calling the rights in *Griswold* and *Roe* rights of privacy invites the rejection of comparable claims on the ground that, after all, they do not rest on any concerns about control over the disclosure of information." Ibid., 664. On Karst's interest in gay rights, see, e.g., ibid., 672 ("As I have argued in connection with the prohibition on homosexual conduct, there is no legitimacy in an effort by the state to advance one view of morals by preventing the expression of another view."); ibid., 682 ("By now it will be obvious that the freedom of intimate association extends to homosexual associations as it does to heterosexual ones."); ibid., 685 ("The chief importance of the freedom of intimate association as an organizing principle in the area of homosexual relationships is that it lets us see how closely homosexual associations resemble marriage and other heterosexual associations."). Nancy Marcus has suggested that "principles of

intimate association underlie the *Lawrence* decision" and that "*Lawrence* is the first actual affirmation of a litigant's intimate associational rights by the Supreme Court since *Roberts*." Nancy Catherine Marcus, "The Freedom of Intimate Association in the Twenty-First Century," 16 *George Mason University Civil Rights and Law Journal* 269, 303, 308 (2006). Laura Rosenbury and Jennifer Rothman argue similarly that the majority's "shift from sex acts to relationships aligns Lawrence with the right to intimate association already articulated by the Court in other contexts." Laura A. Rosenbury and Jennifer E. Rothman, "Sex in and out of Intimacy," 59 *Emory Law Journal* 809, 826 (2010). These claims seem undermined by the lack of any mention of intimate association in the *Lawrence* opinion, particularly in light of the fact that the justices had before them both Blackmun's *Bowers* dissent and arguments about intimate association from the *Lawrence* Petitioners. See, e.g., Brief of Petitioners John Geddes Lawrence and Tyron Garner (January 16, 2003), at *11, *12, *15 (citing Karst's article, discussing *Roberts*'s category of intimate association, and asserting that "the adult couple whose shared life includes sexual intimacy is undoubtedly one of the most important and profound forms of intimate association."); Reply Brief of Petitioners John Geddes Lawrence and Tyron Garner (March 10, 2003), at *5 ("The relationship of an adult couple—whether heterosexual or gay—united by sexual intimacy is the very paradigm of an intimate association in which one finds 'emotional enrichment' and 'independently. . . . define[s] one's identity,' and it is protected as such from 'unwarranted state interference.'" (quoting *Roberts*)).

41. *Roberts v. United States Jaycees*, 468 U.S. 609, 618–19 (1984). Although the intellectual debt to Karst is apparent, the similarities between Karst's article and Brennan's opinion have gone relatively unnoticed. Among the few articles making the connection are Marcus, "The Freedom of Intimate Association in the Twenty-First Century," and Collin O'Connor Udell, "Intimate Association: Resurrecting a Hybrid Right," 7 *Texas Journal of Women and the Law* 232 (1998) (suggesting that *Roberts* "lifted the right to intimate association from Karst's article"). Post-*Roberts* cases have made clear that most associations are nonintimate, and few courts have extended the category of intimate association beyond family relationships. See, e.g., *FW/PBS, Inc. v. City of Dallas*, 493 U.S. 215 (1990) (patrons of motel, which limited rental of rooms to ten hours, did not have an intimate relationship protected by the Constitution); *City of Dallas v. Stanglin*, 490 U.S. 19, 24 (1989) (dance hall patrons "are not engaged in the sort of intimate human relationships" that give rise to the protections of intimate association); *Board of Directors of Rotary International v. Rotary Club of Duarte*, 481 U.S. 537 (1987) (relationship among Rotary Club members is not the type of intimate relationship that is constitutionally protected); *Rode v. Dellarciprete*, 845 F.2d 1195, 1205 (3d Cir. 1988) (brother-in-law relationship not protected as intimate association); *Pi Lambda Phi Fraternity, Inc. v. University of Pittsburgh*, 229 F.3d 435 (3d Cir. 2000) (college fraternity is not an intimate association); *Poirier v. Massachusetts Dept. of Correction*, 558 F.3d 92, 96 (1st Cir. 2009) (refusing to extend protections of intimate association to "[t]he unmarried cohabitation of adults"); *Salvation Army v. Department of Community Affairs of State of N.J.*, 919 F.2d 183, 198 (3d Cir. 1990) (intimate association unlikely to cover religious groups because

"most religious groups do not exhibit the distinctive attributes the Court has identified as helpful in determining whether the freedom of association is implicated."); *Swanson v. City of Bruce*, 105 Fed. Appx. 540 (5th Cir. 2004) ("The tight fellowship among police officers, precious though it may be, does not include such deep attachments and commitments of thoughts, experiences, and beliefs or personal aspects of officers' lives sufficient to constitute an intimate relationship."); *Borden v. School Dist. of Tp. of East Brunswick*, 523 F.3d 153, 173 (3d Cir. 2008) ("While the Supreme Court has held that the Constitution protects certain relationships, those protected relationships require a closeness that is not present between a high school football coach and his team."). But see *Louisiana Debating and Literary Ass'n v. City of New Orleans*, 42 F.3d 1483 (5th Cir. 1995) (extending right of "private association" to private club); *Anderson v. LaVergne*, 371 F.3d 879, 882 (6th Cir. 2004) (assuming for summary-judgment purposes that a dating relationship between two police officers qualified as an intimate association because the two were monogamous, had lived together, and were romantically and sexually involved); *Akers v. McGinnis*, 352 F.3d 1030, 1039–40 (6th Cir. 2003) (concluding that some types of personal friendships may constitute intimate associations).

42. Alexis de Tocqueville, *Democracy in America*, trans. Henry Reeve (New York: D. Appleton, 1899), 511. Indeed, as Nancy Rosenblum has argued: "The onus for cultivating the moral dispositions of liberal democratic citizens falls heavily on voluntary groups such as the Jaycees and their myriad counterparts." Nancy Rosenblum, "Compelled Association: Public Standing, Self-Respect, and the Dynamic of Exclusion," in *Freedom of Association*, ed. Amy Gutmann (Princeton: Princeton University Press, 1998), 76.

43. Peter L. Berger and Richard John Neuhaus, *To Empower People: From State to Civil Society* (Washington, D.C.: American Enterprise Institute Press, 1976).

44. *Roberts v. United States Jaycees*, 619; *Planned Parenthood of Southeastern Pa. v. Casey*, 505 U.S. 833, 851 (1992) ("At the heart of liberty is the right to define one's own concept of existence, of meaning, of the universe, and of the mystery of human life."). On the expressive attachments that people form with groups, see Richard W. Garnett, "The Story of Henry Adams's Soul: Education and the Expression of Associations," 85 *Minnesota Law Review* 1851 (2001) ("The simple act of associating can itself be a form of expression. We often join clubs, affiliate with parties, donate to organizations, and even subscribe to magazines, simply to *say something*.").

45. The constitutional protections offered by intimate association are today almost completely redundant of those found in the right of privacy. See, e.g., *Flaskamp v. Dearborn Public Schools*, 385 F.3d 935, 942 (6th Cir. 2004) ("Whether called a right to intimate association or a right to privacy, the point is similar: 'choices to enter into and maintain certain intimate human relationships must be secured against undue intrusion by the State because of the role of such relationships in safeguarding the individual freedom that is central to our constitutional scheme.'" (quoting *Roberts v. United States Jaycees*, 468 U.S. at 617–18 (1984))); *Montgomery v. Stefaniak*, 410 F.3d 933 (7th Cir. 2005) ("The freedom of intimate association receives protection as a fundamental element of personal liberty, and as

such is protected by the due process clauses." (internal quotations omitted)); *City of Bremerton v. Widell*, 146 Wash. 2d 561, 51 P.3d 733 (Wash. 2002) ("[Our] cases have held that the right of intimate association stems from the right of privacy, which normally applies only to familial relationships, and extends only as far as the principles of substantive due process permit." (citations omitted)).

46. *Roberts v. United States Jaycees*, 618, 622. Lower courts have generally adopted Brennan's instrumental gloss on expressive association. See, e.g., *Salvation Army v. Department of Community Affairs of State of N.J.*, 919 F.2d 183, 199 (3d Cir. 1990) ("The [Supreme] Court has not yet defined the parameters of the right to associate for religious purposes, but it has made it clear that the right to expressive association is a derivative right, which has been implied from the First Amendment in order to assure that those rights expressly secured by that amendment can be meaningfully exercised. Thus, there is no constitutional right to associate for a purpose that is not protected by the First Amendment." (citations omitted)); *Wine and Spirits Retailers, Inc. v. Rhode Island*, 418 F.3d 36, 50 (1st Cir. 2005) ("in a free speech case, an association's expressive purpose may pertain to a wide array of ends (including economic ends), but the embedded associational right protects only collective speech and expressive conduct in pursuit of those ends; it does not cover concerted action that lacks an expressive purpose."); *McCabe v. Sharrett*, 12 F.3d 1558, 1563 (11th Cir. 1994) ("The right of expressive association . . . is protected by the First Amendment as a necessary corollary of the rights that the amendment protects by its terms. . . . [A] plaintiff . . . can obtain special protection for an asserted associational right if she can demonstrate . . . that the purpose of the association is to engage in activities independently protected by the First Amendment."); *Willis v. Town of Marshall, N.C.*, 426 F.3d 251, 261 (4th Cir. 2005) ("a constitutionally protected right to associate depends upon the existence of an activity that is itself protected by the First Amendment"); *Schultz v. Wilson*, 304 Fed. Appx. 116, *3 (3d Cir. 2008) ("A social group is not protected unless it engages in expressive activity such as taking a stance on an issue of public, political, social, or cultural importance."). But see *Deja Vu of Nashville, Inc. v. Metropolitan Government of Nashville and Davidson County, Tennessee*, 274 F.3d 377, 396 (6th Cir. 2001) (First Amendment protects "entertainers and audience members' right to free expressive association" at an adult establishment because "they are certainly engaged in a 'collective effort on behalf of shared goals'" and "the dancers and customers work together as speaker and audience to create an erotic, sexually-charged atmosphere, and although society may not find that a particularly worthy goal, it is a shared one nonetheless.").

47. *Roberts v. United States Jaycees*, 623. Brennan also emphasized that "there can be no clearer example of an intrusion into the internal structure or affairs of an association than a regulation that forces the group to accept members it does not desire." Ibid. The most commonly asserted elements of the test require that a statute subject to strict scrutiny must be narrowly tailored and use the least restrictive means to further a compelling government interest. See, e.g., *United States v. Playboy Entertainment Group, Inc.*, 529 U.S. 803, 813 (2000) (summarizing strict scrutiny test); *Sable Communications of Cal., Inc. v. FCC*, 492

U.S. 115, 126 (1989); *First National Bank of Boston v. Bellotti*, 435 U.S. 765, 786 (1978). For Brennan's hints toward strict scrutiny, see *Roberts v. United States Jaycees*, 626 (the state achieved its interest through "the least restrictive means"); ibid., 628 (the "incidental abridgement" of protected speech is "no greater than is necessary."). The dissenting justices in *Dale* appear to have equated the *Roberts* test of "means significantly less restrictive" to strict scrutiny. See *Boy Scouts of America v. Dale*, 530 U.S. 640, 680 (2000) (Stevens, J., dissenting) ("We also held [in *Roberts*] that Minnesota's law is the least restrictive means of achieving [the state's compelling] interest."). Justices Souter, Ginsburg, and Breyer joined Justice Stevens's dissent. Ibid., 663. But in some ways, *Dale* only adds to the ambiguity of the test the Court applies in freedom of association cases. See ibid., 658–59 (rejecting "the intermediate standard of review enunciated in *United States v. O'Brien*, 391 U.S. 367 (1968)" but noting that under the proper analysis, "the associational interest in freedom of expression has been set on one side of the scale, and the State's interest on the other."). For examples of courts that have construed *Roberts* as requiring less than strict scrutiny, see, e.g., *Tabbaa v. Chertoff*, 509 F.3d 89, 105 (2d Cir. 2007) ("*Roberts* does not require the government to exhaust every possible means of furthering its interest; rather, the government must show only that its interest 'cannot be achieved through means *significantly less restrictive* of associational freedoms.'" (quoting *Roberts*)); *Hatcher v. Board of Public Educ. and Orphanage for Bibb County*, 809 F.2d 1546, 1559 n.26 (11th Cir. 1987) ("The balancing of interests is necessary because '[t]he right to associate for expressive purposes is not . . . absolute.'" (quoting *Roberts*)); *Every Nation Campus Ministries at San Diego State University v. Achtenberg*, 597 F.Supp.2d 1075, 1083 (S.D. Cal. 2009) ("state action that burdens a group's ability to engage in expressive association [need not] always be subject to strict scrutiny, even if the group seeks to engage in expressive association through a limited public forum." (quoting *Truth v. Kent Sch. Dist.* 542 F.3d 634, 652 (9th Cir. 2008) (Fisher, J., concurring)); *Chi Iota Colony of Alpha Epsilon Pi Fraternity v. City Univ. of N.Y.*, 502 F.3d 136, 139 (2d Cir. 2007) ("The mere fact that the associational interest asserted is recognized by the First Amendment does not necessarily mean that a regulation which burdens that interest must satisfy strict scrutiny."). Cf. *Forum for Academic and Institutional Rights v. Rumsfeld*, 390 F.3d 219, 247 (3d. Cir. 2004) (Aldisert, J., dissenting) reversed by *Forum for Academic and Institutional Rights v. Rumsfeld*, 547 U.S. 47 (2006) (describing *Roberts* as having announced a "'balance-of-interests' test").

48. For the kind of argument on which these claims are based, see Ludwig Wittgenstein, *Philosophical Investigations*, trans. G. E. M. Anscombe (Oxford: Blackwell, 1968). Justice O'Connor's concurrence explicitly refers to "nonexpressive association." See *Roberts v. United States Jaycees*, 638 (O'Connor, J., concurring) ("this Court's case law recognizes radically different constitutional protections for expressive and nonexpressive associations"). Richard Epstein argues that the distinction between expressive and nonexpressive association "is indefensible both as a matter of political theory and constitutional law." Richard A. Epstein, "The Constitutional Perils of Moderation: The Case of the Boy Scouts," 74 *Southern California Law Review* 122 (2000).

49. Nancy L. Rosenblum, "Compelled Association: Public Standing, Self-Respect, and the Dynamic of Exclusion," in *Freedom of Association*, ed. Amy Gutmann (Princeton: Princeton University Press, 1998), 78; Soifer, *Law and the Company We Keep*, 40; Kateb, "The Value of Association," 55; Koppelman, *A Right to Discriminate?* 24; Jason Mazzone, "Freedom's Associations," 77 *Washington Law Review* 639, 646. See also ibid., 645 ("Expressive association has shifted the focus away from associating and to the more familiar First Amendment territory of speech and the like.").

50. *Board of Directors of Rotary International v. Rotary Club of Duarte*, 481 U.S. 537 (1987); *New York State Club Ass'n v. City of New York*, 487 U.S. 1, 13 (1988).

51. *Hurley v. Irish-American Gay, Lesbian and Bisexual Group of Boston*, 515 U.S. 557, 560, 566, 568, 573, 575 (1995). Evacuation Day commemorated the day that royal troops and loyalists fled the city during the Revolutionary War. Ibid., 560. Until 1992, the city permitted the council to use the city's official seal, provided printing services to the council, and provided direct funding. Ibid., 561. But GLIB did not contest the lower court's conclusion that the parade did not constitute state action. Ibid., 566.

52. *Boy Scouts of America v. Dale*, 530 U.S. 640, 648 (2000); *New York State Club Ass'n v. City of New York*, 13. *Boy Scouts of America v. Dale*, 655, 650, 651. Justice Stevens challenged Rehnquist's reasoning: "To prevail on a claim of expressive association in the face of a State's antidiscrimination law, it is not enough simply to engage in *some kind* of expressive activity." Ibid., 682 (Stevens, J. dissenting).

53. *Boy Scouts of America v. Dale*, 679 (Stevens, J., dissenting). See Epstein, "The Constitutional Perils of Moderation," 125 ("The Supreme Court's decision in *Dale* did not overtly challenge the conceptual framework established in *Roberts;* indeed, it self-consciously purported to build on it."); Seana Valentine Shiffrin, "What Is Really Wrong with Compelled Association?" 99 *Northwestern University Law Review* 839, 841 (2005) ("The Court's framing of the issues [in *Dale*] grew straight out of Justice Brennan's opinion in *Roberts v. Jaycees*."); Andrew Koppelman, "Should Noncommercial Associations Have an Absolute Right to Discriminate?" 67 *Law and Contemporary Problems* 27, 57 (2004) ("*Dale* is a mess, but the upshot of the mess is that we still have the old message-based rule of *Roberts*."). But see Tobias Barrington Wolff and Andrew Koppelman, "Expressive Association and the Ideal of the University in the Solomon Amendment Litigation," 25 *Social Philosophy and Policy* 101 (2008) ("The decision in *Dale* represented an enormous departure from its predecessors," and "the Court adopted a posture of almost complete deference to an association's claim that an antidiscrimination law's interference with decisions about a small number of members would undermine the group's expressive practice"); Samuel Issacharoff, "Private Parties with Public Purposes: Political Parties, Associational Freedoms, and Partisan Competition," 101 *Columbia Law Review* 274, 297–98 (2001) (arguing that *Dale* eschewed "the functional analysis of *Roberts*"). In 2006, the Court rejected an attempt to expand the scope of *Dale* in *Forum for Academic and Institutional Rights v. Rumsfeld*, 547 U.S. 47 (2006). See generally, Wolff and Koppelman, "Expressive Association and the Ideal of the University in the Solomon Amendment Litigation"; Koppleman, *A Right to Discriminate?*

54. *Chi Iota Colony of Alpha Epsilon Pi Fraternity v. City University of New York,* 502 F.3d 136 (2007); *Chi Iota Colony of Alpha Epsilon Pi Fraternity v. City University of New York,* 443 F.Supp. 2d 374, 376, 377 (2006), reversed by *Chi Iota Colony of Alpha Epsilon Pi Fraternity v. City University of New York,* 502 F.3d 136 (2007).

55. *Chi Iota* (district court), 376, 377, 379, 380. Cf. *Healy v. James,* 498 U.S. 169, 181 (1972) ("There can be no doubt that denial of official recognition, without justification, to college organizations burdens or abridges [the right of individuals to associate to further their personal beliefs].").

56. *Chi Iota* (district court), 381, 389, 395; *Chi Iota Colony of Alpha Epsilon Pi Fraternity v. City University of New York,* 502 F.3d 136, 149 (2007); e-mail from Gregory F. Hauser to John D. Inazu, September 30, 2009 (Mr. Hauser represented Chi Iota in the litigation).

57. *Chi Iota* (district court), 379 (quoting Chi Iota's president explaining that the fraternity members "are not extremely religious, but [they] do talk about things that [they] contribute to the community, an expression of Judaism."); *Chi Iota* (Second Circuit), 141.

58. *Christian Legal Society v. Martinez,* 130 S. Ct. 2971 (2010); *Christian Legal Society v. Martinez,* Petition for Writ of Certiorari, May 5, 2009, 6, 7, 8. CLS specifies that "a person's mere experience of same-sex or opposite-sex sexual attraction does not determine his or her eligibility for leadership or voting membership," but "CLS individually addresses each situation that arises in a sensitive Biblical fashion." Ibid., 8.

59. Petition for Writ of Certiorari, 10; *Christian Legal Society v. Kane,* No. C04–04484, May 19, 2006, *14; *Christian Legal Society v. Martinez,* 130 S. Ct. 2971, 2978 (2010). Hastings did not deny CLS the "use of campus facilities for meetings and other appropriate purposes," which the Supreme Court has called "the primary impediment to free association flowing from nonrecognition." *Healy v. James,* 408 U.S. 169, 181 (1972). Still, nothing in *Healy* suggests that the lack of access to campus facilities for meetings is the only burden caused by nonrecognition, and it is not hard to see how the inability to reserve meeting spaces, to access e-mail lists, or to participate in the student fair could burden associational freedoms. See ibid., 181–82 ("Petitioner's associational interests also were circumscribed by the denial of the use of campus bulletin boards and the school newspaper. If an organization is to remain a viable entity in a campus community in which new students enter on a regular basis, it must possess the means of communicating with these students. Moreover, the organization's ability to participate in the intellectual give and take of campus debate, and to pursue its stated purposes, is limited by the denial of access to the customary media for communicating with the administration, faculty members, and other students. Such impediments cannot be viewed as insubstantial.").

60. *Kane,* *13, *17.

61. *Kane,* *20, *22, *23. Cf. *Christian Legal Society v. Walker,* 453 F.3d 853, 862 (7th Cir. 2006) ("It would be hard to argue—and no one does—that CLS is not an expressive association.").

62. *Christian Legal Society v. Kane,* 319 Fed. Appx. 645 (9th Cir. 2009). The court cited its opinion in *Truth v. Kent Sch. Distr.,* 542 F.3d 634, 649–50 (9th Cir. 2008), which had ruled

that a school district could deny recognition to a high school Bible club that limited its voting members and officers to those who shared the group's beliefs. The Seventh Circuit's opinion is *Christian Legal Society v. Walker,* 453 F.3d 853 (7th Cir. 2006).

63. *Christian Legal Society v. Martinez,* 130 S. Ct. 2971, 2978 (2010). On the tension between public forum analysis and government speech analysis, see, e.g., ibid., 2976 (Hastings's policy "encourages tolerance, cooperation, and learning among students" and "conveys the Law School's decision 'to decline to subsidize with public monies and benefits conduct of which the people of California disapprove.'"). In addition to the doctrinal complications, *Martinez* involved a disputed factual question as to whether Hastings applied an all-comers policy or a policy that prohibited certain kinds of discrimination, including discrimination based upon religion and sexual orientation. The Court remanded on the question of whether Hastings selectively applied its all-comers policy. Ibid., 2995. While this factual question might be important to a public forum analysis, it is less relevant to the freedom of association analysis that the Court should have made. The strength of CLS's constitutional claim to exist as a group should not turn on whether the restriction against it is viewpoint neutral or selectively enforced against it.

64. *Martinez,* 2976. See ibid. ("The same considerations that have led us to apply a less restrictive level of scrutiny to speech in limited public forums as compared to other environments apply with equal force to expressive association occurring in limited public forums."); ibid. ("The strict scrutiny we have applied in some settings to laws that burden expressive association would, in practical effect, invalidate a defining characteristic of limited public forums—the State may 'reserv[e] [them] for certain groups'"). After deciding to pursue a public forum analysis, the viewpoint neutrality of Hastings's all-comers policy was self-evident to the majority. See ibid., 2993 ("It is, after all, hard to imagine a more viewpoint-neutral policy than one requiring *all* student groups to accept *all* comers."); ibid. ("An all-comers condition on access to RSO status, in short, is textbook viewpoint neutral."). Accordingly, the majority "consider[ed] whether Hastings' policy is reasonable taking into account the RSO forum's function and 'all the surrounding circumstances,'" ibid., 2988, and concluded that "the several justifications Hastings asserts in support of its all-comers requirement are surely reasonable in light of the RSO forum's purposes." Ibid., 2991. Ginsburg cited an important article by Eugene Volokh. Ibid., 2985–86 (citing Eugene Volokh, "Freedom of Expressive Association and Government Subsidies," 58 *Stanford Law Review* 1919, 1940 (2006)). Among other things, Volokh's article considers a conflict very similar to the one at issue in *Martinez:* whether a public university can apply antidiscrimination rules to the Christian Legal Society. Volokh, "Freedom of Expressive Association and Government Subsidies," 1935. Ginsburg highlights Volokh's observation that a school may limit official recognition to groups composed only of students, even though this infringes upon the associational freedoms of those who wish to form a group with nonstudents. *Martinez,* 2986. The point is a nice one, but the nonstudent constraint could also be construed as a jurisdictional limit linked far more closely (and less ideologically) to the nature of the public forum than an all-comers

policy. More important, Volokh spends considerable time accounting for the values introduced by the right of association. Volokh, "Freedom of Expressive Association and Government Subsidies," 1935. The majority subsumes this dimension into its speech analysis.

65. *Martinez,* 2984–85 (quoting Brief for Petitioner, 35); Brief for Petitioner, 35; ibid., 18; *Martinez,* 2985 (citing Brief for Petitioner, 18).

66. *Martinez,* 2986. Ginsburg cites *Grove City College v. Bell,* 465 U.S. 555, 575–76 (1984), and *Bob Jones Univ. v. United States,* 461 U.S. 574, 602–4 (1983). "Official recognition" is a term of art that doesn't entail any endorsement of private groups by the state actor. Hastings made clear that it "neither sponsor[s] nor endorse[s]" the views of registered student organizations and insisted that the groups inform third parties that they were not sponsored by the law school. Brief for Petitioner, 4.

Chapter 5. A Theory of Assembly

1. The pervasive adherence of courts to the expressive and intimate distinction in *Roberts* illustrates the entrenchment of the right of association. See Michael J. Gerhardt, *The Power of Precedent* (New York: Oxford University Press, 2008), 100 (discussing the role of "entrenched" judicial decisions that contribute to a "limited path dependency of precedent").

2. Phillip Bobbitt, *Constitutional Fate: Theory of the Constitution* (New York: Oxford University Press, 1984); Neil Siegel and Robert D. Cooter, "Collective Action Federalism: A General Theory of Article I, Section 8," 63 *Stanford Law Review* 115, 155 (2010).

3. I owe the phrase "factions for the rest of us" to Ernie Young.

4. Peter de Marneffe, "Rights, Reasons, and Freedom of Association," in *Freedom of Association,* ed. Amy Gutmann (Princeton: Princeton University Press, 1998), 146. On the importance of informal relationships, see Robert D. Putnam, *Bowling Alone: The Collapse and Revival of American Community* (New York: Simon and Schuster, 2000), 152–53 ("Social networks are the quintessential resource of movement organizations. Reading groups became sinews of the suffrage movement. Friendship networks, not environmental sympathies, accounted for which Pennsylvanians became involved in grassroots protest after the Three Mile Island nuclear accident. Social ties more than ideals or self-interest explain who was recruited to Freedom Summer, a climactic moment in the civil rights movement. Local church connections account for the solidarity that underlies the Christian Coalition.").

5. Sheldon Wolin, *Politics and Vision* (Princeton: Princeton University Press, 2004), 385.

6. Ibid., 524.

7. Ibid., 534, 536, 539, 540, 545, 549.

8. Sheldon S. Wolin, "Democracy, Difference, and Re-Cognition," 21 *Political Theory* 464, 467 (1993). Wolin notes the similarities between his thought and some multiculturalist arguments. Ibid., 480.

9. Ibid., 464.

10. Nancy L. Rosenblum, "Compelled Association: Public Standing, Self-Respect, and the Dynamic of Exclusion," in *Freedom of Association*, ed. Amy Gutmann (Princeton: Princeton University Press, 1998), 75, 92, 90. Examples of contemporary political theorists who support imposing certain consensus norms on illiberal groups include Stephen Macedo, *Diversity and Distrust: Civic Education in a Multicultural Democracy* (Cambridge, Mass.: Harvard University Press, 2000); Brian Barry, *Culture and Equality* (Cambridge, Mass.: Harvard University Press, 2001); Susan Moller Okin, " 'Mistresses of Their Own Destiny': Group Rights, Gender, and Realistic Rights of Exit," 112 *Ethics* 205 (2002). Macedo's arguments are sometimes limited to what he calls "the noncoercive promotion of civic virtue" to further "the constitutional ideals of liberal justice that should unite us all." Stephen Macedo, "School Vouchers, Religious Nonprofit Organizations, and Liberal Public Values," 75 *Chicago Kent Law Review* 417, 418, 423 (2000). He recognizes the value of freedom of association but insists that certain "inward looking" and homogenous groups are "intrinsically problematic in a liberal democratic context" and "the project of promoting a healthy liberal democratic civil society is inevitably a deeply judgmental and non-neutral project." Stephen Macedo, "The Constitution, Civic Virtue, and Civil Society: Social Capital as Substantive Morality," 69 *Fordham Law Review* 1573, 1582, 1593 (2001).

11. Stephen Carter, *The Dissent of the Governed: A Meditation on Law, Religion, and Loyalty* (Cambridge, Mass.: Harvard University Press, 1998), 27; Sheldon S. Wolin, "Fugitive Democracy," 1 *Constellations* 11, 23 (1994). Importantly, Wolin emphasizes that this mode of existence is fleeting and "periodically lost." Ibid. See also Michael Walzer, *Obligations: Essays on Disobedience, War, and Citizenship* (New York: Simon and Schuster, 1971).

12. Nancy L. Rosenblum, *Membership and Morals: The Personal Uses of Pluralism in America* (Princeton: Princeton University Press, 1998), 54. Cf. John Rawls, "The Idea of Public Reason Revisited," 64 *Chicago Law Review* 765, 789 (1997) ("Much the same question arises in regard to all associations, whether they be churches or universities, professional or scientific associations, business firms or labor unions. The family is not peculiar in this respect."). On the feminist critique of Rawls, see, e.g., Susan Moller Okin, *Justice, Gender, and the Family* (New York: Basic, 1989). See also Ruth Abbey, "Back Toward a Comprehensive Liberalism? Justice as Fairness, Gender, and Families," 35 *Political Theory* 19 (2007) ("In his later writings, Rawls tries to incorporate women as full, free, and equal members of the just society. In doing this, he makes his theory of justice as fairness more palatable to feminist-liberals. However, he also makes it harder to contend that justice as fairness could be a purely political doctrine. Rawls comes very close to advocating autonomy for individuals in the domestic, as well as the political, realm.").

13. Rawls, "Public Reason Revisited," 789, 767. Cf. ibid., 789 ("although the principles of justice do not apply directly to the internal life of churches, they do protect the rights and liberties of their members by the constraints to which all churches and associations are subject."). Cf. Robert C. Post, *Constitutional Domains: Democracy, Community, Management* (Cambridge, Mass.: Harvard University Press, 1995), 119–78. Post writes: "The boundaries of public discourse cannot be fixed in a neutral fashion. From the

perspective of the logic of democratic self-governance, any restriction of the domain of public discourse must necessarily constitute a forcible truncation of possible lines of democratic development. Because this truncation must ultimately be determined by reference to community values, the boundaries of a discourse defined by its liberation from ideological conformity will themselves be defined by reference to ideological presuppositions." Ibid., 177.

14. Rawls, "Public Reason Revisited," 800; Chandran Kukathas, *The Liberal Archipelago* (New York: Oxford University Press, 2003), 138; Robert Cover, "Nomos and Narrative," 97 *Harvard Law Review* 1, 17 (1983). Cover specifies that "the term Babel . . . suggests not incoherence but a multiplicity of coherent systems and a problem of intelligibility among communities." Ibid., 17 n.45.

15. John Rawls, *A Theory of Justice* (Cambridge, Mass.: Belknap Press of Harvard University Press, 1971), 386. As Corey Brettschneider argues, "The test for the reasonableness of comprehensive doctrines is substantive and not merely formal," and "nonjustifiable principles expressed in the language of public reason are still nonjustifiable." Corey Brettschneider, "The Politics of the Personal: A Liberal Approach," 101 *American Political Science Review* 22 (2007). On the violence of the law, see generally Robert Cover, "Violence and the Word," 95 *Yale Law Journal* 1601 (1986). Cover begins his article with the pronouncement that "legal interpretation takes place in a field of pain and death." Ibid. He later notes that "the violence of judges and officials of a posited constitutional order is generally understood to be implicit in the practice of law and government. Violence is so intrinsic to this activity, so taken for granted, that it need not be mentioned." Ibid.

16. Wolin, *Politics and Vision*, 17. See Ken I. Kersch, "'Guilt By Association' and the Postwar Civil Libertarians," 25 *Social Philosophy and Policy* 55 (2008) (the right of association is "commonly considered as an instrument for vindicating high-status (First Amendment) rights claims, like freedom of religion and freedom of speech, which, as first-order rights, are defended not as instruments indispensable to the exercise of other rights but rather on their own substantive terms"); Martin P. Golding, "Liberty, Equality, and the Freedom of Association," 13 *Australian Journal of Legal Philosophy* 120 (1989) ("Particular forms of fellowship communality and cultural identity cannot always be understood merely as goals that individuals coincidentally have; they are modes of existence.").

17. The claim is intentionally broad—it is difficult to envision any associative act that lacks expressive potential. William Marshall posits a counterexample: "Tom and Fred walking down the street is, in no meaningful sense, expression." William P. Marshall, "Discrimination and the Right of Association," 81 *Northwestern University Law Review* 77 (1986). But as long as Tom and Fred's stroll reflects a conscious decision to walk with one another, then the act of walking expresses a kind of shared (though perhaps fleeting) affiliation. The meaning of that expression will vary based upon the surrounding circumstances (consider, for example, the expressive meaning if Tom is black and Fred is white and they are walking happily down the main street of a small southern town in the 1950s).

18. *Christian Legal Society v. Martinez* (No. 08–1371), Brief of Gays and Lesbians for Individual Liberty as Amicus Curiae in Support of Petitioner (February 4, 2010), 11 (emphasizing that "many exclusively gay social and activity clubs, retreats, vacations, and professional organizations" have "relied on exclusively gay environments in which to feel safe, to build relationships, and to develop political strategy."); *Roberts v. United States Jaycees*, 468 U.S. 609, 618 (1984). The expressiveness inherent in an act of gathering presupposes an audience of some kind. Thus, for example, the gathering of a secret society would not have an outward expressiveness. Cf. Melville B. Nimmer, "The Meaning of Symbolic Speech under the First Amendment," 21 *UCLA Law Review* 29, 36 (1973) ("The right to engage in verbal locutions which no one can hear and in conduct which no one can observe may sometimes qualify as a due process 'liberty,' but without an actual or potential audience there can be no first amendment speech right."). While Nimmer's observation may be formally correct, it makes little difference in the *application* of an expressive restriction. Any act of self-expression (i.e., expression undertaken without an actual or potential audience) becomes communicative when the state attempts to restrict it. The very determination by a government actor that an act is not "communicative" or not "protected" is an interpretation of the meaning of the act that creates an audience in the government actor restricting the act.

19. *Boy Scouts of America v. Dale*, 530 U.S. 640, 702 (2000) (Souter, J., dissenting).

20. Rosenblum, *Membership and Morals*, 6 ("There are always alternative understandings of an association's nature and purpose, and competing classifications."); Erwin Chemerinsky and Catherine Fisk, "The Expressive Interest of Associations," 9 *William and Mary Bill of Rights Journal* 600 (2001) (discussing the Court's deference to the Boy Scouts' leadership in *Boy Scouts of America v. Dale*). For examples of groups whose meaning and message are not determined by majority vote, see, e.g., *Roberts v. United States Jaycees*, 613 ("The ultimate policymaking authority of the Jaycees rests with an annual national convention, consisting of delegates from each local chapter, with a national president and board of directors."); *United States Constitution*, Art. 2, sect. 2 ("The President shall be Commander in Chief of the Army and Navy of the United States").

21. Chemerinsky and Fisk, "The Expressive Interests of Associations," 608, 609, 611.

22. Andrew Koppelman with Tobias Barrington Wolff, *A Right to Discriminate? How the Case of* Boy Scouts of America v. James Dale *Warped the Law of Free Association* (New Haven: Yale University Press, 2009), 5, 6, 9–10, 11–12, 12–15, 17–18, 19, 20, iii, xi.

23. Koppelman contends that the new right of association in *NAACP v. Alabama* was based exclusively on the right to free speech. Ibid., 17. He makes no mention of Justice Harlan's references to the right of assembly and argues that assembly "has always been understood to mean a right to hold public meetings, not to exclude people from associations." Ibid., 21. Koppelman and I also disagree as to where in the Constitution the Court rooted the right of association in *NAACP v. Alabama*. He contends that "*NAACP v. Alabama* made clear that freedom of association was firmly rooted in the First Amendment."

Koppelman, *A Right to Discriminate?* 18. I have argued that Harlan's opinion never mentions the First Amendment and that Harlan, attempting to balance competing pressures from Frankfurter, Black, and Douglas, obscures the constitutional source of the right.

24. Koppelman claims that the Court "summarily rejected" the right to exclude argument in *Runyon v. McCrary.* Koppelman, *A Right to Discriminate?* 18. But as I noted earlier, the Court struggled to address this issue in the line of cases preceding *Runyon.*

25. Koppelman suggests that the doctrinal framework set forth in *Roberts* was "well-settled" when the Court decided *Dale* sixteen years later. Koppelman, *A Right to Discriminate?* xi. As I suggested in the previous chapter, since *Roberts,* lower courts have been incredibly confused by the Court's categories of intimate and expressive association.

26. *NAACP v. Alabama ex rel. Patterson,* 357 U.S. 449, 460 (1958) ("Effective advocacy of both public and private points of view, particularly controversial ones, is undeniably enhanced by group association, as this Court has more than once recognized by remarking upon the close nexus between the freedoms of speech and assembly." (citing *De Jonge v. Oregon* and *Thomas v. Collins*)); ibid., 462 ("This Court has recognized the vital relationship between freedom to associate and privacy in one's associations. When referring to the varied forms of governmental action which might interfere with freedom of assembly, it said in [*Douds*]: 'A requirement that adherents of particular religious faiths or political parties wear identifying armbands, for example, is obviously of this nature.' Compelled disclosure of membership in an organization engaged in advocacy of particular beliefs is of the same order."). For other scholars who link the right of association to the right of speech, see, e.g., Michael Stokes Paulsen, "Scouts, Families, and Schools" 85 *Minnesota Law Review* 1917, 1919 (2001) ("The First Amendment freedom of expressive association . . . is firmly rooted in the Constitution's text and internal logic. The First Amendment protects 'the freedom of speech.'"); Richard Epstein explicitly rejects the connection between association and assembly in *NAACP v. Alabama.* See Richard A. Epstein, "Should Antidiscrimination Laws Limit Freedom of Association? The Dangerous Allure of Human Rights Legislation" 25 *Social Philosophy and Policy* 131 (2008) ("[Justice Harlan's] use of 'assembly' . . . leaves the impression that the association right has an explicit textual foundation in the First Amendment. Instructively, the word 'assembly' does not appear in the First Amendment, which references only 'the right of the people peaceably to assemble, and to petition the Government for a redress of grievances.' Even if the second clause is not a limitation on the first, the words 'to assemble' in context read much more naturally as the ability to meet in public to discuss various issues. 'To assemble' does not sound like the right to form associations that meet in private to plan and organize with respect to a full range of 'political, economic, religious or cultural' issues."). These modern interpretations are at odds with those advanced by jurists and scholars at the time the Court first recognized the right of association. See, e.g., *Bates v. Little Rock,* 361 U.S. 516, 527-28 (1960) (Black and Douglas, JJ., concurring) ("The ordinances as here applied violate freedom of speech and assembly guaranteed by the First Amendment which this Court has many times held was made applicable to the States by

the Fourteenth Amendment. . . . One of those rights, *freedom of assembly, includes of course freedom of association;* and it is entitled to no less protection than any other First Amendment right."); Glenn Abernathy, *The Right of Assembly and Association* (Columbia: University of South Carolina Press, 1961), 4, 173, 236–37 (arguing that the right of association falls within an "expanded meaning" of the right of assembly, that association was "clearly a right cognate to the right of assembly," and that the right of assembly "can justifiably be extended to include as well those persons who are joined together through organizational affiliation."); George P. Smith, "The Development of the Right of Assembly: A Current Socio-Legal Investigation," 9 *William and Mary Law Review* 366 (1967) ("the broad concept of a right of association . . . developed largely out of the right of assembly and in part out of due process concepts."); David Fellman, *The Constitutional Right of Association* (Chicago: University of Chicago Press, 1963), 3 ("The broader rights of association have developed, in part, out of the right of assembly, and in part out of broader due process concepts.").

27. *United States Constitution,* Amendment I; *Brandenburg v. Ohio,* 395 U. S. 444, 447 (1969) ("the constitutional guarantees of free speech and free press do not permit a State to forbid or proscribe advocacy of the use of force or of law violation except where such advocacy is directed to inciting or producing imminent lawless action and is likely to incite or produce such action"). On the history of unlawful assembly, see Abernathy, *The Right of Assembly and Association,* 19–49. Abernathy catalogues much of the legal commentary on unlawful assembly from the nineteenth and early twentieth centuries, as well as antecedents from English statutes and commentary. Ibid. For a more recent example of state restrictions on a nonpeaceable group, see *Gallo v. Acuna,* 14 Cal.4th 1090, 929 P.2d 596 (Cal. 1997) (enforcing associational restrictions against criminal street gang).

28. See, e.g., Robert Post, "Prejudicial Appearances: The Logic of American Antidiscrimination Law," 88 *California Law Review* 1 (2000); Jordan D. Bello, "Attractiveness as Hiring Criteria: Savvy Business Practice or Racial Discrimination?" 8 *Journal of Gender, Race, and Justice* 483 (2004). Commercial discrimination against customers also exists. See, e.g., Miriam A. Cherry, "Exercising the Right to Public Accommodations: The Debate over Single-Sex Health Clubs," 52 *Maine Law Review* 97 (2000); Michael R. Evans, "The Case for All-Female Health Clubs: Creating a Compensatory Purpose Exception to State Public Accommodation Laws," 11 *Yale Journal of Law and Feminism* 307 (1999). Discriminatory online dating services raise a related concern. Commercial online dating services regularly engage in de facto discrimination based on more suspect characteristics, even if they remain technically open to all customers. See, e.g., jdate.com ("the Premier Jewish Community Online for Dating Jewish Singles") (last visited July 7, 2010); adamforadam.com ("we build a community for gay men looking for friendship, romance, dating or a hot hookup") (last visited July 7, 2010); blackpeoplemeet.com (the "fast and easy way to connect with black singles near you") (last visited July 7, 2010).

29. Joseph William Singer, "No Right to Exclude: Public Accommodations and Private Property," 90 *Northwestern University Law Review* 1283 (1996) (arguing that historical

understanding of public accommodation includes not only inns, restaurants, gas stations, and places of entertainment but also retail stores); *Roberts v. United States Jaycees,* 626; *Boy Scouts of America v. Dale,* 530 U.S. 640, 657 (2000). Jonathan Mitchell notes that "as a matter of state law this holding was a reach, even in light of the state legislature's instructions to 'liberally [construe]' the antidiscrimination laws." Jonathan F. Mitchell, "Reconsidering *Murdock:* State-Law Reversals as Constitutional Avoidance," 77 *Chicago Law Review* 1365 (2010). See ibid. ("The state supreme court essentially equated membership associations with 'places of public accommodation'; that conclusion does not fit the statutory language. New Jersey's [antidiscrimination law] also prohibits places of public accommodation from discriminating based on 'creed,' 'age,' 'sex,' and 'gender identity or expression.' Classifying the Boy Scouts as a 'place of public accommodation' would prohibit the Scouts from setting minimum ages for Scoutmasters, requiring its members to believe in God, or excluding women or girls from membership or any leadership position. The state supreme court never addressed these implications of its ruling."). The ways in which a line between commercial and noncommercial extends the reach of antidiscrimination norms into commercial but noncoercive groups is rarely addressed in contemporary scholarship on matters of group autonomy.

30. *Roberts v. United States Jaycees,* 636 (O'Connor, J., concurring) (positing a dichotomous distinction between "commercial" and "expressive" associations and noting that "an association should be characterized as commercial, and therefore subject to rationally related state regulation of its membership and other associational activities, when, and only when, the association's activities are not predominantly of the type protected by the First Amendment."); Brief for Petitioner, 2, *Christian Legal Society v. Martinez,* No. 08–1371 (Jan. 2010).

31. Koppelman, *A Right to Discriminate?* xii, 74. For an approach similar to the contextual analysis that I suggest, see Robert K. Vischer, "The Good, the Bad, and the Ugly: Rethinking the Value of Associations," 79 *Notre Dame L. Rev.* 949, 973 (2004) ("Judicial deference to an association's expression of identity does not preclude the application of antidiscrimination statutes to all associations. Where the association excludes certain segments of society from economic or political participation in the community, the statute may still be enforceable.").

32. Koppelman, *A Right to Discriminate?* xi, xii, xiii.

33. Koppelman, *A Right to Discriminate?* 20. The district court assumed that CLS qualified as an expressive association because Hastings did not dispute that characterization. *Christian Legal Society v. Kane,* No. C04–04484 (May 19, 2006), at *20.

34. Koppelman, *A Right to Discriminate?* 24.

35. Andrew Koppelman, "Should Noncommercial Associations Have an Absolute Right to Discriminate?" 67 *Law and Contemporary Problems* 57 (2004). See *Bob Jones v. United States,* 461 U.S. 574 (1983) (upholding denial of tax-exempt status to private university and private secondary schools that discriminated on the basis of race); *Grove City College v. Bell,* 465 U.S. 555, 559 (1984) (noting that Title IX's restrictions on gender discrimination trumped the petitioners' First Amendment rights because "Congress is free to attach

reasonable and unambiguous conditions to federal financial assistance that education institutions are not obligated to accept."). Despite the Court's denial of government benefits in *Bob Jones* and *Grove City*, the constitutional distinction between the financial benefits in these cases and the subsidies in official recognition cases like *Martinez* is far from clear. On the one hand, the Court has equated the grant of tax-exempt status with a government subsidy. See *Regan v. Taxation with Representation* 461 U.S. 540 (1983) ("A tax exemption has much the same effect as a cash grant to the organization of the amount of tax it would have to pay on its income."); *Texas Monthly, Inc. v. Bullock*, 489 U.S. 1, 14 (1989) ("every tax exemption constitutes a subsidy that affects non-qualifying taxpayers, forcing them to become indirect and vicarious 'donors.'"). On the other hand, the Court has specified that the "grant of a tax exemption is not sponsorship." *Walz v. Tax Commission*, 397 U.S. 664, 675 (1970).

36. Koppelman, *A Right to Discriminate?* 118–19. Of all of the litigants to bring cases about group autonomy to the Supreme Court in the past thirty years, the most striking victory was won by the Boy Scouts. And yet the Scouts are arguably the litigants least worthy of the constitutional protections of assembly. As Koppelman has noted, the Scouts are "deeply intertwined with the state, to a degree unmatched by any other youth organization." Andrew Koppelman, "Should Noncommercial Associations Have an Absolute Right to Discriminate?" 47. See ibid., 47–48 (listing examples of the Boy Scouts' governmental support, including a congressional charter, the president of the United States serving as the organization's honorary president, the use of military equipment without charge, and the use of military facilities). Koppelman also notes that "athough the Boy Scouts are not an actual monopoly, they have enormous market power." Ibid., 49. See ibid. ("Membership in the Boy Scouts has a nationally understood meaning. If you tell someone you are an Eagle Scout, no further explanation is necessary. No other youth organization has such universal recognition of such enormous cultural resonance.").

37. Amy Gutmann, "Freedom of Association: An Introductory Essay," in *Freedom of Association,* ed. Amy Gutmann (Princeton: Princeton University Press, 1998), 13. The underlying facts and circumstances in the contextual analysis that I propose become more difficult to sort out with groups that maintain both local and larger regional or national identities. Consider the Boy Scouts: Should the focus of the overreaching of private power be at the local or the national level? I find this to be a deeply complicated question, made even more problematic by the quasi-public nature of the Boy Scouts at the federal level. In some ways, the kind of power exerted by the Boy Scouts has been made possible by its national identity. On the other hand, the effects of this power will vary by locality, and local Scout troops might reflect the core understanding of assembly that I have articulated in this book. As Laura Rosenbury has argued: "If one considers the individual groups in which the Boy Scouts functions—the troops and dens, consisting of anywhere from eight to twenty boys—then the Boy Scouts organization shares at least four characteristics of many families. First, like families, the troops are relatively small groups. Second, minors are the focus of both groups. Third, the Boy Scouts seeks to instill

values in young people, a primary family function. Fourth, both the Boy Scouts and families allegedly seek to instill values about gender and sex, aspects of identity that are foundational to state definitions of marriage and the family. When one considers all four characteristics together—when the Boy Scouts is seen as a series of small groups made up of children and mentors performing a function traditionally performed by the family about subjects that are at the core of state definitions of family—it is plausible to conclude that the Boy Scouts constitutes a family-like intimate association." Laura A. Rosenbury, "Between Home and School," 155 *University of Pennsylvania Law Review* 833, 861–62 (2007). Rosenbury nevertheless calls for "limited inclusion-oriented, or pluralism-enhancing, regulations." Ibid., 895. In the context of *Boy Scouts of America v. Dale*, "this normative approach would mean that the Boy Scouts would not be permitted to exclude Dale as a troop leader, because the state of New Jersey has decided, in passing its public accommodations law, that discrimination against homosexuals in spaces like the Boy Scouts is at odds with the state's conception of civil society." Ibid.

38. *Thomas v. Collins*, 323 U.S. 516 (1945); Aviam Soifer, *Law and the Company We Keep* (Cambridge, Mass.: Harvard University Press, 1995), 77, 78. I have otherwise written this dissent to reflect the context in 1984 and have avoided citing events, case law, and scholarship that unfolded after that time.

Conclusion

1. Cf. Tabatha Abu El-Haj, "The Neglected Right of Assembly," 56 *UCLA Law Review* 543, 588 (2009). ("We seem to have forgotten that the right of assembly, like the right to petition, was originally considered central to securing democratic responsiveness and active democratic citizens. We now view it instead as simply another facet of the individual's right of free expression, focusing almost exclusively on the question of whether the group's message will be heard."); Timothy Zick, *Speech out of Doors: Preserving First Amendment Liberties in Public Places* (New York: Cambridge University Press, 2008), 325 ("Our long tradition of public expression, dissent, and contention, from the earliest activities in the colonies to present-day peace activists, agitators, and dissenters, has been possible owing to relatively open access to embodied, contested, inscribed, and other places on the expressive topography.").

2. *Communist Party v. Subversive Activities Control Board*, 367 U.S. 1, 137 (1961) (Black, J., dissenting).

3. C. Edwin Baker, *Human Liberty and Freedom of Speech* (New York: Oxford University Press, 1989), 134 (original emphasis).

INDEX

Abernathy, Glenn, 94–96; *Right of Assembly and Association*, 94, 95–96
abolition movement, 1, 6, 20, 33, 34–35, 110, 157, 178
absolute rights, 8, 75, 151
ACLU (American Civil Liberties Union), 69, 80, 90
act-message distinction, 124, 231n11
Addams, Jane, 45
Adler v. Board of Education (1952), 70–71, 94; dissenting justices, 212–13n13
African Americans: activism-communism conflation and, 8, 63, 64, 77–78, 91–92, 96; assembly curbs on, 6, 8, 20, 27, 30–33, 164; Court application of assembly rights to, 61; federal protection from state actions against, 38; Progressive Era rights

activism of, 44, 45–46, 49; southern violence against, 36–39. *See also* Civil Rights Movement; racial discrimination; segregation
African Methodist Episcopal Church v. City of New Orleans (La. 1860), 32
agrarianism, 109, 157
Alabama, 32, 37, 78–79. See also *NAACP v. Alabama ex rel. Patterson*
Alien Registration Act. *See* Smith Act
Alpha Epsilon Pi, Chi Iota Colony, 144–45, 150, 188n5
Amar, Akhil, 6
American Anti-Slavery Society, 34
American Baptist Convention, 80
American Bar Association, 54–55, 115
American Civil Liberties Union, 69, 80, 90